Contemporary Performance InterActions

Series Editors
Elaine Aston, Lancaster University, Lancaster, Lancashire, UK
Brian Singleton, Samuel Beckett Centre, Trinity College, Dublin, Ireland

Theatre's performative InterActions with the politics of sex, race and class, with questions of social and political justice, form the focus of the Contemporary Performance InterActions series. Performative InterActions are those that aspire to affect, contest or transform. International in scope, CPI publishes monographs and edited collections dedicated to the InterActions of contemporary practitioners, performances and theatres located in any world context.

More information about this series at
https://link.springer.com/bookseries/14918

Lena Šimić · Emily Underwood-Lee

Maternal Performance

Feminist Relations

palgrave
macmillan

Lena Šimić
Edge Hill University
Ormskirk, UK

Emily Underwood-Lee
University of South Wales
Cardiff, UK

ISSN 2634-5870 ISSN 2634-5889 (electronic)
Contemporary Performance InterActions
ISBN 978-3-030-80225-7 ISBN 978-3-030-80226-4 (eBook)
https://doi.org/10.1007/978-3-030-80226-4

Cover illustration: Publicity image for Grace Surman, *Motherload* (2016)
Cover image: Gary Winters

This Palgrave Macmillan imprint is published by the registered company Springer Nature Switzerland AG
The registered company address is: Gewerbestrasse 11, 6330 Cham, Switzerland

Acknowledgements

This book has been in the making since 2015, first laterally, then in a much more directed way from 2017, and we finally signed the contract with Palgrave in 2018. We would like to thank the series editors of Contemporary Performance InterActions, Elaine Aston and Brian Singleton, and all the team at Palgrave for entrusting us with this project.

Thank you to the Arts and Humanities Research Council for funding our 'Performance and the Maternal' research project and to our colleagues at the University of South Wales and Edge Hill University for their support.

We are thankful to Georgina Biggs for her work throughout the Performance and the Maternal research project and our advisory circle members: Aleksandra Nikolajev-Jones, Alice Entwistle, Carolyn Wallace, Dyana Gravina, Jennifer Verson, Prue Thimbleby, Ruth McElroy, Vicky Karkou, and Zoe Gingell.

Since 2015 we have done a number of interviews with artists working around maternal themes, presented our work at numerous conferences including: 'Motherhood and Creative Practice: Maternal Structures in Creative Work' at South Bank University in London, 'Theorizing Motherhood in Academia' at Museum of Motherhood, Manhattan College, New York, 'Mothernists II: Who Cares for the 21st Century?' at the Royal Danish Academy of Fine Art and Astrid Noacks Atelier in Copenhagen and Maternal Attitude at the University of South Wales and MADE Gallery in Cardiff. We have also edited 'On the Maternal' for *Performance*

Research journal and curated *Live Art and Motherhood: A Study Room Guide on Live Art and the Maternal*, as part of the Live Art Development Agency collection. By naming these events and publications, we would like to extend our deepest thank you to all the organizers, artists, scholars, and contributors; without you, your ideas and our mutual exchanges, this book would not have been possible. You have inspired us and helped us grow in our thinking and scholarship.

There are so many to thank and we will not attempt an exhaustive list here; however, we do want to acknowledge a few specific artists, scholars, and practitioners: Amanda Coogan, Bobby Baker, Bryony Kimmings, Catriona James, Courtney Kessel, Deirdre Donoghue, Elena Marchevska, Elina Brotherus, Emily Steel, Eve Dent, Fern Smith, Grace Surman, Hannah Ballou, Hannah Buckley, Helena Walsh, Jessica Olah, Jodie Hawkes, Helen Sargeant, Lara Stevens, Lenka Clayton, Lisa Baraitser, Liz Clarke, Lizzie Philps, Lois Keidan, Luca Rutherford, Lucy Sexton, Lynn Lu, Maddy Costa, Marni Kotak, Megan Wynne, Nanna Lysholt Hansen, Nathalie Anguezomo Mba Bikoro, Patrick Fitzgerald, Paula McCloskey, Paula Varjack, Peggy Shaw, Rachel Epp Buller, Roberta Mock, Third Angel, Tracy Breathnach-Evans, Savitri D., and Quarantine.

Enormous gratitude to Julene Knox for her extraordinary proofreading, to Stuart Lee for his insightful comments, and Elaine Aston for her invaluable observations.

Final thanks to our grandmothers Betty, Ellen-Ruth, Jelena and Magdalena, our mothers Geraldine and Nela, and our children Lillian, Evelyn, Neal, Gabriel, Sid, and James.

Praise for *Maternal Performance*

"*'Motherhood is lived in the moment and in all of time' state Lena Šimić and Emily Underwood-Lee in their dazzling book on maternal performance that defies categorisation. Putting into conversation the complex histories of feminist theorising about motherhood, and an array of contemporary maternal performance, this extraordinary work is inventive, personal, strident, scholarly, political and profound in equal measure, and quietly moving in unexpected ways.*

Through an engagement with maternal loss, grief, embodiment, birth, maintenance and care, as they are performed, and perform us, Šimić and Underwood-Lee weave a deep maternal relational sensibility between theory and practice, and between one another, in a way that is truly generous and generative of new ways of thinking about maternal futures."

—Lisa Baraitser, *Professor of Psychosocial Theory, Department of Psychosocial Studies, Birkbeck, University of London, UK*

"*What a joy to read a text that so fully embodies the idea of maternal performance, not only through extensive scholarly inquiry but also through conversational, relational, and epistolary engagement between the authors. Lena Šimić and Emily Underwood-Lee offer an important model of feminist maternal scholarship alongside nuanced understandings of what maternal performance can entail.*

I found the format incredibly engaging, as the authors moved between scholarly voices and subjective maternal voices and even into epistolary exchange in the penultimate chapter. The shifts in voice helped me further engage in the performance works discussed. And I so appreciated the sudden shift to pandemic lockdown contexts in the maintenance chapter. A real maternal performance in action!"

—Rachel Epp Buller, *Associate Professor in Visual Arts and Design, Bethel College, US*

Contents

List of Figures

CHAPTER 1

Beginnings (1 Month)

Maternal Connections

A beginning is never really possible. We are confined by our history, our bodies, our socialization, and the choices we have made. This awareness of our contexts feels especially important to us when working within the field of the maternal. We come from mothers and produce mothers; the maternal is cyclical and interconnected.

Motherhood is lived in the moment and in all of time, connecting us and expanding us beyond ourselves. Motherhood is also only definable in relation to our other (be that other a child, our own mothers, our chosen family, our communities, or the more-than-human world that cares for us and for whom we may or may not care). The maternal precludes us from ever starting anew as if we were free subjects, and yet it is precisely in the idea of natality that we can seek our freedom as capacity to begin anew, as political theorist Hannah Arendt asserts: 'Because they are initium, newcomers and beginners by virtue of birth, men [*sic*] take initiative, are prompted into action' (1958, p. 177). While Arendt asserts that it is the capacity for beginning of the individual that is the primary condition of being human, it is mothers who are placed in a position to hold the space of those new beginnings, to initiate new beginners, while holding onto themselves too, in between the past, in terms of connectedness to the historic and the family lineage, and the new lives ahead. The maternal

L. Šimić and E. Underwood-Lee, *Maternal Performance*, Contemporary Performance InterActions,
https://doi.org/10.1007/978-3-030-80226-4_1

paradoxically engages us in between the idea of freedom, as capacity to begin anew, and interconnectedness and responsibility to the wider world, which we foreground in this opening. In *Mothers: An Essay on Love and Cruelty* (2018) Jacqueline Rose writes: 'You are born into the slipstream of your mother's unconscious – as a therapist once said to me' (pp. 109–110). We are interconnected through our mothers, and our mothers' mothers, and all the mothers that came before. Yet, as mothers, we bring forth new human beings, and marvel at their capacity for new beginnings, their own freedom. The mother figure brings together, in one moment and one body, all the new beginnings that preceded her and all those beginnings that will follow, collapsing time and relations together.

As artists and scholars, we have further lineage too—we are also a part of the larger body of work and context in relation to maternal performances and studies. We are therefore indebted to both our mothers as well as our feminist and maternal performance foremothers. The Performance and the Maternal research project,[1] from which this book emerges, has grown from our mutual desire to map and theorize multifaceted maternal performances, to pay tribute to the work of various performance practitioners who have tackled the subject, and to pay deep attention to their working methodologies and performance aesthetics. These include (in the order of discussion in the book): Helena Walsh, Emily Steel, Amanda Coogan, Fern Smith and Patrick Fitzgerald, Elina Brotherus, Hannah Ballou, Aleksandra Nikolajev-Jones, Quarantine, Marni Kotak, Third Angel, Tracy Breathnach-Evans, Lenka Clayton, Lizzie Philps, Grace Surman, Megan Wynne, Liz Clarke, Jessica Olah, Hannah Buckley, Courtney Kessel, Peggy Shaw, Nanna Lysholt Hansen, Lynn Lu, Paula Varjack, Catriona James, Maddy Costa, Luca Rutherford, and Bryony Kimmings. While discussing, theorizing, and analysing the working processes and performances of the aforementioned artists we reflexively engage with our own lived experience of mothering, performance making, and writing. We started this research project and our collective thinking on the maternal in 2015, but have had our own paths in maternal studies and feminist performance for over two decades.

Our Subjective Maternal Maps

***Lena**: Since my involvement in maternal studies and my work as an artist around maternal themes, from 2004 onwards, I have been struck by how often the main reference points for scholars working around art and the* *maternal are Mary Kelly and Bobby Baker, and in particular two works: Kelly's* Post-Partum Document *(1973–1979), a six-year exploration of the mother/child dyad, and* Drawing on a Mother's Experience *(1988), which was, in Baker's words, created 'in order to make sense of the first eight years of motherhood, before moving on'* (Baker and Barrett 2007, p. 47). *I am indebted to* Post-Partum Document, *which has inspired my arts practice during maternity leaves, and* Drawing on a Mother's Experience, *to which I have returned again and again, almost compulsively, in my pedagogical work with students, asking them to acknowledge and consider not themselves, but their mothers.*

Beyond Kelly and Baker, I want to return to the moment when I first saw M.O.M. Marks of Motherlands *(2007) by Helena Walsh at the 'Intimacy Across Digital and Visceral Performance' conference at Goldsmiths University, London. This was one of those moments when I was truly unsettled by the experience of viewing performance art, in this case by its maternal theme and its brutality on the body: the performer enacting brutality on her own maternal body. I was eager for this performance; I was at the time working on my own artwork* Contemplation Time *(2007–2008), which was about processing my maternity leave with my son Sid. I was delighted that there was a piece about motherhood at this conference, and moreover that it was tackling issues of national identity, the question of the 'motherland'. I have also always had quite a problematic relationship to my own homeland, the newly created country of Croatia, something I have explored in my video artworks, and which ended up being a part of* Sid Jonah Anderson by Lena Šimić, *a live art event in Carlisle in 2008. I didn't know Helena Walsh but as I was waiting to enter the George Wood Theatre where the piece was to be performed, I chatted away to my then partner saying how I would love to interview Walsh, and talk to her after the performance.*

We entered the darkness of the studio and we sat on the floor, I seem to remember. Walsh was stark naked as she entered the stage, which was full of plastic baby bottles and brittle brushes placed in an orderly manner. A video projection came on in the background, images of milking cows, of rural Ireland. I can't seem to remember if there were any images of the Troubles, but it was clear that this was a piece about war, devastation, failures of the body, of the motherland. Walsh was marching around the stage as a soldier, later on bandaging her breasts, filling her mouth with some gauze, sucking her fingers in the process of doing it, gagging even. At one point she placed one of the baby bottles next to her sex, inviting it to act as a dildo, an inadequate phallus. In the final act of the piece, she started cleaning herself with a brittle brush, pushing it into her vagina. She squatted on the floor, her legs wide open, and stuck the brush into herself, penetrating herself, cleaning herself. The brush was pulled out stained with blood. All throughout the piece I was unnerved. The final action unsettled me further. What is this? Motherhood? How can it be this bad, this violent? Is this what motherhood produces? Is this what this artist feels about becoming a mother? There were references in the piece about mastitis and her failure to breastfeed, interspersed with images of milking cows. All was so raw, so mechanical and brutal. Following the piece I could hardly speak. I quickly told my partner we better go, I wasn't going to speak to this artist, this was one of the most devastating and shocking pieces I had ever seen.

It was much later on that I was more able to process the performance, try to understand why such violence was necessary upon the body by the artist herself, in public moreover. After all, it is only in public where artwork has a capacity to become a part of discourse, of knowledge, of exposure of maternal realities and brutalities. Eventually, I became friends with Walsh and we have collaborated on a number of projects, supporting each other's work. M.O.M. Marks of Motherlands *toured to Art Workshop Lazareti in Dubrovnik, my hometown. This was an artistic exchange that I helped organize and for which I am glad. Unfortunately, I did not see the piece in my hometown on tour, but in some ways I have contributed to spreading a particular version of real maternal experience into the public sphere, exposing the ideal myth of motherhood internationally too.*

The shock of the maternal is such that the new mother is catapulted into the land of overwhelming love, pleasure and pain, jouissance, ambivalence, depression. M.O.M. Marks of Motherlands *did something to me, viscerally, through my body. It was a kind of shock, a break, an interruption which needed to happen in order for me to process the performance, and eventually decide to research its field in depth. The first task was to map a number of maternal performances which were lived maternal experiences made public. For that shock I am deeply grateful to Helena Walsh, her courage as well as the brutality of her maternal aesthetics. It was through the analysis of Walsh's work, my own* Sid Jonah Anderson by Lena Šimić *(2008) created during my maternity leave, and through Jess Dobkin's* The Lactation Station *(2006), which looked at the topic of breastfeeding in a much more humorous and communal manner, that I started formulating some thoughts around labour and violence in maternal performance works. I was seeking my own understanding and insertion into a maternal performance context.*

Emily: *I threw myself into maternal performance making as an instinctive response to having my first child in 2008. At that time, I found inspiration not within a maternal tradition but more in a feminist tradition of making autobiographical performance, and yet I could not see my new maternal self reflected within that tradition. To me, it seemed that the maternal and feminism were often at odds. The domestic seemed tame and unimportant; I felt that my desire to carry, birth, and raise a child was an obstacle to my professional and political actualization. All the performances I had thought about, watched, and admired were about the 'big' issues (for example Annie Sprinkle's engagement with sex positivism or Eddie Ladd's examination of gender). And then, shortly after the birth of my first daughter, Lena sent me a copy of Phyllis Chesler's* With Child (1998) *and my parameters immediately shifted. I was pleased to read a representation of maternal experience with which I could identify, different in the specifics of time, place, and culture, yet something that resonated with me and allowed me to negotiate my maternal identity in relation to another's opening up of the domestic space into the public realm. Andrea Liss'* Feminist Art and the Maternal *(2009) further introduced me to the work of many mother/artists and encouraged me to begin to examine how the world could be viewed through the lens of the maternal, to think and act 'm/otherwise'. Here I could find strength in my maternal subjectivity and 'unleash the maternal taboo'* (Liss 2009, p. xvi), *not as a means of promoting maternal experience as more profound, more feminine, or more feminist, but instead as a subjectivity that is important and worthy of consideration.*

Liss' deeply moving interlude in her book, during which she describes how her son 'coax[ed her] back to life' (p. 122) when she experienced breast cancer, was particularly pertinent as I was wrestling with my own breast cancer treatment at the time. The shock of motherhood and the shock of cancer coalesced and I suddenly became aware that my maternal life, my cancer, and my feminism were inextricably intertwined. With my consciousness raised (the allusion here to the consciousness raising of second wave feminism is very much deliberate) I remembered encounters I had had with the Magdalena Project's 'Mothers of Invention' (1995) years earlier and sought out reports about that event, which helped me realize I could be a feminist and speak about the maternal. I watched Jill Greenhalgh's The Threat of Silence *(2010) and was reminded of the cyclical, ongoing nature of maternal life and experience. I devoured the script of Peggy Shaw's*

To My Chagrin *(2003), realizing I could find my own maternal identity through performance practice and academic study.*

When I was diagnosed with cancer while pregnant, I began writing immediately; these writings, which took the form of letters to my unborn child, later became the basis for a performance, Patience *(2008). Jackie Stacey has written about the privilege of being an academic and being able to turn to one's own research skills in order to understand whatever crisis we might happen to be living through at that time* (1997, p. 3). *So too with performance, I turn to works by artists that I admire and to making my own practice in order to understand better the shock of motherhood. It is through making and thinking about artwork that I have been able to engage with that shock, this new state which overwhelms, delights, and destroys in equal measure. Now my children are older, I have moved beyond the new and yet it is still through performance that I seek to understand the maternal.*

In June 2015 we found ourselves resting on the chairs in a classroom, after a series of papers at the 'Motherhood and Creative Practice: Maternal Structures in Creative Work' international conference at South Bank University, organized by Elena Marchevska and Valerie Walkerdine. It was getting towards the end of the second day, and we were tired. We started discussing the overall conference—its massiveness, its ambition, its creativity, all somehow impossible to contain. We felt slightly alone in our performance studies discipline—it seemed the work was so much further ahead in other fields. Our conversation evolved along these lines: *I'd love to know more about performance and motherhood. Could we call that 'maternal performance'? Yes, how about thinking about 'maternal performance' specifically? Let's do that, try to understand the maternal in relation to the performance artform. Okay.*

Two years later, in 2017, we published our *Manifesto for Maternal Performance (Art) 2016!*, which followed Mierle Laderman Ukeles' *Manifesto for Maintenance Art 1969!* and its two-part structure (Šimić and Underwood-Lee, pp. 131–139). Ukeles has, alongside Kelly, Baker, Greenhalgh, Shaw, and Chesler, been one of the major influences for our project. The lines such as 'The sourball of every revolution: after the revolution, who's going to pick up the garbage on Monday morning?' and 'Maintenance is a drag; it takes all the fucking time (lit.)' became etched into our consciousness. We found resonance in Ukeles' proclamations:

> I am an artist. I am a woman. I am a wife.
> I am a mother. (Random order).
> I do a hell of a lot of washing, cleaning, cooking,
> renewing, supporting, preserving, etc. Also,
> (up to now separately) I 'do' Art.
> Now, I will simply do these maintenance everyday things,
> and flush them up to consciousness, exhibit them, as Art. (Ukeles 1969)

This was daily life as art, moreover it was performance. We divided our *Manifesto for Maternal Performance (Art) 2016!* into IDEAS and MATERNAL PERFORMANCE JOURNAL. All our IDEAS emerged from the JOURNAL, the messiness of the daily. Our *Manifesto* was born out of our mothering practices and, importantly, collaboration. We were always writing in relation to one another. The process of writing and living the *Manifesto* very much related to our daily experience of mothering, which is made obvious through the JOURNAL section of the work, and our personal histories of performance making.[2] In the following pages of this book, we turn our eyes towards other performance makers and their maternal practices, while, in our position as scholars, attempting not to lose sight of our own methodology as mother/artists.

Contexts and Questions

> But what then is 'the maternal'?
> Is it a physical thing?
> Is it the ability of some bodies to carry life and give birth?
> Is it a concept connecting various notions to each other?
> Is it a metaphor for something else?
> For me the maternal includes all of these, but perhaps most of all it functions as a system of seeing, thinking, and relating to the world. A system which completely breaks away from the binaries of the feminine/masculine oppositions through the maternal body's pivotal role to natality and otherness.
>
> (Donoghue and McCloskey 2013)

The maternal is contested both as a term and a condition, definitions and arguments abound. Previously we have stated 'For us, motherhood refers to the lived experience of mothering regardless of our route to it, whereas the maternal refers to the study of and representations of motherhood'

(Šimić and Underwood-Lee 2016, p. 3). We stand by this definition as a central tenet in our consideration of the maternal in performance. In this first chapter we bring together some of the arguments, methodologies, and practices that are brought forth by a consideration of maternal performance. We predominantly examine work by mother/artists working within the medium of performance. We also engage with the work of childfree practitioners who have addressed maternal themes or employed what we have come to name maternal methods in their work. We define maternal methods and approaches as artistic endeavours that are primarily concerned with a relation to an other and are directed towards that other with careful intent. In our *Manifesto for Maternal Performance (Art) 2016!* (Šimić and Underwood-Lee 2017b) we set out our IDEAS, or propositions. One of them reads: 'Day 2. Maternal performance relies on the other' (p. 131). We also state: 'Day 27a. Maternal performance others' (p. 132). It might be arguable that all performance is inevitably relational, but what is particular about a maternal method is that inclination towards the other. Maternal comes into being, it exists, because of its potential to be in relation. We are also keen to foreground feminist approaches and relations.

We employ the term 'mother/artists' to describe diverse practitioners, a phraseology employed by Eti Wade (2016), Andrea Liss (2009), and many of the artists in this book. The term has gathered strength through its usage in various exhibitions, and social media networks.[3] The term 'mother/artists' functions as an empowerment of a statement as well as a strategic outcry, similar to the way in which Ukeles proclaimed her own position as an artist, woman, wife, mother. In many of the cases we explore, the term 'wife' is redundant, but woman, mother, and artist firmly stand. Moreover, it is the term 'mother' that we have come to interrogate, rather than the still contested term 'woman'. In *Women in Performance: Repurposing Failure* (2020) Sarah Gorman writes about a number of women performance practitioners who, despite working with postmodern strategies in performance making, and creating work in contemporary times, occupy strategically defined subject positions and embrace identity politics (Gorman 2020, p. 4). In discussing the examples of women's contemporary performances, Gorman follows on from the feminist tradition of Luce Irigaray and Rosi Braidotti and their assertion of sexual difference as ontological, which then becomes a political strategy in marking one's particular lived experience as well as activist collective endeavours (p. 11). Despite the ever-present fear of returning women to essentialism, Gorman identifies the potential for agency that is offered by an understanding of bodily difference:

> However, the artists I discuss are liberated by a departure from the pressure to ascribe to particular feminist or gender theorists and take to the stage in order to actively claim a position of agency. They can be seen to adopt an essentialist belief in ontological difference as political strategy and as a result their position is in keeping with that of Irigaray and Braidotti. The artists detail interlocking experiences of oppression, celebrate their cause and unapologetically rekindle an agenda for identity politics. (p. 11)

As part of our research for this book we interviewed a number of artists and our starting point was always to ask if they identified with the term 'mother/artist'. This kind of question is leading, and can be seen as setting a path towards a similar kind of return to identity politics, a reaffirmation of one's position either as an artist, as a mother, or as both. The responses are varied and revealing. Some of the artists we interviewed stated a strong affiliation with the term and self-identified as mother/artists, for example Aleksandra Nikolajev-Jones describes herself as a 'maternal artist' (Nikolajev-Jones with Underwood-Lee 2020), while other artists rejected the label as pigeonholing their work. Nathalie Anguezomo Mba Bikoro explained:

> I ... feel that we should not tokenise the term [mother/artists] as something exclusive. Just as we are not exclusively BIPOC [Black, Indigenous, and people of colour] artists but we choose to weave through language, queering that which identifies our current positionalities. We are moving beings, we are artists. The maternal experience is a means for me which is about empowering my existence, enhancing my spiritual practice and elastifying understandings of resistance, strength and allyship. (Anguezomo Mba Bikoro with Šimić and Underwood-Lee 2020, p. 2)

The complexity in adopting the term 'mother/artist' is further explored by Amanda Coogan:

> It is a little tricky because there are lots of layers to identity, as well as layers to being an artist. So, certainly, inspiration for a piece has to come from what I know and where I am. I want to say, crisis, but it is actually also the crises of becoming a mother.

> Even from the very early days when you are totally shocked, when your body is all over the place, your hormones are all over the place, and you're thinking in a different way… all of these things become really important to the creation and making of a piece of work. Then there is another level, which is the professional level. I'd be a little wary of saying, 'No I can't do that exhibition because I am needed at home with my family.' My prime focus is to negotiate, from the start, in a different way. Being a mother/artist is absolutely like the bricks and mortar, the foundations of my work. (Coogan with Šimić 2017, p. 2)

Coogan here highlights the complex intertwining of biology, domestic labour, the politics and the pragmatics of showing work in the public domain, and the performance of a maternal identity, but overall she comes back to an approach that is informed by a desire to do things differently, to imagine a maternal method and inspiration that move away from the patriarchal and inform every aspect of our life and work. This approach might be viewed as a feminist relation—feminist because it rejects the patriarchal, and relational as it involves negotiating a different way of working in and with her community, which in turn will lay the path for other artists to have a more ethical, relational, feminist encounter. Coogan uses the word 'negotiation' when describing her focus, a different way of approaching her performance making. It is this maternal approach that has informed the selections we have made within this book. Furthermore, the maternal negotiating position, in both Coogan's and Anguezomo Mba Bikoro's cases in the context of their arts making practices, makes explicit a need for feminist relations, those which thrive on the sense of justice and equality as well as the recognition of our differing material conditions.

How is it that we approach the term 'mother' or 'mother/artists'? We hope to be able to work through these complex terms by addressing the doing, the making, the creating, and the active process of being a mother, or mother/artist, rather than a fixed biological position. Alison Stone usefully reinterprets Irigaray's conception of sexual difference to argue that any progressive philosophy of gender must incorporate a sexed dualism but must also recognize that all bodies are never confined to a singular identity or position. Drawing from this proposition, and addressing Judith Butler's well-known critiques of Irigaray, Stone proposes 'an ontology of bodily multiplicity' (2006, p. 87). Such an ontology would acknowledge biological experience and gendered categories of sex, while not limiting or confining those categories (p. 122).

While we cannot get away from the biological acts of pregnancy and birth, which both hold an important personal and political dimension in our understanding of identity, we want to understand mothering as an activity that is inclusive and can take up many different forms. Mothering is a site of never-ending political and personal production. While it is fluid and changing over time, generations and geographies, its discourse must be informed by situatedness in a specific time and place, since mothering is undertaken by specific bodies, marked by certain experience and contexts.

As well as an approach to doing, maternal works can be those that consider the situations around the act of carrying a child in utero, raising children, caring for our others, or being cared for. We consider works from a range of perspectives: those who identify as mothers, those who choose not to mother, those unable to mother, and those who are mothered. A useful example of the power of performance to open not just a generalized political consideration of the maternal, but also a specific and highly charged debate with direct reference to legal frameworks, can be found in *19 Weeks* by Emily Steel. *19 Weeks* (2017) is a play about the author's decision to terminate her pregnancy. The show website describes Steel's decision thus: 'In 2016, playwright Emily Steel had a termination after her baby was diagnosed with Down Syndrome' (*19 Weeks*, n.d.). *19 Weeks* was originally produced as a live performance that premiered at the Adelaide Fringe in Australia in 2017 and was subsequently produced as a radio play by BBC Wales and broadcast on Radio 4. In *19 Weeks* Steel shares a story that is hugely under-represented within the field of maternal performance. Her play invites us to have compassionate understanding for a decision that is portrayed within the play as at once difficult and easy, filled with sadness but not regret, emotional and clear-headed. Steel talks in the play of her certainty about wanting to get pregnant and then of her clarity that this particular pregnancy, with these particular test results, could not continue. Abortion is still a loaded topic and the moral and legal frameworks are constantly in debate. The year of 2017 marked the fiftieth anniversary of the UK Abortion Act 1967 and there have been frequent debates in Parliament and public since the commencement of the act in order to attempt to refine it and to open up or to limit bodily autonomy. A cursory glance at the US media will show that US abortion law was an even hotter topic under the Trump administration, with all too frequent attacks on state-funded clinics 'promoting' abortion. It is also worth noting here that abortion is still illegal in the UK after twelve weeks and it is only 'exceptions' that the various legal frameworks permit, although in practice these exceptions are now applicable in almost all pregnancies within Northern Ireland, England, Wales, and Scotland up to twenty-four weeks of pregnancy. When set against this background, *19 Weeks* can be seen as a bold and important political work that enables us to reflect on the power of art and performance to make a space where we can consider some of the most complex and incendiary aspects of the maternal. *19 Weeks* humanizes abortion—it makes it not a political issue to be debated but a real-life event for one woman and her family, full of emotion and complexity. The decision to terminate a pregnancy here is difficult but necessary and we, as listeners, are asked to empathize with the central protagonist. We use 'maternal performance' to bring to light the stories of particular artists working through their own maternal experience. Thus, within this book we consider works that are either maternal in their approach or aesthetics, deal with maternal themes within their content, or are made by self-identified mother/artists, and many of the works we consider are maternal in all of these ways in a complex intermingling of structure, approach, identity, and themes.

We choose to use the term 'maternal' over 'parental' deliberately. There is a significant pull towards the term 'parental' in order to escape certain essentializing arguments that conflate mothering and the responsibility for care with women, and women with those that have the capacity to bear children; however, we believe that 'parental' obfuscates the significant contemporary and historic gendered labour that has been done by mothers over the centuries as well as makes invisible the birthing body of the mother. We do not believe that mothering is dependent on a capacity to birth or that all those who birth are women, and a driving force in our research for this book has been to move from this essentialized position to understanding mothering and the maternal as thought and action, rather than primarily through the lens of biology. Nonetheless, we acknowledge that the majority of mothering work has been and is still done by women, as Simon Kelly and Adele Senior point out (2020, p. 3). Kelly and Senior argue for the use of 'parental' as a means of marking the intersection between the act of mothering, the ecological, and the shared labour within a family unit or community. They argue for a parental ethics that is in direct opposition to neo-liberal economies of labour, a position with which we have much sympathy; however, our project here is to understand the specificity of maternal performance and feminist relations. Within this complex negotiation between recognizing the ontology of birthing and mothering bodies, including the gendered division of caring labour, and seeking to de-essentialize mothering, we use 'maternal' much as we use 'feminist'—recognizing that you do not have to have a uterus to be maternal and you do not have to be a woman to be a feminist.

The crux of our project lies in ethics, in the way we relate to one another, which is imbued with feminist urges towards equality, acceptance of difference and reciprocity. It is therefore paramount that we highlight not only examples of 'maternal performance' but also 'feminist relations'. Those take centre stage in the public maternal performances that we discuss in this book, as well as artistic methodologies in making work. Since maternal performance is always about relations, we seek to understand those as primarily feminist, meaning cognizant of different positions of power between us, striving to be just and equal while at the same time transparent and respectful about our differences. Hence, we highlight in our title for this book both maternal performance and the feminist relation it engenders.

The main research aim of this project is to map and theorize some of the current performance practice and studies activity around the maternal. Our choices are, of course, subjective. Our responses are also subjective. We have considered the work that we have been drawn to or that has been brought into our field of vision since 2015, through the maternal discussions that have taken place in the research for this book or that we have been made aware of because it has gained currency within conversations about feminist maternal art within the informal and formal networks of which we are members. We are not aiming for this publication to be an exhaustive catalogue of the history of maternal performance; instead, we have chosen work that engages with particularly knotty problems, intriguing conceptions, or challenges our own ideas around maternal performance. Our thinking about the maternal is in the context of a proliferation of mother/artist exhibitions, networks, and performances internationally, many of which are featured in this book, as well as our own positions as mother/artists/scholars. We recognize that our own context and background still shape the work we chose to explore here and the lens through which we view it. The artists we write about come from an international context and predominantly the territories of Northern Europe and the USA. The limits of our own geographical location and language barriers have informed our choices about the work we have engaged with. Many of the artists are migrants, which might reflect our own position (Lena is a migrant to the UK, a country she was not born into, and Emily is English-born and living in the devolved, bilingual nation of Wales). We have tried to make sure we write about artists who are living regionally as well as in capital cities. We note that the majority of artists we write about in this book are white, cis-gendered, academically and economically privileged, and do not present as disabled. We propose that an examination of the diversity of maternal performance is an area that must be given more attention in future research, something we have tentatively begun across our Performance and the Maternal project, particularly through the inclusion of more artists of colour in the curated section of our website for this research project, which includes interviews as well as documentation of workshops, fora, and online performances.

We acknowledge that there is a gap in our engagement with maternal performances made by mother/artists who belong to the global majority. In her examination of the priorities for feminist action, *feminist theory: from margin to center*, originally published in 1984, bell hooks notes that motherhood has not historically been top of the list of problems that black women have to contend with:

> Had black women voiced their views on motherhood, it would not have been named a serious obstacle to our freedom as women. Racism, lack of jobs, lack of skills or education, and a number of other issues would have been at the top of the list – but not motherhood. (2015, p. 133)

The reasons identified by hooks may contribute to the disproportionate whiteness of maternal art, with global majority artists engaging with more pressing concerns before having the luxury of considering their maternal relations, or, as hooks also identifies, it may be that motherhood is romanticized by white women. Hooks highlights that black thinkers and artists who are dealing with a legacy of colonial essentialism and racism reject the un-nuanced celebration of the maternal (p. 136). It is also possible that artists of colour may be making maternal performance work and we may just have failed to see it, as have so many white scholars, programmers, and others who have ignored or not paid attention to the work of artists from beyond their own sphere of reference or canon. As Robin DiAngelo has pointed out, defensiveness is often a mark of 'white fragility' and can be seen as being apologist for our own racism (2011, p. 57). We must therefore not attempt to defend our position but to ask ourselves how we perpetuate the whiteness of maternal art, and offer that we will continue to try to do better. One of the crucial questions that has come up through our organization of a series of online maternal fora is yet again that of whether the maternal art context is too white. We had been aware of whiteness in maternal performance and art since working on our *Live Art and Motherhood: A Study Room Guide on Live Art and the Maternal* for the Live Art Development Agency (Šimić and Underwood-Lee 2016), and we are grateful to Jess Dobkin for frankly raising the issue once again, in her email correspondence with us in connection to us organizing an online Maternal Performance (Artist Forum) in October 2020. Furthermore, we are aware that in-depth questions ought to be asked in terms of intersectionality, some of which we have started unpacking through our forum 'Migration and (Maternal) Citizenship' in October 2020 (Performance and the Maternal, n.d.). While it is evident that mothers are as diverse as the human population, different kinds of questions arise around the identity of mother/artists and their representations and aesthetics: Who are they? Whose voices are privileged in the art world and the academy? What barriers exist? What structures need to be dismantled and reimagined? How are we contributing to a process of canonization and repeating a particular perspective on who mother/artists are?

The overarching research drive for this book has been to try to better understand some of the complex and diverse experiences of mothering, mothers, and the maternal that are presented to us in performance as maternal approaches and performance aesthetics. We are driven to explore such aesthetics. Following on from this research aim, a number of research questions emerged, including: What is specific about maternal performance, as opposed to other artforms? What processes, strategies, and methodologies are used by performance practitioners and mother/artists working with maternal themes? What, if any, are distinct maternal performance aesthetics? What is the history of the relationship between motherhood and feminism? How is the maternal life/art dyad informed by both performance practice and theory? How is maternal subjectivity framed in both representations of motherhood and of being mothered? What can a maternal sense of subjectivity offer in performance encounters? How are the maternal and ecology connected? What are our maternal futures? How is maternal art able to contribute to change in the material and social conditions in which women mother? We do not attempt to provide definitive answers to our questions but instead aim to open up areas for discussion and engagement. We explore how other artists and scholars have approached these areas with genuine curiosity. Maternal subjectivity must continuously reinvent itself; the ongoing, unending, and relentless nature of the maternal means a conclusion is always contingent.

Feminism and the Maternal

In naming the book *Maternal Performance: Feminist Relations* we wanted to underline and probe the theoretical and practical tensions between motherhood and feminism which Simone de Beauvoir outlined in *The Second Sex* (1988) back in 1949, and which Judith Butler usefully queers in her reading of de Beauvoir (1986, p. 42). Despite Butler's now decades-old challenge to the compulsory heteronormativity as reinforced in certain constructions of mothering and the nuclear family, the view that a woman's sense of freedom and autonomy is at stake from the moment she enters a biological cycle of reproduction and becomes a mother still remains, and is something we have both felt acutely. One of the prevailing sensations upon becoming a mother is a sudden lack of independence. This rings true in the 2020s as much as in the 1950s. Throughout this book, we argue that feminist maternal performance is a vehicle through which mother/artists, as well as artists working around maternal themes, seek to readdress their agency, those of their mothers and carers, those that they care for, and possibly even reaffirm freedom and autonomy in the acts of performance and art making. Maternal performance, in any case, allows for a reassessment of relations with others, which offers a possibility to recreate and form those in a feminist manner. We are eager to attend to pressing maternal matters through feminist approaches in performance making.

Our scholarly response to this desire to unite performance studies and feminist thought is to employ a multiplicity of theoretical perspectives and to bring together the fields of feminist philosophy, performance studies and maternal studies (Cavarero 2000, 2011; Haraway 2016; Howie 2010; Arendt 1958; Young 2005 [1990], 1997; Tyler 2013; Rose 2018; Benjamin 1988, 1998; Kristeva 1980, 1981, 1984, 1985; Baraitser 2009, 2017; Irigaray 1981; Irigaray et al. 2008; Simone de Beauvoir 1988 [1949]).[4] This connection of feminism and motherhood can be traced from Adrienne Rich's seminal work *Of Woman Born* (1988 [1976]), which distinguishes between motherhood as institution and mothering as experience, through to the more recent work of Bracha L. Ettinger (*The Matrixial Borderspace*, 2006), Lisa Baraitser (*Maternal Encounters: Ethics of Interruption*, 2009), Andrea Liss (*Feminist Art and the Maternal*, 2009), Alison Stone (*Feminism, Psychoanalysis and Maternal Subjectivity*, 2012), and Jacqueline Rose (*Mothers: An Essay on Love and Cruelty*, 2018). Amber E. Kinser in *Motherhood and Feminism* (2010) usefully charts the evolution of feminist thinking in relation to motherhood. She notes that feminism has had a long and complex history in terms of the relationships between feminist thought and motherhood, and highlights that feminism cannot be seen as a movement that has one cohesive perspective on motherhood, with feminist thinkers occupying a multiplicity of positions in regard of the maternal. Kinser writes: 'There has been no single, unified monolithic response coming from feminism about motherhood, or anything else for that matter' (p. 2). What she does propose is that feminist thinkers are united in relation to motherhood by their concern with the 'empowering' or 'oppressive' nature of motherhood in relation to power and agency (p. 2). Similarly, in the editorial of the first edition of the *Studies in the Maternal* journal, Lisa Baraitser and Sigal Spigel note:

> There is no doubt that motherhood has remained a problematic issue for feminism and feminists. Whether viewed as embodied practice, theoretical construct or social relation, the maternal challenges hard-won feminist notions of autonomy whilst at the same time serving as the nodal point [for challenging and reworking feminist debates]. (2009, p. 1)

In the more recent tenth-anniversary edition Baraitser and Spigel reflect on the decade of the exploration of the maternal. In particular, they examine the move that they note over those ten years from the maternal as a matter to be examined in terms of the social positioning and construction of the mother, to their current call for a reinvestigation of the structural inequalities that come to play in the maternal, particularly as highlighted by the global understanding of care that has developed in relation to the COVID-19 pandemic and the Black Lives Matter movement (2020, p. 2). They envisage maternal studies taking 'a reflexive turn to the politics of Afrofuturism' as well as re-evaluating the notion of 'dependency as structural to the human subject' (p. 6).

Performance Studies and the Maternal

We realized that in spite of this theoretical activity in terms of maternal and feminist studies, the theorization of maternal artforms, and performance in particular, is still lacking in the field of performance studies (which is not the case within disciplines such as sociology, cultural studies, philosophy, feminist studies, visual arts, and psychology).[5] Previous studies have been carried out in relation to the maternal in fine art practice including *Feminist Art and the Maternal* (2009) by Andrea Liss and *Maternal Bodies in the Visual Arts* (2014) by Rosemary Betterton. We are indebted to Liss for her clear cataloguing of the history of maternal art. Particularly helpful for our project in this book is Liss' insightful analysis of the durational, manual, and bodily elements that occur in so much maternal art, which she notes evokes 'highly skilled and time and labor intensive work performed by mothers' (2009, p. 5). Motherhood has also been examined in relation to playwriting by Jozefina Komporaly (*Staging Motherhood: British Women Playwrights, 1956 to the Present* [2006]).[6] It is also important to mention here edited collections including *The M Word: Real Mothers in Contemporary Art* (2011) by Myrel Chernick and Jennie Klein, and *Reconciling Art and Mothering* (2012) by Rachel Epp Buller, which both deal with the maternal in the visual arts. *Performing Motherhood: Artistic, Activist, and Everyday Enactments* (2014) by Amber E. Kinser, Kryn Freehling-Burton, and Terri Hawkes, as well as *The Maternal in Creative Work: Intergenerational Discussions on Motherhood and Art* (2020) by Elena Marchevska and Valerie Walkerdine and *Inappropriate Bodies: Art, Design, and Maternity* (2019) by Rachel Epp Buller and Charles Reeve deal with the artistic and social dimensions of the maternal. Our study here is carried out in relation to the fields of performance studies and live art.

In this book, *Maternal Performance: Feminist Relations*, we move away from the scripted theatrical text as the locus of meaning. Our focus of study is performance art and live art. Although both performance art and live art are performed mediums often staged within theatre settings, they are perhaps more akin to the visual arts than to the theatrical text and many of the practitioners that we have considered within this study are more often located within a fine art tradition (for example Elina Brotherus, Marni Kotak, and Lenka Clayton among others). The laborious, durational practice of maternal art is perhaps even more acute in performance works, where the artwork can only exist as the performer offers their body to the audience as the site of meaning in a relational encounter between at least one audience member and one performer.

Our aim in this book is to chart and theorize the multifaceted outputs of artists working in the fields of live art and contemporary performance. Throughout this book we will argue that these disciplines, which focus on the body of the creator in a (mostly) live encounter with an audience, enable us to explore the embodied and bodily experience of the maternal, which is dependent on the one in a maternal role making actions directed towards another.[7] Live art is notoriously resistant to definition, indeed many assert that the strength of live art is that the form is constantly reinventing itself and evolving and thus is best defined as an attitude to doing or approach. Dominic Johnson extends this resistance to definition stating that performance art is an 'anti-medium' (2015, p. 1) or 'the archetypal anti-form' (2015, p. 5). The Live Art Development Agency assert:

> The term Live Art is not a description of an artform or discipline, but a cultural strategy to include experimental processes and experiential practices that might otherwise be excluded from established curatorial, cultural and critical frameworks. Live Art is a framing device for a catalogue of approaches to the possibilities of liveness by artists who chose to work across, in between, and at the edges of more traditional artistic forms. (Live Art Development Agency, n.d.)

Live art focusses on an approach to practice rather than being a limiting or rigid formal concern, much akin to the 'maternal approach' we have used when defining maternal performance. The work we have included in this book takes a maternal approach, but we have not been as open in our choices as the definition offered by the Live Art Development Agency invites. We have limited ourselves to considering work that falls broadly within the discipline of performance and which privileges the body of the artist making real actions in a specific time and place as the site of meaning. Johnson argues that live artists take radical approaches in utilizing their bodies and lives within their artworks:

> Performance artists have, variously: remodelled their bodies, through surgery, body modification or anomalous daily practices; become polymaths, folding every practice of their life into the continuous endeavour of artistic becoming; extended the duration of performance actions well

> beyond conventional limits, to last many months, or years; or found other means to expose the interior workings of their creative, imaginative, emotional, sexual or medical lives. (2015, p. 1)

When we read this quote by Johnson, we are struck by the affinities with both maternal art and the daily lived experience of mothering—mother/artists' bodies are 'remodelled' through pregnancy, birth, and the daily physical activities of care; our maternal lives overspill boundaries and permeate all that we do as we perform motherhood in the public domain and mine our maternal life for our art making; the 'extended duration' of the life-long activities of caring, and our 'creative, imaginative, emotional, sexual … medical' maternal lives are exposed in our performance practices. Mother/artists' maternal bodies are employed as a transgressive site of meaning, allowing a renegotiation of what it is to mother and what is a maternal act. The leaking breasts, bloody uterus, or other similarly oozing maternal bodies of some mother/artists, and the negotiation of shit, blood, and pus that is so often a daily part of caring for a dependent other, offer us bodies and actions that are as radical as the most cutting-edge performance art when placed in the public domain for consideration as the site of meaning.

The question of what is and should be public and the politics of care are brought to the fore when the maternal moves out of the home and into the public performance space. This move into performance allows us to reframe motherhood, not as a private action confined to the home but as a more complex collapsing of the immanent and transcendent in one moment. Simone de Beauvoir provides a robust critique of motherhood in *The Second Sex* (1988). De Beauvoir argues that motherhood is a site of women's oppression and a 'misfortune to have been biologically destined for the repetition of Life, when even in her own view Life does not carry within itself its reasons for being, reasons that are more important than the life itself' (p. 96). According to de Beauvoir, women cannot affirm their existence through their reproductive role as they are confined to the private, domestic sphere, the one of immanence in de Beauvoir's understanding, rather than public life and transcendence. Yet, woman still longs for transcendence. De Beauvoir writes: 'For she, too, is an existent, she feels the urge to surpass, and her project is not mere repetition but transcendence towards a different future' (p. 96). We would suggest that 'the kingdom of life, of immanence' (p. 97) as de Beauvoir calls it, might be just the right place to be. We perform our domestic and maternal actions in order to make them enduring, worthwhile, and open for discussion and debate.

We have argued previously that performance is particularly well placed to explore the maternal due to synergies regarding performance's uniquely durational, embodied, and relational qualities (Šimić and Underwood-Lee 2017a, p. 3). Maternal performance both within daily life and within our artworks must take place over an extended period of time, as we will explore more in our chapter Maintenance, influenced by Lisa Baraitser's analysis of maternal time as 'time that pools' (2017). Maternal performance is predicated on the body of the mother, who must perform the actions of the artwork, carry out the daily labour of child-rearing and often grow new life in her uterus, and birth the new subject into the world. Moreover, as we have outlined above, maternal performance is always in relation to an other, be that the other who we mother or are mothered by or the other of the audience. To this we would also add that maternal performance creates a space of community where audience members are not only in relation to a performer but also to one another. Further, maternal performance mirrors maternal life in its ephemerality. Peggy Phelan's oft-cited work *Unmarked* (2003) argued that performance, by its very nature, disappears, to live on only in the minds of the people who were present in that encounter at that time. Performance documentation exists but always misses something of the actual event. So it is with the maternal—the baby that was mothered disappears as the child grows, the actions we performed are equally fleeting and soon become only apparent in our memories and in the growing child, who stands as a testament that we have kept another alive.

The performance or live art work offers us a chance to consider the maternal in a form that both mirrors our maternal relations and offers a chance for those relations to be critiqued, made strange, or reimagined. Performance and live art are public and relational, the majority of artistic practices work through performers' encounters with one another and audiences. Moreover, performance as a discipline offers us the chance to both reflect how things are and to consider how we might want them to be, or as Richard Schechner has repeatedly asserted, performance offers us the space to consider the broad aspects of doing, thinking, history, contemporary politics, and action (2013, p. 7). The attitude of experimentation and innovation that is central to live art offers us a place to debate and challenge our maternal experience in an artform that uniquely parallels the embodied, oozing, transgressive maternal body. We see examples of this mirroring of form and content again and again in the maternal performance that we have examined in this book, for example in Tracy Breathnach-Evans' birthing of a new experience in *Cord*, which we explore in our Birth chapter, in Lenka Clayton's pushing of maternal limits as her child exits the frame of the camera, as discussed in our Aftermath chapter, or in Lynn Lu's relational, caring encounters and Nanna Lysholt Hansen's making compost of the audience, which we explore in our Futures chapter.

At the 'Mothernists II: Who Cares for the 21st Century?' international symposium at the Royal Danish Academy of Fine Art and Astrid Noacks Atelier in Copenhagen in 2017 we asked participants, a self-selected group of women with an interest in art and the maternal, maternal processes, and ethics—what they saw as the alliances between performance and the maternal. We already had a strong sense that the maternal and performance both engage with risk, duration, a deeply embodied practice, and a relationality with an other, but a number of other complementary areas were raised, such as: a lack of predictability, interruption as a generative space, the mess of the daily, embracing fear, revealing the emotional, foregrounding exhaustion, collaboration, body-horror, excess, and the never-ending. This could easily be read as a description of either maternal practice or contemporary performance practice. These are the words we hear again and again—it seems to us that what the most avant-garde performance practitioners bring to the space, mothers have always lived. In making these personal experiences explicit in maternal performance, the artists we feature in this book present us with a place where we can see ourselves as both mothers and artists and exhale with a deep sigh at the relief of recognition and identification.

The oozing, transgressive maternal body is not only portrayed but embodied in Amanda Coogan's durational performance piece *Yellow* (2008), which was the first piece the artist developed following the birth of her son, emerged from the highly demanding laborious task-driven domestic sphere, and got transformed into an intense aesthetic experience. In the artist's own words, the piece 'oozes' from the birthing body and carries that body into the highly structured formal space of the gallery. The private is aestheticized and made public. The audience is subjected to a durational encounter with the 'oozing body'. While the artist develops her own personal aesthetic form, namely through the format of a heightened time-based performance, what rings true is the affirmation of domestic labour, a kind of repetitive, endless, relentless, task-driven, sense of the world. In her article 'Not Just "A Life Within the Home": Maternal labour, art work and performance action in the Irish intimate public sphere' EL Putnam contests de Beauvoir's assertion that 'women's labour produces nothing' and acknowledges that 'Coogan draws from women's labour to produce performance art – an aesthetic encounter that constitutes something' (2017, p. 66). Film works by Grace Surman and Megan Wynne, which we explore in our Aftermath chapter, invite us into the artists' homes as they play with their children. The action of entertaining the child collides with the making of art in these works. Both Surman's *I Love My Baby and My Baby Loves Me* (2010) and Wynne's *Affirmation (I Am A Professional Artist)* (2018) are made in the artists' kitchens using the objects they find around their home. Here the private home as well as private maternal activity is made public and we are offered an invitation to view the daily, ongoing, unrelenting yet joyful toil of maternal life. As a transformation from everyday life to an aesthetic experience, maternal performance offers us something new, something affirmative and critical; it asks us to reinvent ourselves as mothers, scholars, and artists and to consider our maternal labour a worthy subject for art.

Our desire to write about performance and the maternal is personally driven; we find ourselves as mothers working within performance studies striving towards a better understanding of ourselves, our communities that are forged through experience, and our representations. Maternal activity is necessarily as old as humanity—the business of mothering and thinking about the maternal is not new and yet each generation of mothers continually reinvents the how and why of both the way we mother/are mothered and the way we think about the maternal as if for the first time. We make representations of these experiences in performance, standing on the shoulders of our feminist mothers, developing representations and articulations of maternal experience, and drawing on traditions, and yet also reinventing anew. In this book we explore the work of artists who choose to make performances about their maternal relationships and experiences through various stages of mothering as represented in performance.

Maternal Methodologies

There are as many maternal subjectivities as there are mothers; there are a variety of maternal representations and each mother/artist working from her own circumstances and situation develops her very own aesthetics. However, we are keen to pull these maternal performance worlds together, to learn from them and better understand our socio-political frames as mothers in the world. Imogen Tyler asks us to consider the collective thinking invoked by a maternal engagement with the world, what she terms 'a maternal commons', when she discusses political protests by mothers (2013, p. 107). Tyler further develops her arguments concerning 'maternal commons' in her article with Lisa Baraitser where they state that recognition of what we share is 'a political act' (Tyler and Baraitser 2013, p. 23). Our attempt to engage with this 'maternal commons' is foregrounded in our collaboration and our conversations with artists, scholars, and practitioners with an interest in the maternal within this book and through research gatherings centred around conversations. *Maternal Performance: Feminist Relations* has been researched through conversations with each other and a number of mother/artists—collaboration here is a deliberate feminist strategy in order to bring a multiplicity of voices to the fore. It is also a political act that recognizes that in these hyper neo-liberal times, where the individual is paramount, collaboration and collectivity, what Tyler names 'maternal commons' offer us a new way of engaging with the world that takes responsibility for and cares for the other.

Just as we define performance as maternal due to its approach, our tactical collaboration might be considered a maternal methodology of researching and writing, and is a method we have developed throughout our Performance and the Maternal research. Our chosen methodology aims to counter the traditional patriarchal construction of the sole author working in isolation; instead a maternal methodology attempts to converse and write in relation to the (often absent) other, acknowledging our status as humans, who are always in relation to one another. As we have already noted, the maternal is predicated on relating to and reliance on the other. Jessica Benjamin writes of the constant conflict between dependence and independence in the formation of the psyche of both child and mother: neither mother nor child can formulate a subjectivity in isolation and instead must constantly negotiate in response to their other, and it is this interdependence that we might experience as maternal love (Benjamin 1988). Further this sense of relationality can be extended out into all our social interactions and engagements with the world (Benjamin 1988). Our choice to work as collaborators and to foreground our collaboration is a deliberate attempt to be in relation. Following this methodology, this book highlights the collaborative nature of the co-authoring process as well as the shared experience of coming to an understanding through the conversing process with each other and our chosen mother/artists. A singular authorial voice is replaced by co-authorship; through the process of co-writing we have developed a 'maternal commons' which nevertheless allow for the specificity of our singular and mutual personal experiences. Through the writing our subjective voices are privileged, while at the same time we have attempted to outline recurring themes and approaches in maternal performance making and thinking. In practice, this involved a writing on, through, and over each other's words in order to reach a collaborative 'we' voice, which is mostly evident in Beginnings and New Beginnings, our tender conclusion. We send our formal writings back and forth, annotating and changing them along the way. This is, of course, an approach that all co-authors must adopt—the difference here is that we aspire to make visible this particular writing practice with, to, and for one another in our final book, often in the form of correspondence.

While this introductory chapter Beginnings is written in a more academic register, outlining our contexts and framing the writing theoretically, the following seven chapters carry our subjective maternal voices. They are written in relation, in correspondence with one another, with more poetic and journal-style registers, letters too, hopefully opening up maternal and feminist theories as well as responding to the chosen performances in our specific maternal voices, visceral and affective, and unique to us both. We remain committed to the idea of the specificity of mothering each individual child, and through that commitment we seek our own specific maternal writing voices, in relation to one another, through the everyday experience of mothering but also inspired and moved by the brave and courageous work of mother/artists on stage. In the seven chapters, which loosely follow a line of mothering stages—Loss, Pregnancy, Birth, Aftermath, Maintenance, Generations, and Futures—we foreground the relational process and expose the duality of our collaborating voices. Our book closes not with a conclusion but with an opening out of New Beginnings.

We come to this book as feminist women who have struggled both personally and professionally with our choices regarding if, when, and how to mother. We recognize that choice here is a privilege that is not afforded to all; many find themselves in positions where motherhood is forced upon them or denied to them, and many are unable to mother for a myriad of medical, social, legal, cultural, and economic reasons. We know we are lucky that the time, context, and bodies we were born into enable motherhood to be something about which we have the option to choose. We brought our own questions into conversation with artists also wrestling with these conflicting emotional and political demands on a daily basis. Feminist concerns around equality, the distribution of labour in childcare and the household, lived experience, as well as deeply material understandings of our embodied differences in contexts and circumstances, have guided us in this research. Conversations happened through research gatherings, artist interviews, and online fora, all of which allowed us to come to knowledge together, in relation to one another, as mother/artists supporting one another's struggles and finding mutual understanding.[8] We link these qualities to a maternal dyadic relationship as articulated by Benjamin (1988) or to Tyler's 'maternal commons' (2013) as we have discussed above. Thus, we propose this as a specifically maternal methodology of writing and researching. Beyond the relational, the maternal parallels with our research methods include: an embrace of the daily lived experience of the maternal and maternal time, an affirmation of the generative power of maternal experience as a space for reflection and research, an openness of process, and a performance of care, both for each other within our research and for our wider families and communities (with performance indicating both a public showing and an act of doing).

Our approach is not new; it draws on the long history of feminist writing, and particularly feminist letter writing, and on the famous rallying cry 'The Personal Is Political' issued by Carol Hanisch in 1970.[9] Rachel Epp Buller, in a chapter that we co-authored with her, briefly charted this history of letter writing as a form of feminist exchange (Epp Buller et al. 2019). Epp Buller has also addressed this subject elsewhere, for example in her rather beautiful exchange with Derek Owens (Epp Buller and Owens 2018). In the introduction to our own chapter with Epp Buller, she notes that epistolary forms of writing offer a space 'in which deep listening and genuine care offer radical possibilities for transforming academic writing and relationships' (2019, p. 332). We wonder what the radical potential of our chosen form of writing in this book might be.

Our work with Epp Buller was not the first time we have used a maternal methodology to co-author. For our *Manifesto for Maternal Performance (Art)! 2016* (2017b) we employed a similar form and sent JOURNAL entries back and forth daily. These entries formed the basis for our *Manifesto* assertions, our IDEAS; they blurred the lines between our personal lives, our scholarly research, and our performance practices. They also opened up maternal time. We each wrote one entry a day for forty days for our *Manifesto* and stated this was 'to mirror the 40-week gestation period during which a human mother carries her child' (p. 131). Here, in this book and its nine chapters, we have chosen to write our first draft in the nine months between November 2019 and August 2020 to again reflect a 'normal' gestational period. Each chapter was then redrafted in nine days. There is something of an ironic wink to our use of 'normal' here—just one of our combined ten pregnancies conformed to the medicalized 'normal' length arriving exactly at the projected due date. We also hold between us three miscarriages, an abortion, one baby born prematurely at thirty-two weeks, one early at thirty-eight weeks, two late at forty-one weeks, and one late at forty-two weeks. Even with babies born on their due date, this nine-month notion is nonsense as it counts weeks before conception and does not take account of the vagaries of the Gregorian calendar. We also recognize that, although we have all come to life through gestation in the womb of someone, there are many, many other routes to maternal life. Nine months is poetic, however, and something about it feels right. It allows us to take a metaphoric approach to our writing, think about maternal time, and to embrace the idea that things beyond just biological babies are gestated. Needless to say that the research, interviews, gatherings, and fora with mother/artists and numerous drafts of the chapters have already been in the making and have been presented as papers at various conferences and symposia since we began the Performance and the Maternal project in 2015. However, having this tight frame of nine months in writing has given us a structure and certain limits within which we can operate as mother/scholars as well as mother/artists. Just as our children need limits, so does this academic book, this writing. And of course, the persistent question 'how do you find the time to write?' (so eloquently reiterated by Carolyn Jess-Cooke during her presentation on 'Motherhood and Ambivalence' at the 'Motherhood and Poetry' symposium at Birkbeck in November 2019) remains unresolved. Does the writing, having the time to write, always come second, after childcare, after other academic obligations such as teaching and administration? Why is writing secondary? In order to come to our maternal writing we realize we need to structure it, create time for it, take care of it, cherish it, and open it up. This links to the notions of maternal time and our need to carve it out, fight for it, make space for it.

We write through, in spite of, and inspired by interruption, failure, and distraction. Our family lives and working lives blend. We are inspired to make our private, family space visible in our writing, something which has become more apparent culturally with the pandemic of COVID-19. Taking this personal approach beyond our art practices and into our scholarly writing is encouraged not least by Lisa Baraitser's 'anecdotal theory' approach. Baraitser asks us to explore what is it like 'to be exposed to incessant crying, incessant demands, incessant questioning, incessant interruption?' (2009, p. 11). Our own mothering is in relation to our older children, to our communities, to our practice. These different mothering spheres and times may not expose us anymore to the crying invoked by Baraitser but they still demand, interrupt, and question, unsettling us, challenging us, and inspiring us to investigate more deeply.

Maternal Performance: Feminist Relations is structured as a series of seven chapters that focus on specific performances in order to explore a particular theme. Most often, we write these chapters together; however, occasionally we employ our individual voices as either Lena or Emily, which are presented in italics as in the section on subjective maternal maps above. Including this introductory Beginnings and our contingent conclusion, titled New Beginnings, the book contains nine sections, again representing the gestation period for the human child. Topics in this book include reproductive rights, subfertility, abortion, birth stories, maternal labour, temporality, action vs. representation, the art/life dyad, the private/public conundrum, domesticity, mother–daughter relationships, ecology, and more-than-human subjectivity in relation to the maternal. The thematic arrangement loosely follows the various stages of mothering.

In Loss we are informed by feminist psychoanalytic perspectives (Melanie Klein and Luce Irigaray) to argue that loss is an inherent part of the maternal, which requires that we are open to the loss of our other. In particular, we explore the loss of the mother through Fern Smith and Patrick Fitzgerald's 2003 performance *This Imaginary Woman* and reproductive technology and the loss of an imagined maternal identity through Elina Brotherus' photography series *Annonciation* (2009–2013). We then move into our Pregnancy chapter and examine how Hannah Ballou's *goo:ga* (2016), Aleksandra Nikolajev-Jones' ongoing *Gravida* project (2012–), and Quarantine's *Spring.* (2016–2017) open up the representation of the pregnant body on stage. For our theoretical perspective in Pregnancy we draw on Julia Kristeva's 'Stabat Mater' (1985) and Iris Marion Young's propositions on pregnant embodiment (2005 [1990]). Our next chapter deals with the interconnected stories that surround birth, particularly focussing on Adriana Cavarero's notion of 'relational narratives' (2000) as read through Marni Kotak's *The Birth of Baby X* (2011), Third Angel's *Partus* (2015), and Tracy Breathnach-Evans' *Cord* (2016). The post-partum period, which we term Aftermath, is explored in our next chapter through the lens of maternal jouissance as drawn from Julia Kristeva's and Luce Irigaray's extensions of Lacanian thinking. We see jouissance enacted in the works of Lenka Clayton (2013), Lizzie Philps (2013), Grace Surman (2010), and Megan Wynne 2013, 2018).

The second part of our book moves into the later stages of maternal life. Here we deal with maintenance, generations, and futures. In Maintenance we explore the ongoing, temporal qualities of the maternal, drawing on Lisa Baraitser's monograph *Enduring Time* (2017) in order to examine Jessica Olah's *2 340 Peanut Butter and Jelly Sandwiches* (2016), Liz Clarke's *Cannonballista* (2017–2018), and we return to Grace Surman's practice to explore how it has evolved as she moves to representing her mothering of older children in *Performance with Hope* (2017). We examine the relational, wave-like connectedness of the generations through the lens of Gillian Howie's careful attention to intergenerational feminist relationships (2010). Howie's thinking allows us to examine the grandparent–grandchild performances of Peggy Shaw (2003) and Hannah Buckley et al. (2015), and the ongoing mother–daughter performance by Courtney Kessel with her daughter Chloé. Our penultimate chapter takes the form of a correspondence on potential maternal futures and our thoughts about how our feminist relations might inform our interactions with the more-than-human world. We are assisted in our thinking here by Donna J. Haraway's *Staying with the Trouble* (2016) and by performances by Nanna Lysholt Hansen (2014–2018), Lynn Lu (2013, 2015), and TheBabyQuestion, a collective formed by Paula Varjack, Luca Rutherford, Catriona James, and Maddy Costa in order to explore the choices and lack of choices about remaining childfree. We end the book not with a concluding chapter but with a call for New Beginnings, in doing this we hope to open out the unending, ever-changing nature of the maternal and to draw some final thoughts about what performance might have to offer to an understanding of maternal action.

We hope that this book will bring maternal performance some of the prominence it deserves. We also hope it speaks to you about your own very specific maternal experiences, whatever they may be.

Notes

1. Performance and the Maternal built on our work in the field from 2015 to 2021, and not least on our eighteen-month research project funded by the Arts and Humanities Research Council, which included the production of this book, as well as a number of maternal performance fora and interviews with artists, all of which are documented on our website https://performanceandthematernal.com/. Previous to that, the project had been funded internally by Edge Hill University and the University of South Wales.
2. We have discussed our individual performance careers in more detail previously (see Šimić and Underwood-Lee 2020).
3. Examples of networks and exhibitions include the collaborative blog and exhibition *The Egg, the Womb, the Head and the Moon* (2013–2014); the m/other voices foundation [*sic*]; the Cultural ReProducers, Creative Collaborative Mothers, and Mothers Who Make networks; the Mother House Studios; the *Artist as Mother as Artist* (2016) exhibition; and the A.M.M.A.A—the Archive for Mapping Mother Artists in Asia, alongside the many works featured in this book and other performances.
4. The field of maternal studies in the UK can broadly be traced from the establishment of the MaMSIE network in 2007 and the publication of the first edition of the *Studies in the Maternal* e-journal in 2009. Demeter Press specializing in publishing on motherhood (in collaboration with the Motherhood Initiative for Research and Community Involvement) in Canada, the emergence of terms such as 'Mothernism' (Lise Haller Baggesen) and 'New Maternalism' (Natalie Loveless), as well as the founding of the *Journal of Mother Studies* (2016) supported by the annual conferences at the Museum of Motherhood in the US and the establishment of the Archive for

Mapping Mother Artists in Asia in 2016 are other notable examples of the international development of maternal studies.

5. See Šimić, L. (2018) 'Encountering Performing (M)Others: Feminist maternal practice in contemporary performance', in *Contemporary Theatre Review*, special issue 'Feminisms', 28.3. for a more extensive overview of maternal performance practice and theory.
6. Komporaly's *Staging Motherhood: British Women Playwrights, 1956 to the Present* (2006) is principally an attempt to catalogue and theorize writing by women playwrights from the 1950s to the early twenty-first century. Komporaly charts thematic trends as well as exploring the material conditions and institutional structures within which women's writing for the stage about motherhood is presented and received. Her important work takes a historical perspective and examines the barriers that have impacted on women playwrights through the latter half of the twentieth century and into the new millennium. She draws parallels between the various waves of feminist activism, feminist critical thought, the content of women's plays about motherhood, and the social and material conditions affecting mothers. Komporaly makes an important case for an opening up of the term 'motherhood' to include topics such as infertility, the parental, adoption and other routes to motherhood, childcare, and more (p. 168). We draw on her work in this area to consider the maternal as action and lived experience rather than biological status.
7. Several of the works we examine are documents in film or photography (for example works by Grace Surman and Elina Brotherus). Although these works do not bring the audience and performer together in a live encounter, we include them here as documents of a live performance for camera, which again speaks to our understanding of performance as engaging us in a bodily experience.
8. Interviews with artists, recordings of the forum series, and other resources are available at https://performanceandthematernal.com/.
9. Hanisch notes that the title 'The Personal Is Political' was attributed to her paper by Shulie Firestone and Anne Koedt, the editors of *Notes from the Second Year: Women's Liberation*, the book in which her essay was published (Hanisch, 'Women of the World Unite: Writings by Carol Hanisch', 2006).

References

19 Weeks. n.d. *19 Weeks*. https://www.19weeks.com/. Accessed 11 Dec 2020.

Anguezomo Mba Bikoro, Nathalie with Lena Šimić, and Emily Underwood-Lee. 2020. *Performance and the Maternal*. https://performanceandthematernal.files.wordpress.com/2020/12/nathalie-anguezomo-mba-bikoro.pdf. Accessed 18 Dec 2020.

Arendt, Hannah. 1958. *The Human Condition*. Chicago: The University of Chicago Press.

Baraitser, Lisa. 2009. *Maternal Encounters: The Ethics of Interruption*. London and New York: Routledge.

Baraitser, Lisa. 2017. *Enduring Time*. London: Bloomsbury.

Baraitser, Lisa, and Sigal Spigel. 2009. Editorial. *Studies in the Maternal* 1 (1): 1.

Baraitser, Lisa, and Sigal Spigel. 2020. Editorial. *Studies in the Maternal* 13 (1): 1–7.

Barrett, Michèle, and Bobby Baker. 2007. *Bobby Baker: Redeeming Features of Daily Life*. London: Routledge.

de Beauvoir, Simone. 1988 [1949]. *The Second Sex*, trans. H. M. Parshley. London: Picador.

Benjamin, Jessica. 1988. *The Bonds of Love: Psychoanalysis, Feminism and the Problem of Domination*. New York: Pantheon Books.

Benjamin, Jessica. 1998. *Shadow of the Other: Intersubjectivity and Gender in Psychoanalysis*. New York and London: Routledge.

Betterton, Rosemary. 2014. *Maternal Bodies in the Visual Arts*. Manchester: Manchester University Press.

Butler, Judith. 1986. Sex and Gender in Simone de Beauvoir's Second Sex. *Yale French Studies* 72: 35–49.

Cavarero, Adriana. 2000. *Relating Narratives: Storytelling and Selfhood*. London: Routledge.

Cavarero, Adriana. 2011. Inclining the Subject. In *Theory after 'Theory"*, eds. Jane Elliott and Derek Attridge. London and New York: Routledge.

Chernick, Myrel, and Jennie Klein. 2011. *M Word: Real Mothers in Contemporary Art*. Toronto: Demeter Press.

Chesler, Phyllis. 1998 [1979]. *With Child: A Diary of Motherhood*. New York: Four Walls Eight Windows.

Coogan, Amanda with Lena Šimić. 2017. Interview with Amanda Coogan. *Performance and the Maternal*. https://performanceandthematernal.files.wordpress.com/2020/10/amanda_coogan.pdf. Accessed 16 Oct 2020.

DiAngelo, Robin. 2011. White Fragility. *International Journal of Critical Pedagogy* 3 (3): 54–70.

Donoghue, Deirdre, and Paula McCloskey. 2013. *m/other voices*. https://www.mothervoices.org/art-research-and-theory/. Accessed 12 Dec 2017.

Epp Buller, Rachel. 2012. *Reconciling Art and Mothering*. Farnham, Surrey: Ashgate.

Epp Buller, Rachel, and Derek Owens. 2018. "Our Hopes Lie in a Time of Alliances": Epistolary Praxis and Transdisciplinary Composing. In *Something Other*, eds. M. Paterson, M. Costa, and D. Martin. https://somethingother.blog/2018/12/14/our-hopes-lie-in-a-time-of-alliances/. Accessed 8 Nov 2019.

Epp Buller, Rachel, and Charles Reeve. 2019. *Inappropriate Bodies: Art, Design, and Maternity*. Bradford, CA: Demeter.

Epp Buller, Rachel, Lena Šimić, and Emily Underwood-Lee. 2019. The Body in Letters: Once Again, Through Time and Space. In *Inappropriate Bodies: Art, Design, and Maternity*, eds. Rachel Epp Buller and Charles Reeve. Bradford, CA: Demeter.

Ettinger, Bracha L. 2006. *The Matrixial Borderspace*. Minneapolis: University of Minnesota Press.

Gorman, Sarah. 2020. *Women in Performance: Repurposing Failure*. London and New York: Routledge.

Hanisch, Carol. 2001 [1970]. The Personal Is Political. In *Radical Feminism: A Documentary Reader*, ed. B. A. Crow. New York: New York University Press.

Hanisch, Carol. 2006. Women of the World Unite: Writings by Carol Hanisch. http://www.carolhanisch.org/CHwritings/PIP.html. Accessed 8 Nov 2019.

Haraway, Donna J. 2016. *Staying with the Trouble: Making Kin in the Chthulucene*. Durham, NC: Duke University Press.

hooks, bell. 2015. *Feminist Theory: From Margin to Center*. London and New York: Routledge.

Howie, Gillian. 2010. Feminist Histories: Conflict, Coalitions and the Maternal Order. *Studies in the Maternal* 2 (1): 1–12.

Irigaray, Luce. 1981. And the One Doesn't Stir Without the Other, trans. Hélène Vivienne Wenzel. *Signs* 7 (1): 60–67.

Irigaray, Luce, Stephen Pluháček, and Heidi Bostic. 2008. Thinking Life as Relation. In *Conversations*, eds. L. Irigaray and S. Pluháček. London and New York: Continuum.

Johnson, Dominic. 2015. *The Art of Living: An Oral History of Performance Art*. Basingstoke and New York: Palgrave Macmillan.

Kelly, Simon, and Adele Senior. 2020. Towards a Feminist Parental Ethics. *Gender, Work and Organization*. https://doi.org/10.1111/gwao.12566. Accessed 2 Feb 2021.

Kinser, Amber E. 2010. *Motherhood and Feminism*. Berkeley, CA: Seal Press.

Kinser, Amber E., Kryn Freehling-Burton, and Terri Hawkes. 2014. *Performing Motherhood; Artistic, Activist and Everyday Enactments*. Bradford, CA: Demeter Press.

Komporaly, Jozefina. 2006. *Staging Motherhood: British Women Playwrights, 1956 to the Present*. Basingstoke: Palgrave.

Kristeva, Julia. 1980. *Desire in Language: A Semiotic Approach to Literature and Art*, trans. Thomas Gorz, Alice Jardin, and Leon S. Roudiez. New York: Columbia University Press.

Kristeva, Julia. 1981. Women's Time. *Signs* 7 (1): 13–35.

Kristeva, Julia. 1984. *Revolution in Poetic Language*, trans. Margaret Walker. New York: Columbia University Press.

Kristeva, Julia. 1985. Stabat Mater. *Poetics Today* 6 (1/2): 133–152.

Liss, Andrea. 2009. *Feminist Art and the Maternal*. Minneapolis: University of Minnesota Press.

Live Art Development Agency. n.d. What Is Live Art. http://www.thisisliveart.co.uk/about/what-is-live-art/. Accessed 21 Nov 2019.

Marchevska, Elena, and Valerie Walkerdine, eds. 2020. *The Maternal in Creative Work: Intergenerational Discussions on Motherhood and Art*. London and New York: Routledge.

Nikolajev-Jones, Aleksandra with Emily Underwood-Lee. 2020. Interview with Aleksandra Nikolajev-Jones. *Performance and the Maternal*. https://performanceandthematernal.files.wordpress.com/2020/10/aleksandra-nikolajev-jones.pdf. Accessed 15 Oct 2020.

Performance and the Maternal. n.d. Maternal Forums. https://performanceandthematernal.com/maternal-forums/. Accessed 2 Feb 2021.

Phelan, Peggy. 2003. *Unmarked: The Politics of Performance*. London: Routledge.

Putnam, E.L. 2017. Not Just "A Life Within the Home": Maternal Labour, Art Work and Performance Action in the Irish Intimate Public Sphere. *Performance Research* 22 (4): 61–70.

Rich, Adrienne. 1988 [1976]. *Of Woman Born: Motherhood as Experience and Institution*. New York and London: W. W. Norton & Company.

Rose, Jacqueline. 2018. *Mothers: An Essay on Love and Cruelty*. London: Faber.

Schechner, Richard. 2013. No More Theatre PhDs? *TDR—The Drama Review—A Journal of Performance Studies* 57 (3): 7–8.

Šimić, Lena, and Emily Underwood-Lee, eds. 2016. *Live Art and Motherhood: A Study Room Guide on Live Art and the Maternal*. London: Live Art Development Agency.

Šimić, Lena, and Emily Underwood-Lee. 2017. On the Maternal—Editorial. *Performance Research* 22 (4): 1–4.

Šimić, Lena, and Emily Underwood-Lee. 2017. Manifesto for Maternal Performance (Art) 2016! *Performance Research* 22 (4): 131–139.

Šimić, Lena, and Emily Underwood-Lee. 2020. Returning to Ourselves: Medea/Mothers' Clothes and Patience One Decade On. In *The Maternal in Creative Work: Intergenerational Discussions on Motherhood and Art*, eds. E. Marchevska and V. Walkerdine. London and New York: Routledge.

Stacey, Jackie. 1997. *Teratologies: A Cultural Study of Cancer*. London and New York: Routledge.

Stone, Alison. 2006. *Luce Irigaray and the Philosophy of Sexual Difference*. Cambridge: Cambridge University Press.

Stone, Alison. 2012. *Feminism, Psychoanalysis and Maternal Subjectivity*. London and New York: Routledge.

Tyler, Imogen. 2013. *Revolting Subjects: Social Abjection and Resistance in Neoliberal Britain*. London: Zed.

Tyler, Imogen, and Lisa Baraitser. 2013. Private View, Public Birth: Making Feminist Sense of the New Visual Culture of Childbirth. *Studies in the Maternal* 5 (2): 1–27.

Ukeles, Mierle Laderman. 1969. *Manifesto for Maintenance Art 1969!* Proposal for an exhibition 'Care', originally published in Jack Burnham (1971) 'Problems of Criticism', *Artforum*, 41. http://www.queensmuseum.org/wp-content/uploads/2016/04/Ukeles_MANIFESTO.pdf. Accessed 19 Sept 2020.

Wade, Eti. 2016. Motherhood and Art Practice: Expressing Maternal Experience in Visual Art. In *The Mother in Psychoanalysis and Beyond: Matricide and Maternal Subjectivity*, ed. R. Mayo and C. Moutsou. London and New York: Routledge.

Young, Iris Marion. 1997. Asymmetrical Reciprocity: On Moral Respect, Wonder, and Enlarged Thought. *Constellations* 3 (3): 340–363.

Young, Iris Marion. 2005 [1990]. *On Female Body Experience: Throwing Like a Girl and Other Essays*. Oxford: Oxford University Press.

Performances and Artworks Cited

Baker, Bobby. 1988. *Drawing on a Mother's Experience* [performance].

Buckley, Hannah, Brown Elsie, and Rowland Hill. 2015. *Untitled (Elsie and Hannah)* [film].

Clayton, Lenka. 2013. *The Distance I Can Be from My Son* [film].

Coogan, Amanda. 2008. *Yellow* [performance].

Dobkin, Jess. 2006. *The Lactation Station* [performance].

Greenhalgh, Jill. 2010. *The Threat of Silence* [performance].

Kelly, Mary. 1973–1979. 'Post-Partum Document' [exhibition].

Magdalena Project, The. 1995. *The Mothers of Invention* [gathering].

Philps, Lizzie. 2013. *Maternity Leaves* [photography].

Shaw, Peggy. 2003. *To My Chagrin* [performance].

Šimić, Lena. 2007–2008. *Contemplation Time* [mixed media].

Šimić, Lena. 2008. *Sid Jonah Anderson by Lena Šimić* [performance].

Steel, Emily. 2017. *19 Weeks* [performance and radio play].

Surman, Grace. 2010. *I Love My Baby and My Baby Loves Me* [film].
Underwood-Lee, Emily. 2008. *Patience* [performance].
Walsh, Helena. 2007. *M.O.M. Marks of Motherlands* [performance].
Wynne, Megan. 2013. *My Puppet* [film].
Wynne, Megan 2018. *Affirmation (I Am A Professional Artist)* [film].

CHAPTER 2

Loss (2 Months)

The Place of Parting

The maternal is about relations, it is about the other, it extends beyond the self. When we open ourselves up to the other, we become vulnerable to their absence. The maternal must therefore contain loss within itself. The maternal is always in extension, expanding itself towards the other, the impossible other who might not respond, might be out of reach, and might have left. The maternal is dependent on the other and their state. Loss can be construed as a state of exile—we have moved from and can never return to a previously inhabited or imagined state of being, just as we can never return to our united subjectivity with our own mother. Luce Irigaray names the parting of the subject from the mother: 'The first place in which we develop and move, from which we receive oxygen, warmth and food is our mother from whom we part by being born' (2017, p. 39). In *To Be Born* (2017) Irigaray contemplates the individual's necessary journeys of becoming, of effectively being reborn again from and despite one's family, origins, and social preconditions. In such a consideration the maternal is framed as a place of loss, necessarily a place of parting, a site of exile and a lost union to which we can never return. Beyond the maternal loss engendered by separation, we extend our examination in this chapter into the realms of grief, and the acute articulation of loss that we find therein.

L. Šimić and E. Underwood-Lee, *Maternal Performance*, Contemporary Performance InterActions,
https://doi.org/10.1007/978-3-030-80226-4_2

Autobiographical performance and art often speak from a place of loss. Some artworks and performances that have staged a maternal loss include the already mentioned *19 Weeks* (2017) by Emily Steel, which explores the decision to undergo an abortion; Ana Alvarez Errecalde's *Duelo* (2020), in which she marks the death of her son through poetry and photographs of herself and her partner in the depths of their grief; and Clare Parry-Jones' *Angel C* (2013), inspired by her experience of miscarriage. Kirsten Hudson's article 'Taste My Sorrow' (2014) opens up the event of stillbirth while discussing Hudson's newly developed complex artistic forms as she seeks to perform pregnancy loss. There are certain challenges in seeking the 'appropriate' aesthetics through which loss can be conveyed, maternal loss in particular. The topic of maternal loss is still often taboo and the appropriate form in which to discuss it is difficult to find. In this chapter we have chosen to examine works that deal not with the death of a child, but with the loss of a maternal identity and with the death of the performer's mother. We wonder why we go to these works rather than those that deal directly with the loss of a child—perhaps it is something too terrible for us both to consider? Certainly, when we have not personally experienced the death of a child it is difficult for us to write from that perspective; instead we have chosen to write about works that speak more closely to our own personal experiences, with Lena reflecting on her identity as a daughterless mother and Emily as a motherless daughter.

In this chapter we turn to close readings of two significant and deeply personal artworks. Emily discusses Fern Smith and Patrick Fitzgerald's performance *This Imaginary Woman* (2003) and Lena considers Elina Brotherus' *Annonciation* (2009–2013) photography series. We are choosing to read *This Imaginary Woman* and *Annonciation* as maternal performances of loss, not only because of the subject matter (that is, a daughter's story of the death of her mother or a woman's experience of IVF) but also because we believe they push us into an encounter that is based on reciprocity and empathy, which is in and of itself a maternal encounter. Through experiencing these works we are able to look out through another's eyes, finding an empathic and compassionate portrayal of loss with which we identify. We are reminded of our status as always in relation to our other, the other of the one we have lost and the other with whom we find commonality or identification.

Creativity and Grief

This Imaginary Woman and *Annonciation* both deal with grief, a very particular form of loss. At its basic definition grief is a response to loss, usually a loss that comes from the death of someone or something that is important to us (Smith and Fitzgerald's work focusses on the death of her mother and Brotherus contemplates the death of her imagined identity as a biological mother). Grief can be thought of as a stage in mourning in which there is a strongly felt emotional movement towards the lost object, in this case the dead mother and the unconceived child. Sigmund Freud's pivotal essay from 1918 'Mourning and Melancholia' (Freud in Bokanowski et al. 2009) distinguishes between mourning, which is a natural process with an end in sight, and melancholia, which affects the ego in much deeper, even pathological, ways. In Freud's words: 'Mourning is regularly the reaction to the loss of a loved person, or to the loss of some abstraction which has taken the place of one, such as one's country, liberty, an ideal, and so on' (Bokanowski et al. 2009, p. 44). However, 'when the work of mourning is completed the ego becomes free and uninhibited again' (p. 46).

Mourning, in this Freudian construction, is something that can be progressed through, and the works that we examine in this chapter take us with their creators as they embody that process. Grief here is not to be wallowed in and the spectators are not asked to pity the protagonists. Instead, we are actively engaged in coming to an understanding of loss through these performances. Alessia Ricciardi notes that Freud defines mourning as 'sorrow work' and draws our attention to the durational elements of his thesis, and Freud's focus on sorrow as a process that involves labour, which moves it from simply an emotion to an activity (Ricciardi 2003, p. 6). Jacques Lacan takes up and reinterprets Freud's use of mourning as a task that we can 'accomplish' (1977, p. 38), emphasizing mourning as an active process with an end-goal. It is our contention in this chapter, that through these maternal performances of loss we can move together with the artists into a better understanding of our own necessary encounters with maternal loss as part of the activity of the maternal.

Grief, as already mentioned, is a part of mourning, and it is in that context, in that activity, that we situate our critical analysis of Smith and Fitzgerald's and Brotherus' work. In her discussion on mourning Melanie Klein writes:

> Thus, while grief is experienced to the full and despair at its height, the love for the object wells up and the mourner feels more strongly that life inside and outside will go on after all, and that the lost loved object can be preserved within. At this stage in mourning, suffering can become productive. (1940, p. 143)

This productivity is evident in the works we explore here, where suffering has been transformed into considered performance and photography; thus the pain and suffering experienced in grief have engendered the creation of art, or, as Klein would put it, have propelled people to creativity. Discussing mourning and creativity Maria Cristina Melgar writes: 'In mourning the creativity of the psyche straddles the border between the unknown and what is known, between what is lost and what is about to be resumed' (2009, p. 168). The finished artwork or maternal performance allow for that ambiguity, that border to be visible, while pushing towards a new understanding, a new known. It is precisely because the works we are exploring here deal with the immediacy and emotional response to loss, and harness it as part of the creative process, that we will employ the word 'grief' over the more commonly used terms 'mourning' (within psychoanalytic discourse) and 'bereavement' (within therapeutic contexts). Despite our assertion that these works deal with particular moments of grief rather than the entirety of mourning, they still are acts of agency on the part of the performers, who, in making representations of their grief, are enabling us as spectators to travel through the mourning process.

Smith and Fitzgerald's *This Imaginary Woman* is a public chronicle of Smith's work through the stages of grief as she has learnt them while training as a bereavement counsellor (Smith 2006, p. 13). The display of raw emotions which is employed in the performance makes it a most eloquent expression. Brotherus also appears to make work situated in the moment of grief. There is an immediacy to her work, which seems to be taken at the time of experience rather than restaged for reflection. Brotherus explores her reactions to loss, to the lost object, a child, an idea of a child, an idea of herself as a biological mother. Grief can be viewed as an instance where the mind is unable to contain and control itself or maintain rational reasoning: the confusion of the emotional and physical sensations of grief, the flowing of tears, the involuntary rage and depression, all serve to illustrate the lack of control we have over both our physical bodies and our emotional selves. While grief can be understood as a momentary reaction to loss, it is transient and it passes. In the case of creative outputs, what happens at the end of the emotional process is the framing of the photographic moments, or the staging of performance, a kind of curation, an edit of grief.

It is our contention that loss, as the name of the chapter indicates, is a stage and an inevitable part of the cycle of mothering, be it through infertility, subfertility, miscarriages, and abortions, children leaving home, as well as mother's and children's deaths. Here we explore two specific examples of loss that we personally relate to and find compelling. Our theorizing of maternal loss is unavoidably and unashamedly personally informed and we are finding our way to an understanding of ourselves through the particular pieces we examine by these artists—Smith and Fitzgerald and Brotherus. What follows are contemplative responses on the two artworks from Emily and Lena.

Emily on Fern Smith and Patrick Fitzgerald's *This Imaginary Woman*

As I write this it is the eve of the twenty-fifth anniversary of my own mother's death. I am just a little off two years younger than she was when she died. There should be some way to mark this anniversary, some ritual that I can perform. Especially on this quarter century occasion. But I find the appropriate rites are still out of my reach. I have tried to create numerous rituals and borrowed, stolen, or remembered acts from both the cultures I was born into and those that I have come across, but none of it feels like it means anything or has anything to do with my mother, our relationship over the eighteen years in which we both inhabited one space and breathed the same air, or with my own subjectivity as a motherless daughter. A nursing professional, who was involved in the care of my mother while she lived the last days of her life, suggested that I ask one of my mum's friends if I could call them whenever I would have rung my mum. These suggested phone calls could mark rites of passage or help me on days when I needed to see myself reflected through the eyes of an older woman. At the time I thought this a stupid and insensitive idea—how could anyone possibly replace or stand in for my mum? Now I rather regret not following this recommendation, at least it would have been a concrete action I could take. Too much time has passed for this to be meaningful now. These days, the closest I come to marking significant moments in relation to my mother's life and death is sending a quick text to my siblings to say I am thinking of them and to acknowledge the date. Nothing more, as I do not want to say too much for fear of upsetting the others. I suppose this is a technologically aided ritual of sorts, just like lighting a candle it shows we have not forgotten.

This Imaginary Woman *is a 'requiem' for a woman 'who wasn't famous or important to most of us, but she lived, died and left people behind''* (Smith and Fitzgerald 2003). *It is a marker of transition and it is an acknowledgement of life and death. Smith has described the show as a moment of change when she had to find a way to live as 'no longer the child of my mother''* (Smith and Ralph 2019). *I have tried many times to make performance about my mother, or to write about her, but this chapter is the closest I have come to speaking publicly about my mum in any form. Performance should be the obvious method for me to mark my own mother's life and death—my mother was incredibly proud of her brief career as a professional actor in her twenties and nurtured in me a love of theatre from my infancy, although she would find my current tastes in performance more than a little esoteric. Performance is always where I have turned to process my difficulties. Performance would also provide the ritual that I so keenly feel the lack of in my life and especially on this anniversary date. Despite all of this, which feels so incredibly compelling to me, I have still never managed to make my own show for or about my mother and I doubt that I ever will. When I read back over my writing for this chapter I am struck by how much I hide behind my academic position to avoid sharing too much, perhaps the grief is still too acute. And so, I turn with gratitude to Fern Smith, who has shared her experience in* This Imaginary Woman *and articulated her own version of that which I have never managed to say.*

This Imaginary Woman *is a one hour and twenty minutes show created and performed by Fern Smith, a performance maker, and Patrick Fitzgerald, a medical doctor and musician. I witnessed the show live at Chapter in Cardiff in 2003, just over nine years after my own mother had died. The performance charts Smith's recollections of her mother's life, illness, and death through the performance of fifteen songs. Each song can be seen as a performance of a different stage of the grieving process as Smith embodies it. As the audience enter the auditorium for a performance of* This Imaginary Woman *they are greeted by an empty white stage, the only objects in the space are a guitar, piano, and microphone. When the audience have settled, Patrick Fitzgerald enters the space; he is dressed in a suit but carries himself with an air of informality. Fitzgerald provides musical accompaniment during the show and also serves as something of a narrator. In the gentle and reassuring but authoritative tone we can imagine him using in his day job as a medical doctor he asks that everyone turn off their phones and informs the audience that this is going to be a performance about death. He tells us that it is the creators' intention that the performance will offer a space for the audience to reflect on their own experiences of grief and states, 'we hope this is a space where you can think about the largely hidden process of death and with that in mind the auditorium will remain open after the show has finished'. When Smith enters, she makes a remarkable figure—athletic, muscular, clothed in a long black coat, underneath which is a sparkling and beaded black evening dress. Smith takes centre stage throughout as she sings each song while performing deceptively simple poses and postures.* This Imaginary Woman *was released as both a performance and a CD of songs, although it is only the live performance that I am considering in this discussion, and which I am constituting here as another iteration of maternal loss.*

In both the performance and CD publicity Smith and Fitzgerald describe the show as a requiem for Smith's mother. I was deeply affected on a very personal level when I first watched the performance. This was the first time I saw presented to me some of the things I had been experiencing in relation to my own mother's death and I was overcome with a sense of recognition. I had, for a long time, enjoyed Smith's work, but in previous shows it was always the visceral form and political content that had spoken to me. Through this show, I came to understand some of my own experience of losing my mother and to hear what I had found impossible to articulate presented before me. It was, in no small part, through experiencing this performance in 2003, and analysing it years later, that I became able to find a framework for understanding my own subjectivity as a motherless daughter. When I first witnessed this show I read it through the lens of my own particular grief at that time. In 2003 my emotions were still too raw for me to consider the wider ramifications of the work, but as I return to it now, in 2020, I am issued a sharp reminder that all those we love will one day die. Other bereavements have affected me over these seventeen years since I first saw the work and I know there will be more—the intersubjectivity on which we depend, and which is first formulated through the reciprocal gaze of mother and child, will be wrenched from me again and again. The passage that follows combines my recollected response to the work as I first encountered it in 2003 and my current response to the documentation as I watch it now.

Smith's grief exceeds the limits of her body at every turn, thrown across the audience through her vocal utterances and represented on the stage in the contorted movements she performs, moving in postures and falls that appear as if she is unable to contain the physical tension held in her muscles. Smith's grief is not neat or ordered; it is chaotic, loud, and unruly. Smith's performance of grief serves to remind us of the fragility of our psychic ego. In his lecture 'Desire and the Interpretation of Desire in Hamlet' Lacan explores the impact of grief on our understanding of the Real and the Symbolic (1977, pp. 35–39). *He argues that grief makes the ultimate phallus of the object of desire since that object is only attainable through our memories. However, at the very moment grief creates the ultimate object of desire it also destroys that phallus, since the object itself must be replaced by memories. The objectified other collapses in on itself and disappears all at once. Lacan terms the confusion between the Real and the Symbolic which he finds in grief 'the hole in the Real' (p. 38). Richard Armstrong draws on Lacan, Freud, and others to argue that grief is utterly unutterable and impossible to contain within the realm of the Symbolic (that is, language). Armstrong argues that 'grief manifests itself in affects, which are too inexpressible, too uncontainable, too awful for verbal articulation'* (2012, p. 11). *Grief not only breaks down the Symbolic; it also literally renders us outside language. It can leave us without words, or grief-stricken. We are struck dumb by the power of our emotions; the mind and the body are united in their inability to psychically or physically contain our grief. The failure of language is repeatedly found in* This Imaginary Woman, *which has myriad references to silence and voicelessness. In the song 'Hang on to My Voice' Smith addresses her grief directly, stating: 'you took my words and I disappeared'. Following Lacan, I receive* This Imaginary Woman *as a visceral demonstration of the 'hole in the Real'. For most of the show, I recognize a grief that is not contained in an orderly narrative form. In Smith's performance, the unutterability of the loss of the mother is most articulately demonstrated.*

Smith and Fitzgerald use music to express a version of grief that is beyond language. When I listen to Smith's words they become simply sounds, language disintegrates in my reception of Smith's vocal utterances just as the Symbolic disintegrates in grief. During the song 'Relief' Smith sings a scream and, as the song ends, she breathes deeply, panting from the effort of the scream, falls down, and weeps. Smith communicates through guttural, throaty songs and screams. During a personal conversation I had with Smith she cited P J Harvey and Patti Smith as influences—female musicians known for their vocal experimentation and innovation. Smith's body is always held in tension, unbearably still or intensely taut as she moves around the stage. During the song, 'This Proud Strong Woman', Smith holds a lunge position while her arms are outstretched in what looks like a phenomenal act of physical control and strength. During the performance there is also an emphasis on the sound of Smith's breath as she pants, sighs, and exhales into the microphone. Smith's body is forever foregrounded in the performance, with the sound of the words she sings, whispers, sobs, or screams always taking precedence over their logical meaning. The song 'Voiceless' is completely comprised of a scream which becomes stronger then frailer through the piece. Smith's bodily performance of grief continually asserts itself. During 'Funeral' Smith repeats the words 'forever and forever, as your body went into the fire' again and again until the words themselves become meaningless and the song becomes a highly fluent corporeal expression of distress that functions outside of language. I am pushed to think about the funeral of my own mother, not a cremation, but a moment of recognition that is so strong for me that I want to yell across the auditorium.

Despite the appearance of overwhelming emotion, Smith's performance is remarkably controlled. The precision and difficulty of the physical and vocal exertions she performs mean that these actions must be meticulously rehearsed and require immense physical and vocal skill and training. The dexterity with which Smith performs these acts and repeats them on a nightly basis marks this display as a performance.Smith's appearance *of loss of control in reality requires enormous bodily and vocal rigour; however, despite the careful construction and virtuosity of this performance, we know that Smith is performing* her story *of the loss of her mother and in that sense this autobiographical performance becomes all too authentic. Even though this performance is clearly marked as a performance it still has the power to show me Lacan's 'hole in the Real' and invoke the attendant horror that we must experience when confronted in this way. Smith and Fitzgerald make manifest the deepest moment of grief in their performance and allow me a glimpse of the moment I became undone and might become undone again. The wonder of* This Imaginary Woman *for me is that I am able to glimpse this most unruly and uncontainable place within such a contained and structured performance and therefore am always brought back to safety.*

Margrit Shildrick argues that the disabled body reminds the 'normatively embodied … of the impermanence of their morphological status' (2009, p. 4). *This threat is also present in* This Imaginary Woman. *Smith appears in this performance as the epitome of physical fitness, lean and athletic and clothed in a tight-fitting sleeveless dress that displays her impressive arm and leg muscles; nonetheless, she is performing the vulnerability we all have both to experiencing the death of a loved one and to our own mortality. Further, Smith is discussing her mother's death after a long and disabling illness (her mother suffered with multiple sclerosis and this is described in depth within the show); thus* This Imaginary Woman *offers a double threat as it makes me consider my own death and the potential we all have of succumbing to disease, and the possibility (or perhaps the certainty) of having to witness death and disease in others* (Fig. 2.1).

Lacan noted that '[t]he one unbearable dimension of possible human experience is not the experience of one's own death, which no one has, but the experience of the death of another' (1977, p. 37). This Imaginary Woman *exposes me to all that is most fearful: death, grief, the collapse of the ego, the breakdown of intersubjectivity, and the breakdown of the Real and the Symbolic.This overspilling of psychic boundaries serves to make Smith the other but does not allow me to simply look on her from a safe distance. My own vulnerability is reflected back at me and I identify with that other as myself. Smith does not become the other that marks difference and so affirms our own normality; instead, she is the threat of the other we will all, at some stage, become.*

Although Smith is performing a version of what are undoubtedly traumatic events, her performance of threat is not a performance of trauma. Peggy Phelan notes that the rehearsal and repetition of trauma is an essential component of the healing process in psychoanalysis (1997, pp. 44–72).[1] *This process of recalling trauma in order to heal is markedly different from the performance of threat in that one follows the logic of recollection and the other of premonition. Although* This Imaginary Woman*'s content is based on recollections of events, it is the element of premonition that marks this performance as threat and links it to the hole in the Real—this is what we may become rather than what we have already been. In this show I see not only the grief I have faced at my own mother's death but also all the other deaths and losses I will have to deal with. I am reminded through this performance that grief is something I will face again and again; it will live within me and I must learn to accommodate loss. Although I am challenged to face my own fears of maternal loss when watching* This Imaginary Woman, *I find I am also able to find resolution and community. Facing my vulnerability to loss through Smith and Fitzgerald's work is something I experience as a form of healing. It is seventeen years since I watched this show live and yet I still return to it again and again.* This Imaginary Woman *is unequivocally one of the most extraordinary and brilliant performances I have ever encountered.*

Fig. 2.1 Fern Smith in Fern Smith and Patrick Fitzgerald, *This Imaginary Woman* (2003) (Image by Graham Mathews)

Elaine Aston, writing about autobiographical works that explore the mother's life and death from the perspective of the daughter, notes that identification with the grieving daughter is a profoundly moving experience for audiences regardless of their own position. Audiences are able to look through the eyes of another and experience the undoing nature of grief or the 'hole in the Real', to return to a Lacanian formulation. Aston follows Butler to argue that this engenders an empathetic response that can prompt a collective, and therefore political, understanding (Aston 2007, p. 136). *When watching* This Imaginary Woman *I was able to see my own experience of losing my mother reflected for me, not because the particularities of Smith and my stories were the same, and not because Smith and I reacted identically to our personal maternal loss, but instead because I was able to see an experience of maternal grief and to identify. Yes, of course this is a terrifying prospect, but it is also a moment of recognition where I can see that, despite the wrenching separation caused by the loss of my mother, I am not alone—this grief is shared and I can find empathy, understanding, and community.* This Imaginary Woman *allows me to explore the maternal through its subject matter, but more than this, it understands something essential about the maternal—that we can find community with another, find compassion and understanding, and that we are never in isolation but are always in a reciprocal maternal relationship, not just to the mother who carried us or the child we might carry in our own womb, but to humanity and beyond. Watching Smith and Fitzgerald's performance, I was able to understand my own experience and to see my loss reflected, re-establishing intersubjectivity as I was being reminded of how that intersubjectivity had been ripped from me.*

Fitzgerald and Smith create a safe space in which to enable their audience to experience threat and yet still feel that they have been 'looked after' and are seen. Smith and Fitzgerald further take care of their audience through following a pattern of grief as a process with resolution and acceptance as its final state.[2] *As the performance ends, Smith moves out of her portrayal of grief—she puts on the coat in which she had entered the space, but which had been discarded throughout the show to reveal a stunning black cocktail dress, and sings one final song, titled 'Ice Skating'. This song is performed in a major key and is sung tunefully and softly; in this it is markedly different from the earlier songs expressing grief. This change in the tone of the performance signals a move away from the rawness of grief and into resolution and acceptance. Smith then walks off the stage. The attendance shown for the audience and the careful choreography of a journey through the stages of grief allow us to step through the 'hole in the Real' in safety. This care enabled me to move further into a reflection on my own grieving state knowing that I could be okay, I would be brought back, that there would be resolution, that rather than ever moving beyond grief, I can find resolution through acceptance and learning to live with grief and loss as part of my experience of being open to the maternal and to the other.*

Lena on Elina Brotherus' *Annonciation*

Performance is immediate. It is raw and in need of a reaction, in the here/now in front of the audience. It forces you to be present, or absent. It forces you towards a response and immediacy. This aligns it to grief. Performance is demanding. You are confronted by it. It screams at you. The form of performance art asks of you, begs of you, needs of you—all that physicality, all that presence. The audience is affronted. Yet, it is hard to talk about loss, to witness it even, to be in its presence, to sit by it, collectively, in public space. How do we experience loss in maternal performance? Should we be grateful to Brotherus and Smith for confronting us with their grief, the rawness, the immediacy of it? How do we move with them, so intimately, so publicly?

Am I cheating here when deciding to write about Elina Brotherus' Annonciation (2009–2013) *photography series in which she charts five years of undergoing IVF treatment, unsuccessfully? Can* Annonciation *be considered a durational performance? Ought I to name it as such, frame it as performance, or is it 'just' autobiographical photography, the documentation of a durational performance? Does an exhibition opening function at a performative level when we all collectively confront the artist's world as presented to us at that mutual moment?*

Why am I concerned with these questions? Because the artform matters in relation to the theme of loss. The enquiry we have set out in this book is about the capacity of the performance artform to hold the maternal, to contain its leakage, its trauma. We are keen to ask questions of the alliance between performance and the maternal. Thinking about loss and performance at the same time, I wonder what is lost through the form itself? What is the performance artform incapable of? Is some kind of deeper, subjective (as opposed to collective), highly individualized contemplation on the subject of the maternal lost in the insistence of performance and theatre for the collective experience of addressing various issues? Do such issues not inevitably become 'watered down' somehow, since they are to be received collectively, in a community of strangers, and not individually, in the privacy of one's bedroom when reading a book, or on a walk through a gallery? Can the collective hold the maternal, the intimate, the raw, the lost? How can one be intimate in a collective? Does one allow oneself to become lost in it? Is it only through religious, mystical, and spiritual practices that move us beyond consciousness that we can feel affected in a collective, in the togetherness of a community?

It is from precisely the capacity of being in a communal response, as a group of people who have most likely randomly gathered, that the performance artform gains its strength. On the other hand, mothering is a highly individual, and oftentimes lonely, experience, as is the 'trying to get pregnant' stage, including all its failures and successes. All this happens behind closed doors, more often than not with a woman being the main protagonist. It is her body which becomes a battleground. Bringing these intimate and private mothering experiences out into the public sphere, regardless of which artforms they are in, is a kind of public outcry, a space of hearing.

Annonciation *is a story of 'false annunciations about waiting for an angel who never shows up'* (Brotherus 2013)*—a series of thirty-two photographs, ranging from portraits with flowers, to images of a bruised belly, medications, a naked body on the bathroom floor expecting, waiting in vain, interspersed with images of calendars and IVF treatment days, ovulation and period cycles for 2008, 2009, 2010, 2011, 2012, and 2013. This is staged life, moments of it, in loss, in longing, in disappointment, with tears. Brotherus photographs and performs her grief; she stages it and possibly, by making it public, gains some agency over her story of infertility. She writes:*

> *What we learn about the subject in the media – documentaries, interviews, articles and TV programs on infertility – they all have a happy end. In reality, the success stories are rare, but they are the ones we hear of. For the rest of us, this biased broadcasting is upsetting. It's as though the general public should not see the inconsolable reality but instead a cathartic 'per aspera ad astra' Hollywood story.* (Brotherus 2013)

Brotherus brings her experience of pain and loss into the public realm. I first encountered the work through the 'Home Truths: Photography and Motherhood' exhibition, which took place at the Photographers' Gallery and the Foundling Museum from 11 October 2013 to 5 January 2014 in London. It was a lonely experience. I was pregnant at the time with my fourth child.

I also saw the photographs from the project at the 'Odgajanje budućnosti' ('Bringing up the Future') exhibition at SC Gallery in Zagreb, running between 22 February and 4 March 2017, in a new context. I attended its opening. By this point the artist had long completed the personal process of IVF treatment.

Later on, I found myself looking over the thirty-two photographs, again and again, in the solitude of my desk chair, opening the catalogue from the 'Home Truths' exhibition, or on the artist's own web page.[3] *As I encounter these false annunciations, these mini performances, staged photographic experiences, I am struck by how they linger in between the unknown and the known, to go back to Melgar's discussion of the psyche in mourning and creativity* (2009, p. 168). *In this annunciation an angel does not appear, but a carefully considered skilled artform does. Art holds the space of loss. Is it there instead of loss? Is art transfigured and productive of grief? Does it become a substitute, an imaginary child, possibly even a new loved object? An act of performing loss, an act of staging a photograph that holds a space of loss, reframes it, reconfigures it as an affective outcry, possibly even as agency as well as a potential for engagement and a deeper understanding of infertility and failed IVF treatments.*

In an interview with Ellyn Kail, Brotherus notes that her photographs are not therapy work. She states:

> *I used to think that I could deal with my problems by making photos. Later, I realized that despite the photo, the problem remains and needs to be verbalized – that's what therapy is. But photographs can underline moments in life and make them visible. Photography can occupy [space] and give [you] something meaningful to do. ... It can be rewarding and satisfying to get at least an image, if you see what I mean. And in the end, I got a dog too.* (Kail 2016)

There is a confrontational self-portrait of Brotherus from 2013, in which she shows her middle finger to the viewers. The title of the photograph is 'My Dog Is Cuter Than Your Ugly Baby' (2013). *Clearly artwork is not aligned to therapy work in this case, but it is 'something meaningful to do' which inevitably becomes a part of the process, of one's narration of life and loss within it. Artwork might be there as a by-product of grief, but it does not stand in for therapy work, which is yet to be addressed, verbalized through a different format. Nevertheless, the artworks influence deeper public understanding of maternal loss, ask us to confront it and come to accept that we ought to live beside it, live with the experience of it. Maternal loss is no longer an invisible private matter.*

The photograph 'Annonciation 30, Last one in my line' (2012) features a woman in a red coat, her back to us, facing the city, removed from its buzz, its liveness. There is a fence and water in between her and the city, a gap between them; the city remains out of her reach, an impossible destination. Brotherus is the last one in her line. She came to a decision, a knowledge, a recognition. This is 2012. This particular photograph comes after twenty-nine others, some of which are much more raw, painful, open: the artist is exposed in her vulnerability, in her grief. In others she is seen clutching her arms with a smiling hope on her face, or naked with tears running down her cheeks, or seated on a lonely chair in an empty space, on the bathroom floor, at times curled up on a sofa, alone.

These photographs are markers in time, punctures, but also moments of decision, both the decision of the exact moment at which to press the shutter button of the camera, and also the decisions in the editing process and the exhibiting space. These photographs give form to and frame loss; they are contained. With the creation of an artwork, the process of artworking and artmaking, comes a new understanding of the autobiographical material exhibited. The form shapes the content, however raw that content might be. Artwork might help us arrive at a kind of end, the completion of a process of making at least. In Motherhood Lost: A Feminist Account of Pregnancy Loss in America (2003) *Linda L. Jayne writes about the 'miscarriage years' and notes how she had 'experienced these losses as an assault on my sense of self. The losses forced me to revise the story of my life and my account of myself' (p. 6). Yet, both Jayne and Brotherus gain something from the losses in terms of their identity, a new knowledge as an academic or a new artistic practice. While this does not stand in for the agony of the losses themselves, a new identity sits beside them, with them.*

There was a knowledge I came to, with my four sons, the last one born in 2014, that I would not have a daughter. I was thirty-nine and my last birth, although incredibly quick, slightly over an hour, included shoulder dystocia and retained placenta (Šimić 2014). *I had exhausted myself bodily; in the past women died in childbirth from post-partum haemorrhage often caused by retained placenta. I had a medical intervention, and was not in any real danger, but remembering my violent miscarriage a year earlier made me realize that my body had had enough. This is before considering the emotional, material, planetary, and financial implications of having another child. At thirty-nine I knew my limit, something I had struggled with throughout my life when it came to children and love (always wanting and needing more). In that sense I also felt myself to be the 'last one in my line'—the maternal line had ceased with me. Not having a daughter also felt like a feminist loss. Upon hearing I had yet another boy, a mother at the school gates told me: 'You get what you can handle.' These lines have somehow remained with me, although I have been able to unpick the sense of injustice and determinism of such a phrase. How fair is it to think thus, to have a feeling of no power over one's destiny, particularly when it comes to subfertility, infertility, miscarriages, abortions, and many other instances of maternal grief?*

It is, of course, quite different to think about my mothering experience of having four children, four boys, and Brotherus' journey. Yet, there is a loss present in my mothering self, my woman self, which informs my identity, as a daughterless mother. The loss of one identity creates another. Loss inhabits our lives. And with loss, there is a fantasy of an end. Can there ever be a resolution, something akin to a conclusion, to coming to terms? Brotherus' penultimate image is called 'Annonciation 31, The End', the artist staring into the whiteness of the snow, a pose similar to the image before, except there are no skyscrapers, no city life. The artist 'returns' to nature, or rather landscape, possibly her homeland. Yet this image is not the last one.

The very final image is the artist's face, a portrait, and a simple note of place and time, Helsinki 04.03.2013. All three images, 30, 31, and 32, frame the ending. This artwork creates a narrative, a story with an end. The artist stares back at us in the final image, with her decision to stop IVF treatment, with the loss as well as determination. It is through art that the decision is also made—the artwork provides the end, the last image, the frame. From my audience perspective Annonciation *stands in for a kind of closure instead of loss without the end. There is something comforting in this activity.*

And of course, this particular series of photographs are not the end of Brotherus' creativity and oeuvre. In many ways, her artwork is just beginning, her career spreading ahead of her with many different projects following on from Annonciation. *A different kind of care for the other is exhibited in her series of photographs* Carpe Fucking Diem (2011–2015), *which she frames as 'an attempt to reconstruct the meaning of life for a future that is not what I imagined it to be'* (Brotherus 2015). *Humour as well as connectedness to the natural world play a substantial part in this new series of photographs. A different future is possible—the artist can and does reimagine herself.*

Annonciation *showcases the bitter process of going through IVF treatment. The final images arrive at the outcome—the loss of an imaginary child, the decision to stop with IVF—but also they complete this particular story, give the artwork its meaning, its outcome. The project is completed. One story ends, and yet,* Carpe Fucking Diem, *a new photography series, has already been happening beyond the frame of* Annonciation, *overlapping for three years. Our phases in life and creativity are not crystal clear; one artwork leads into another. The clean-cut end is impossible; living with loss is what becomes available.*

Living with Maternal Loss

In 'Womb Envy: Loss and Grief of the Maternal Body' (2007) Catherine B. Silver refers us back to Kristeva's *Revolution in Poetic Language* and reminds us that '[f]or Kristeva the turning away from phallic language into poetic intuitions and art is a way to access the deep substratum of grief and sensuality where the experience of loss becomes soothing and self-repairing rather than pathological' (Silver 2007, p. 417). While art making in itself is not equated with therapy work, its processes are contained in a certain time which might coincide with the time of mourning. Returning to Freud, we are reminded that mourning passes like the process of making artworks and performances, while melancholia is a condition which might affect one's ego and become pathological. To make art out of loss, because of loss, about loss, and to be productive about it, the artist will probably have resolved, to a certain degree, their own mourning process, and not entered into a melancholic state. Art is about a desire to communicate outwards, it seeks its audiences. The forms of both Smith and Fitzgerald's and Brotherus' artworks are well considered, even when the content might be messy and raw, brought about from the experience of grief.

Writing on her blog entitled *Emergence*, under the entry 'Creating Space for Change' in December 2019, Smith reflects on *This Imaginary Woman*:

> I became convinced that sometimes a life begins with a death. The last words of 'This Imaginary Woman' were: 'I will live' and this was the promise I charged myself to keep, in honour of the life of my mother Pearl Isobel, Stanley. I made a pact with myself to live deliberately, consciously, with gratitude and with awe at this transitory gift called life. Something

> changed in me then and the process of change has continued to play out in an unending cycle of many smaller and larger deaths and rebirths. My work has changed, friendships have shifted, my home and the landscape I see out of my window has changed beyond recognition many times since then. I knew that there was a healing process to be done and a growing up and a becoming more and more the person I was born to be. I was no longer the child of my mother. It was about time I became an adult. And what did I want to have learned before I died. (Smith and Ralph 2019)

It is through maternal loss that a new space opens up, a space of becoming anew, of being reborn. Irigaray writes: 'Without a continual movement of backwards and forwards between one's beginning and one's end, no one can accomplish one's own becoming' (2017, p. 38). One's own becoming takes place through transformative events such as the loss of one's mother, or imaginary child—as is the case for the two artists we have discussed here—which allows for an emergent new sense of being as well as living. The close and intimate exploration of the maternal, through art, pushes us towards a deeper re-examination of our own lives, and the way we ought to act and live. We must all experience loss, as Irigaray notes, our first loss is the moment we are expelled from our mother's womb. To be born into a subjectivity as a biological mother we must also experience our separation from the child we have carried within us. To be born into a maternal sensibility we must accept our interdependence and vulnerability to the inevitable loss of the other. Any philosophy or ideology that seeks to position the self in relation to the other, as our call for maternal ways of understanding ourselves and our contexts throughout this book does, must also acknowledge that loss and grief are inevitable. Brotherus and Smith and Fitzgerald, through maternal performance, potentially allow us to come to terms with our loss and grief, to be born anew, and to understand our vulnerability. Maternal performance forces something ajar, something painful but affectively open.

Notes

1. Phelan draws on Lacan's analysis of *Antigone* to explore how tragic theatre always presents multiple deaths; in her analysis characters rehearse their deaths over and over again, enabling a repeated playing out of the threat of death (Phelan 1997, p. 14). This repetition is also present in *This Imaginary Woman* where Smith sings of

all the ways her mother died before her death: 'she died before she died … the loss of my healthy beautiful mother'.

2. This care for the audience and following of the stages of grief is informed by Smith's training as a Cruse bereavement counsellor (Smith 2006, p. 13).
3. See https://www.elinabrotherus.com/photography#/annonciation/.

References

Armstrong, Richard. 2012. *Mourning Films: A Critical Study of Loss and Grieving in Cinema*. London: McFarland.

Aston, Elaine. 2007. A Critical Step to the Side: Performing the Loss of the Mother. *Theatre Research International* 32 (2): 130–142.

Bokanowski, Thierry, Letitia Glocer Florini, and Sergio Lewkowicz (eds). 2009. *On Freud's 'Mourning and Melancholia'*. London, New York: Routledge.

Brotherus, Elina. 2013. Annonciation. *Elina Brotherus*. http://www.elinabrotherus.com/photography#/annonciation/. Accessed 13 Oct 2020.

Brotherus, Elina. 2015. Carpe Fucking Diem. *Elina Brotherus*. http://www.elinabrotherus.com/photography#/carpe-fucking-diem/. Accessed 13 Oct 2020.

Hudson, Kirsten. 2014. Taste My Sorrow: Caught Horribly, Somewhere, Between the Pregnant and the Maternal. *Performance Research* 19 (1): 41–51.

Irigaray, Luce. 2017. *To Be Born: Genesis of a New Human Being*. London: Palgrave Macmillan.

Jayne, Linda L. 2003. *Motherhood Lost: A Feminist Account of Pregnancy Loss in America, the Cultural Construction of Miscarriage and Stillbirth in America*. London, New York: Routledge.

Kail, Ellyn. 2016. Carpe Fucking Diem: One Photographer's Courageous Discussion of Involuntary Childlessness. *Feature Shoot*, 13 January. https://www.featureshoot.com/2016/01/carpe-fucking-diem-one-photographers-courageous-discussion-of-involuntary-childlessness/. Accessed 2 Feb 2021.

Klein, Melanie. 1940. Mourning and Its Relation to Manic-Depressive States. *International Journal of Psycho-Analysis* 21: 125–153.

Lacan, Jacques. 1977. Desire and the Interpretation of Desire in Hamlet. *Yale French Studies* 55 (56): 11–52.

Melgar, Maria Cristina. 2009. Mourning and Creativity. In *On Freud's 'Mourning and Melancholia'*, ed. T. Bokanowski, F.L. Glocer, and S. Lewkowicz. London, New York: Routledge.

Phelan, Peggy. 1997. *Mourning Sex*. London: Routledge.

Ricciardi, Alessia. 2003. *The Ends of Mourning: Psychoanalysis, Literature, Film*. Stanford, CA: Stanford University Press.
Shildrick, Margrit. 2009. *Dangerous Discourses of Desirability, Subjectivity and Sexuality*. Basingstoke: Palgrave Macmillan.
Silver, Catherine B. 2007. Womb Envy: Loss and Grief of the Maternal Body. *The Psychoanalytic Review* 94 (3): 409–430.
Šimić, Lena. 2014. Birth Story. *Performance Research* 19 (4): 24–30.
Smith, Fern. 2006. This Imaginary Woman. *The Open Page* 11: 10–18.
Smith, Fern, and Philip Ralph. 2019. Creating a Space for Change. *Emergence: The Art of Living Blog*. https://emergenceuk.blogspot.com/2019/12/creating-space-for-change.html. Accessed 16 Oct 2020.

Performances and Artworks Cited

Alvarez Errecalde, Ana. 2020. *Duelo* [photography series].
Brotherus, Elina. 2009–2013. *Annonciation* [photography series].
Brotherus, Elina. 2011–2015. *Carpe Fucking Diem* [photography series].
Parry-Jones, Clare. 2013. *Angel C* [performance].
SC Gallery. 2017. 'Odgajanje budućnosti' ['Bringing up the Future'], 22 February–4 March. Zagreb [exhibition].
Smith, Fern, and Patrick Fitzgerald. 2003. *This Imaginary Woman* [performance].
Steel, Emily. 2017. *19 Weeks* [performance and radio play].
The Photographers' Gallery and the Foundling Museum. 11 October 2013–5 January 2014. 'Home Truths: Photography and Motherhood'. London [exhibition].

[illegible], Christine. 2002. *The [illegible] of [illegible]*. Stanford, CA: Stanford University Press.
[illegible], Stephen. 2004. *Dying and Mourning in [illegible]*. Basingstoke: Palgrave Macmillan.
Silvey, Catherine R. 2003. "[illegible]." *The [illegible] Review* 94 (2): 409–430.
Stone, Lena. 2006. "[illegible]." *Performance Research* 19 (4): 28–30.
Smith, Tom. 2003. "[illegible] of Women." *The Open Space* 11: 10–18.
Smith, Tom and Philip Ralph. 2019. "Creating a Space for [illegible]." *The Art of Dying Well*. https://www.artofdyingwell.org/2019/12/[illegible]. Last accessed 16 Oct 2020.

[illegible]

[illegible]. 2020. [illegible].
[illegible]
[illegible]
[illegible]
[illegible]
Smith, Tom and Patrick [illegible]. 2008. *[illegible]*. [illegible]
[illegible]
[illegible]
[illegible]

CHAPTER 3

Pregnancy (3 Months)

Maternal Experience

We started thinking about this chapter through our own lived experiences. In conversation, we remembered that we had both performed on stage while pregnant, but not in a 'maternal performance context'—it just kind of happened. For Lena, this was when touring *Joan Trial* to Odin Teatret, Denmark, and *Medea/Mothers' Clothes* to the University of Winchester, UK, both in 2007. Lena was not visibly pregnant; her pregnant body was still 'in between' the visible and invisible. In 2013, again pregnant, she performed *1994*, a piece about the Yugoslav War and Kurt Cobain. In *1994* she was very visibly seven months 'gone', but being pregnant on stage was still 'accidental'. The performance was not conceived for a pregnant body; the piece clashed with the protruding belly as this show discussed Lena's teenage years and former lovers, and included a list of all the boys Lena had kissed. The planned tour of the performance was abandoned due to the arrival of her fourth baby. Emily found out she was pregnant shortly after receiving confirmation from the Arts Council of Wales that she had successfully secured funding for her performance *Ode to Morten Harket* in 2007. The piece, which was already extensively developed, chronicled her love of the lead singer of A-ha, the Norwegian band who first found fame with their 1985 single 'Take on Me'.

L. Šimić and E. Underwood-Lee, *Maternal Performance*, Contemporary Performance InterActions,
https://doi.org/10.1007/978-3-030-80226-4_3

Emily's costume, a large green dress, was adapted to disguise her pregnancy. Just as Lena had struggled to accommodate her pregnant body in a text about her teenage self, Emily's pregnant body did not fit with this performance, which was about youthful sexuality. We both, separately, came to the conclusion that our pregnant bodies somehow tamed and domesticated our performances and made it feel impossible for us to discuss youthfulness and desire. In 2011, Emily again found out she was pregnant, this time with her second child, while working on her Arts Council of Wales funded performance *Titillation* (2010), which left her wondering if arts council funding might be a useful aid to her fertility. Again, her pregnancy was hidden in the performance, which discussed femininity and breast cancer. For Emily, it was impossible to reconcile her pregnant body with her creative body or to find a way to incorporate her pregnancy into her performance.

We were both pregnant performers but we were not able, in these instances of our practice, to represent our pregnancies. On other occasions we both chose to engage in maternal art. Lena's *Contemplation Time* and *Friday Records* art projects of her maternity leaves with her third child Sid in 2007/2008 and her fourth child James in 2014 consisted of images, recordings, and text. Lena's projects allowed for her mothering practice to be equated with her artistic one as they were both put under the microscope, observed, and scrutinized. This microscopic observation of the maternal is something we notice in the work of many of the artists who are making performances with maternal concerns, including Elina Brotherus' and Fern Smith and Patrick Fitzgerald's complex examinations of absence, as we discussed in our previous chapter, Loss, as well as Hannah Ballou's opening up of the moment of the gender reveal of the foetus in her performance *goo:ga* (2016), as we write about in this chapter.

In conversation, we realized that two of the three performances we decided to write about in this chapter are conceived for pregnant performers' bodies but conceptualized by artists who are no longer pregnant or have never been. *Spring.*, a part of Quarantine's *Summer.Autumn.Winter.Spring.* (2016–2017) quartet of pieces, which Lena will address towards the end of the chapter, and Aleksandra Nikolajev-Jones' ongoing series of performances as part of her *Gravida* project, which Emily will reflect on, are both created for pregnant performers by non-pregnant artists. Hannah Ballou's *goo:ga* is the exception here as it is the performer herself who presents her pregnant body.

For us, this absence of autobiographical work about the state of pregnancy that is conceived, created, and performed while pregnant opens up questions about why we resisted performing our own pregnant bodies and why so much work is only able to capture the pregnant body after the event. There is a simple answer here: pregnancy is fleeting and exhausting, and we only have a few months when visibly pregnant, while production and touring schedules often need to be planned months or years in advance; but more nuanced discussion is necessary, taking into account not only the practical and bodily needs of pregnancy but also the psychic and representational questions opened up by pregnant performance. For our theoretical framework we draw on Julia Kristeva (1985) and Iris Marion Young (2005 [1990]) to propose that the psychic and bodily transition that must occur as the mother transforms through her pregnancy is an unruly occurrence that defies representation.

Julia Kristeva, in 'Stabat Mater', asks us to try to understand the mother psychically and in terms of maternal experience (1985, p. 147). Kristeva invites us to listen to mothers and to consider the fullness and range of their experiences, alongside a consideration of representations of the maternal in art, in order to better understand the condition of the maternal:

> Those interested in what maternity is for a woman will no doubt be able to shed new light on this obscure topic by listening, with greater attentiveness than in the past, to what today's mothers have to say not only about their economic difficulties but also, and despite the legacy of guilt left by overly existentialist approaches to feminism, about malaise, insomnia, joy, rage, desire, suffering and happiness. (p. 147)

The shows we consider in this chapter offer us an opportunity to take up this invitation from Kristeva by presenting the personal stories of the mother on stage; in doing so they certainly 'shed new light' on the topic of pregnancy and the maternal. This is generally the case with many of the performances discussed in this book that present the autobiographical voices of the mother/artists as a means of understanding various maternal states and stages. Kristeva also employs her own personal voice in 'Stabat Mater' in a manner that is not common in her other theoretical writing. 'Stabat Mater' comprises two parts: running alongside the more theoretical writing, in parallel, are experiential bodily words (an *écriture féminine*). Two strands of text present us with the duality of a 'real' mother and her complex existence, in this case through the experiential and the theoretical, which exchange positions at the end of the essay. The ostensible division between the abstract and the lived is broken down in 'Stabat Mater' and the two texts often bleed into one another, their form following Kristeva's conceptual interlinking of maternal experience and theory.

We will take up two points from Kristeva's proposal in 'Stabat Mater': firstly, this invitation to explore both the practical and psychic elements of motherhood alongside an analysis of its representations and, secondly, the notion that pregnancy only becomes representable when frozen and removed from the flow of time and change that is inherent in the act of growing new life. Performance as a live, time-based artform resists this freezing and offers us a chance to extend Kristeva's argument regarding pregnancy as a moment when the corporeal and the temporal combine. We also draw here on Young's conception of pregnancy as a condition in which the mother is doubled in both her subjectivity and her experience of time (2005 [1990]).

On Performance, Pregnancy, and Time

Hannah Ballou's *goo:ga* had a very short life span on stage in 2016, performed only twice, and we both missed seeing it live. We relied on the video documentation footage of *goo:ga* on Ballou's website (Hannah Ballou, n.d.). We might be excused for missing Ballou's show: due to the transitory nature of the pregnant body the touring window was quite short, and so the documentation had to suffice. After all, pregnancy passes, it is ephemeral, even when at times nine months can feel like years; pregnancy escapes the touring schedule. To create and tour a performance while pregnant seems to require that you have determined to create performance about pregnancy before actually getting pregnant (which would probably mean you are an established performance maker already with a developed and specific performance aesthetics and most likely on your second or third or fourth... baby, so the experience is no longer 'a shock'); could get pregnant; could come up with the idea for the pregnant performance (while dealing with the newness of your own body); could apply for funding to develop and tour the work; and could manage to do it all before the baby's arrival. This seems to be something of an impossible task. Yet, Ballou managed to perform *goo:ga* when eight months pregnant. We are astounded by the feat it must have taken to actualize this performance. The wait for our Arts and Humanities Research Council grant for our Performance and the Maternal project alone took nine months.[1] The UK Arts Councils of England and Wales both turn around their small grant applications in six weeks, so it might be possible if you are quick and organized but the systems and funding regimes of contemporary performance practice in the UK do not fit with the time-scale of pregnancy (Arts Council of Wales, n.d.). Touring is even harder because most venues confirm their programme a year or more in advance. Nothing in this system of production is set up to cope with daily changes and flux or with the uncertainty of pregnancy.

Alongside issues of timing around funding and touring, there are also structural concerns that make pregnant performance difficult. Vincent Dance Theatre, in collaboration with Dance UK and Creative and Cultural Skills, carried out research exploring the pressures that pregnancy and early motherhood place on the dancer (Vincent Dance Theatre 2009). Issues that were raised in this research included: the precarity of a dance career, the need to maintain fitness, a lack of institutional support for pregnant dancers and new mothers, and the pressures of touring not being compatible with a family life. All of these pressures combined to create an extremely challenging environment for pregnant dancers. In addition, choreographers and company directors showed nervousness about the health and safety implications of working with pregnant dancers (Vincent Dance Theatre 2009). These institutional, structural, and economic difficulties combine to create a perfect storm that ensures that the pregnant body rarely appears in performance, which is not the case in other artforms.

Pregnancy has regularly been represented in fine art, not just within the images of the Virgin Mary discussed by Kristeva (which we explore later in this chapter), but with whole exhibitions in major cultural institutions dedicated to the history of the representation of the pregnant body, such as recent exhibitions 'Portraying Pregnancy: From Holbein to Social Media' (2020) at the Foundling Museum in London and the twin 'Part 1: Matrescence' (2019) and 'Part 2: Maternality' (2020) at the Richard Saltoun Gallery, also in London. 'Part 2: Maternality' featured Liv Pennington's *Private View* (2002–2010), a large photograph of forty-nine pregnancy tests, numbered and with a short sentence underneath each one of them.[2] The piece was conceived as a performance over a period between 2002 and 2010, and it took place in London, Poitiers, Oslo, and Manchester. Every woman who came to the performance,

Private View, was asked to use the toilet and take a pregnancy test, the results of which were displayed in real time above the bar (Pennington 2002–2010). The resulting 2019 photographic print is the outcome of the opening night of 'Part 1: Matrescence'. The words of various women who took the test, words that they uttered while waiting, are printed underneath each number. #43 read 'Gonna be negative for sure… unfortunately, not that I want to be pregnant'. There is no clear positive pregnancy test among the forty-nine, although one seems to have a very faint second line. Is pregnancy so uncommon? Or is it that pregnant women are keeping away from 'private view' exhibition spaces? They keep themselves in private. This artwork functions as a combination of media, private performance, and documentary photograph of the event.

Kirsten Justesen's series of five photographs entitled *Circumstances* (1973), also featured in the 'Part 2: Maternality' exhibition, sees the artist pose nude and pregnant with her plaster torso, a cast of her pregnant belly and breasts, white and marble-like. There is a contrast with the 'reality' of the artist's body, which is 'alive' even when frozen through the medium of a photograph, and the solidity of the plaster. Now, in the 2020s, there exists a whole industry that works to capture pregnancy portraits and belly casts. This demonstrates how the works and ideas of artists, ideas which were once considered avant-garde, can influence and be taken up within the mainstream. Justesen's work provides us with a sharp contrast between the live and the cast, both frozen in representation, but also revealed through it.[3]

The contrasted frozen sculptural body and frozen live body in Justesen's work return us to our consideration of Kristeva (1985) and Young (2005 [1990]) and their propositions that pregnancy brings together the corporeal and the temporal, or, to use a Kristevan formulation, the symbolic order of time comes together with the pre-symbolic visceral body. The performance makers we discuss in this chapter—Hannah Ballou, Aleksandra Nikolajev-Jones and Quarantine—have all managed to create and show performances that consider the nature of pregnancy. What unites all of the performances, aside from simply their profiling of the pregnant body on stage, is the consideration of the representation of the state of pregnancy. Pregnant performance enables the visceral, unruly body to be shown on stage in all its complexity, both presented and represented in a very particular tight time of developing and producing new life as well as developing, producing, and touring performance work.

Through our consideration of pregnancy in performance in relation to time, we ask questions about the accelerated pace of change of the pregnant body, and how the enigma of pregnant time might problematize the presentation (and representation) of the pregnant body on stage. The inescapable flow of pregnancy ensures we are in a constant state of renegotiation of our subjectivity and thus takes us beyond fixed representation. Pregnancy creates and stops time; it expands it and contracts it at once. We see here a parallel with live performance, which is absolutely reliant on time, as we argued in our Loss and Beginnings chapters. Performance reminds us of its temporal and fleeting qualities by its very essence as a medium that cannot exist beyond the time of meeting between performer and audience at one specific moment and in one specific place. During pregnancy, despite the expansion and growth of one's self and body, this 'special time' is perceived as one of nothingness and waiting. In her chapter 'Pregnant Embodiment: Subjectivity and Alienation' from the oft-cited book *On Female Body Experience: Throwing Like a Girl and Other Essays* (originally published in 1990, republished in 2005) Young writes:

> The dominant culture projects pregnancy as a time of quiet waiting. We refer to the woman as 'expecting,' as though this new life were flying in from another planet and she sat in her rocking chair by the window, occasionally moving the curtain aside to see whether the ship is coming. The image of uneventful waiting associated with pregnancy reveals clearly how much the discourse of pregnancy leaves out the subjectivity of the woman. From the point of view of others pregnancy is primarily a time of waiting and watching, when nothing happens. (p. 54)

Although pregnancy is a time of massive change and evolution, as Young's quote implies, it is also a time of interregnum, caught between times and states—neither pre-maternal or singular nor fully maternal or doubled through the bodily separation of mother and child as the child is expelled from the mother's uterus. Pregnancy is a 'weighted waiting', as Nikolajev-Jones has termed it in personal conversation with Emily; we return to the conception of pregnancy as both heaviness and slowness in our discussion of Nikolajev-Jones' performances below.

Pregnancy and the Challenges of Its Representation in Performance

Kristeva argues that to enter the symbolic realm of language (and of representation and performance) the Western canon has arrested the changing pregnant body so that the fluid maternal form can remain constant long enough to become understood and representable. We extend Kristeva's argument to specifically address the place of performance and the live pregnant body and its unruly uncontainability. For Kristeva, this containment of the pregnant body is the primary goal of art in the Christian tradition; she writes: 'for Freud imagining Leonardo—and even for Leonardo himself—taming the Maternal—or primary narcissistic—economy is a necessary precondition of artistic or literary achievement' (1985, p. 135). In this scenario performers then have two choices: present the pregnant body as beyond representation, never fixed and changing in time, or stop time, at least for the duration of the performance. According to Kristeva, this attempt to freeze the maternal body into a fixed state is enacted in representations of the Virgin Mary. She acknowledges that representations of Mary are culturally and historically specific and charts depictions of Mary in biblical scripture, apocryphal gospels, the Eastern Orthodox church, Dante's *Divine Comedy*, and 'in musical compositions from Palestrina to Pergolesi, Haydn, and Rossi' (p. 144) to name but a few of the examples she includes in 'Stabat Mater'; however, she sees all these various representations as united in an attempt to contain Mary, and thus the mother, in one symbolic meaning. Kristeva suggests that these attempts to freeze the maternal will always fail as they can never encompass all that the maternal figure is.

Fanny Soderback extends Kristeva's 'Stabat Mater' to argue that the maternal is 'a temporal principle that refuses the separation of word and flesh' (2010). The explicit marking of the maternal as an instance where word and flesh combine in Soderback's reading of Kristeva reminds us of the performative qualities of the maternal. The body of the performer brings to light the subject of the mother, lives that subjectivity, and reframes that subjectivity for consideration within the public sphere, as we argued after Hannah Arendt in our Beginnings chapter. Performance collapses the maternal body with maternal representation, and the body of the performer becomes both visceral embodiment and text when read through the lens of performance.

It is interesting to us that in 'Stabat Mater' Kristeva focusses on the written word and musical score, artforms that might be considered more stable than performance. The written word and musical composition create a fixed document, frozen in time at the moment of their creation, at least to some degree.[4] As a distinctly unfixed medium, might performance offer us an opportunity to think the maternal beyond its fixed representation? The visibly pregnant performer on stage brings her transitory and evolving maternal subjectivity together with an embodiment that, according to both Kristeva and Young, is in flux. The live maternal body on stage enacts while exceeding its containment in time or subjectivity and thus the pregnant performer counters orderly or static representation. We both managed to hide our early pregnancies in our performances and yet we both also felt we had to cease to perform these shows as our pregnancies developed. In this chapter we turn to an exploration of how others have carried the risky and unruly pregnant body on stage.

The challenge to representation proffered by the performing pregnant body is further complicated by considerations of who and what is being represented. Young opens her chapter on pregnant embodiment with a stark reminder of the secondary place of the mother to the developing child:

> Pregnancy does not belong to the woman herself. It is a state of the developing foetus, for which the woman is a container; or it is an objective, observable process coming under scientific scrutiny; or it becomes objectified by the woman herself as a 'condition' in which she must 'take care of herself'. (2005 [1990], p. 46)

The mother's subjectivity only emerges in relation to her other. This relational development is further heightened in pregnancy, when the mother and child are not only linked in terms of their subjectivity, but also their physical bodies. Pregnancy belongs to the outside, the child-outsider who is inhabiting the body as well as being governed by social scrutinizing norms—do not drink, do not smoke, rest, eat for two, don't eat too much, watch your step, don't bend too fast. Examples of this scrutiny of the pregnant body abound; in autumn 2020 a proposal was debated in the UK Parliament that this surveillance of the pregnant woman's body and behaviour was further formalized through a record of every alcoholic drink she consumes being kept on both her and her unborn child's medical records (Grover 2020). The pregnant subject is both to take care of herself and to be 'taken care of' by community and state. To become an artist, moreover a performer, to exhibit oneself during this process, to perform on stage, to reveal oneself as a pregnant performer can be conceived as beautiful and bold. It is through this public action, through performance making and pregnant showcases, that mother/artist's or the expectant mother/artist's agency resides. In her performance *goo:ga*, Hannah Ballou presents her pregnant performing self and body with charm and agency, humour, openness, honesty, and suspense. This act is a call for visibility. I am on stage pregnant, and (at one point) naked. Look at me!

On Hannah Ballou's *goo:ga*

Ballou starts *goo:ga* with pregnancy facts, telling the audience that 'white pregnant people love yoga balls' and that 'almond oil helps with stretch marks', before asking an audience member to spread the aforementioned almond oil across her pregnant, tight belly, as she gets close to the chosen audience member in her tiger-patterned bikini. The performance is about getting closer and closer to the audience, a kind of confessional story, with Ballou's pregnant body fully visible—first in the bikini, but later on fully naked, and finally the pregnant belly protruding in her tight bodycon dress. The performer carries her pregnant belly, her new state, in a slightly improvised manner, taking the audience through her stories, culminating with the 'gender reveal'. Brechtian in narrative and form, with the performer speaking at the microphone in front of an audience and no fourth wall, the piece is framed as a kind of critical gender reveal party. The show is interspersed with video footage of 'real' gender reveal parties that have been found on the Internet and which Ballou screens while she commentates on the videos live on stage or which she uses to give the audience something to watch while she leaves the stage to change her costume.

The finale of the performance is when the sex of the baby is revealed, just before Ballou admits (in spite of her admiration of gender-fluid parenting) she would rather have a girl. In true suspense, reveal, and relief fashion, the brown envelope, in which the information on the sex of her baby is contained and which Ballou herself has never opened, is brought onto stage and opened by a member of the audience; the screen is fixed so that it shows an illustration of the revealed gender (a female reproductive system in this case) while the happy couple are on stage with their eyes closed. At the count of three the audience reveal that it is a girl, complete with balloons and music.

In this frame of nothing happening and so much happening at the same time, Ballou is willing to publicly embody her own pregnant subjectivity and thus drafts her own representation. Ballou has already partly lived her pregnancy in front of the audience, who accompanied her for the 'big moments'. Her previous performance, *hoo:ha* (2015), included undertaking a pregnancy test live on stage; *goo:ga* can be seen as a continuation of this series, framed as the gender reveal moment during its first performance, while on the second night the audience gets to choose the baby girl's name from a list of potential monikers (Hannah Ballou, n.d.). Ballou makes public her own pregnancy, while also enabling us to critically come to terms with pregnancy through framing it in performance. Throughout the piece we are faced with a resistance to standard views of pregnancy, confronted with ovulation and pregnancy apps, introduced to critical songs about this new state, and asked to assess cultural perspectives of how celebrities are presented when pregnant, as too fat or too thin.

The famous Demi Moore *Vanity Fair* cover, a well-known nude pregnant photo shoot shot by Annie Leibovitz in August 1991, is projected on the screen behind the performer and then re-enacted live.[5] Ballou swiftly undresses herself, takes off her long dress in one fell swoop, and, completely naked, runs around the stage asking for volunteers to photograph her in the same pose as Demi Moore. This nude body reveal comes as a moment of surprise, and possibly 'too muchness' of the demanding pregnant body taking space. And yet the performer, while aware of this effect, does not do anything to mitigate the audience's discomfort. There is a kind of pretend ease about Ballou as she, pregnant and naked, asks the audience to photograph her. Later on, she checks the photographs for good results and, apparently unhappy with the images she and the audience have produced together, she runs off stage and brings back a packet of donuts, which she starts eating, eventually burying her face among the donuts and lying down, still nude, on the floor asking to be photographed again. This scene presents the pregnant body as a vehicle for both comedy and the erotic gaze. Can we conceive of the pregnant naked body as erotic? Is it allowed, or does it stay fixed as a container, a utility, an instrument? This moment feels incredibly transgressive, especially when presented against the more common cultural images of pregnancy that

Ballou has shared with us throughout this performance and which present the pregnant body as domestic, homely, and chaste in an almost sacred service to the growing foetus. While Ballou does not in any way present her body as erotic in this scene but rather as humorous (while Demi Moore's image is inescapably erotic and sexy), a few audience members decide to take their own photographs of Ballou. What are these photos for? Private moments of erotic pleasure, or a photographic document of a pregnant performance artist who dared to bare it all? Performance artists do dare, after all (Fig. 3.1).

There is something very powerful in Ballou's ability to pull off this show herself, to have her own Demi Moore moment, to get naked on stage, do the shoot live, as if it is a most normal thing to do, dress again, and continue with the piece. Beyond the Moore moment, the show is funny, educational, and straightforward; it enacts agency. Ballou claims

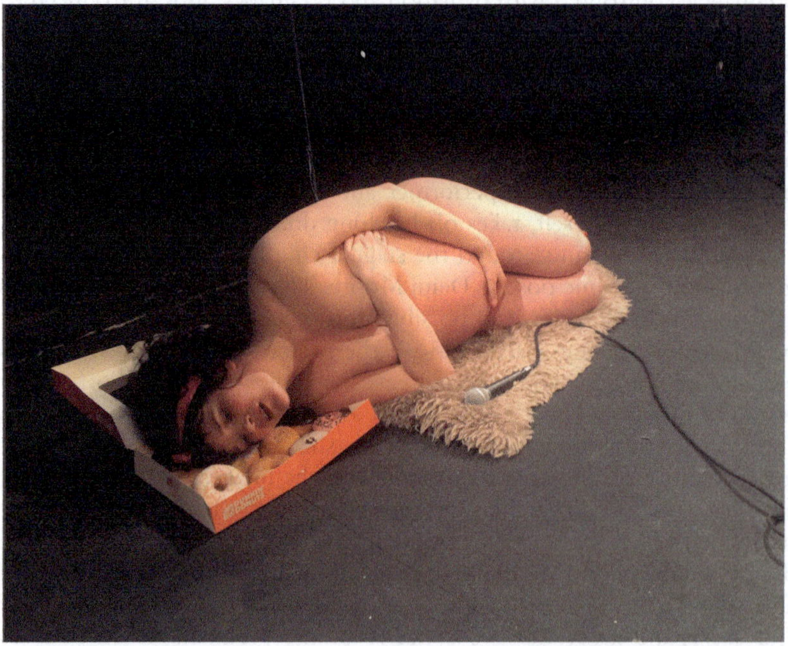

Fig. 3.1 Hannah Ballou in Hannah Ballou, *goo:ga* (2016) (Image by Eugenio Triana)

the stage (at times with her dog and her partner) with humour, through education, through exposure, through charm and stand-up. At the same time Ballou makes pregnancy look glamourous on stage: it is present, embraced, and full on. In this piece Ballou raises issues around gender, pink and blue sex reveal parties, the internalized mentality of boy vs. girl battles, the differences and fantasies of labour ward and birth centre births, one being obstetrician-led, the other midwife-led. Ballou uses her pregnant body as a vehicle to comment on these debates, while also presenting performed framings of her negotiations with maternal subjectivity. Ballou makes public what are more usually the profoundly private moments of pregnancy, bringing them from the domestic bathroom (in the case of the pregnancy test) or the clinic (in the case of the gender reveal) and living these events live on stage with us in real time, moving beyond a frozen or static temporality and enacting agency.

Emily on Aleksandra Nikolajev-Jones' *Gravida*

Aleksandra Nikolajev-Jones describes herself as a 'maternal dance practitioner'. She has been working with the pregnant body in dance for over twenty years and states that her first impulse to work with the pregnant body was in response to the shock she felt when becoming pregnant herself. Her training and experience as a classical ballet dancer had given her a particular sense of her own embodiment and she describes the feeling of 'death' as her body transformed with her pregnancy (Nikolajev-Jones with Underwood-Lee 2020, p. 9). *Nikolajev-Jones' ongoing interest in working with the pregnant body is driven by both a choreographic interest in the altered gravity experienced by the pregnant dancer and also a desire to explore the condition of the maternal and the interlinking of mother and unborn child that is carried within her. Nikolajev-Jones has described choreographing for a duo of pregnant women as creating a dance for not two but four dancers* (March 2013).

When she became pregnant with her third child, Nikolajev-Jones was inspired to work again with the pregnant body and she was successful in obtaining funding from the Arts Council of Wales to undertake research and development during her pregnancy. She has followed this with a number of performances and projects where she has worked with pregnant professional dancers, with community dancers with a relationship to pregnancy, and with midwives. I am hugely impressed by Nikolajev-Jones' tenacity in making pregnant performances. She has found creative solutions to the issues caused by the lack of alignment between the time it takes to get public funding and the duration of pregnancy by applying for small-scale research and development funding that can be processed more quickly or by getting funding in place and then recruiting pregnant dancers. I have not seen Nikolajev-Jones' performances live and am drawing here on our personal conversations and published interview (Nikolajev-Jones with Underwood-Lee 2020), *as well as documentation of her work, which she has generously shared with me. It strikes me that it is particularly revealing that the work of two of the three practitioners with which we engage in this chapter is accessed through documentation. The pregnant performing body evades us, gone before we can catch its representations.*

The pregnant body is fleeting—it disappears at every stage. Every day new embodiments emerge, our physical shape changes, our sensations change, our sense of self changes, our relationship to the foetus we are carrying changes, and before we have had time to stop and consider how we feel a new and strange embodiment has arrived. All bodies are always in transition, never static, even renewing on a cellular level, but this transition is more often than not slow, even imperceptible. In my current bodily state (not pregnant, post-menopausal, and not managing a health crisis) I find that I notice these changes only when I catch a glimpse of myself unexpectedly in the mirror and am surprised by my reflection. Now, when I am caught by my own image in an unexpected window or looking glass, it is my mother I see. Apart from these somewhat shocking moments when I see my mother's face in the mirror or my children see my face in photographs of her, I don't notice the shift in my body on a daily basis, especially as I am now past menopause and so not connected to a monthly cycle of change in my body. The pregnant body is in a state of accelerated evolution, or what Kristeva refers to as the 'endless flux of germinations' (1985, p. 151). *When I was pregnant, I was in a constant state of shock, new sensations emerging all the time. Nikolajev-Jones' evocation of pregnancy as a death of one's former self and former body chimes with my own experience of being pregnant; in order to bring new life into the world and to birth our new maternal embodiment we must say goodbye to the body that we inhabited before pregnancy. Daily, I was surprised by my own body and the transformations it was undergoing as it stretched and contorted. I could not catch hold of myself; my body was overtaken by the act of growing a baby, seemingly controlled by this new life within me rather than something that I knew, understood, or had time to get used to. I am talking here about the pregnancies that resulted in the live births of my daughters; pregnancies that end with a different result have, for me, felt rather different, or certainly feel different in my recollection of them. I enjoyed this constant sensation of newness and surprise in my pregnancies, but it is easy to see how this constant negotiation with embodiment could be challenging. The challenge then, for performance makers that wish to engage with the pregnant body, is to stand still for long enough to consider and perform.*

Aleksandra Nikolajev-Jones' choreography for pregnant bodies, and for bodies that 'have been pregnant' or for those who 'wish to empathize with the pregnant' (Westwater and Jones 2019), *embraces the fleeting and the ungraspable as the very quality that makes the dance interesting. Nikolajev-Jones and I discussed how dancers can work with an 'authentic' body that embraces and celebrates change and transition. She sees this possibility as unique to dance as she proposes that the training and practice of professional dancers allow for an acute awareness, memory, and understanding of bodily states. Of course, Nikolajev-Jones is speaking from her own experience of professional dance practice and pregnancy; the dancers with whom she works may experience this entirely differently. I wonder, what is the specific difference in Nikolajev-Jones' dance and performance training that enables this complex understanding of embodiment? Are dancers generally just so much more aware of their bodies or is this something particular to Nikolajev-Jones? The dancers with whom she has worked have been pregnant and then moved on, not continuing to represent pregnancy within their work, while Nikolajev-Jones has remained with the subject long after her own pregnancies have ended. Nikolajev-Jones tells me that she does not encounter this same level of awareness when she works with non-dancers, which she frequently does. My own understanding of my body in flux is constituted by my experience as a middle-aged, disabled woman living with chronic lymphoedema. Pain, illness, and disability, both physical and mental, are all things I sense as fluctuating. My own awareness of my body is acute: however, my training in how to manage this awareness and move through and beyond it is very different to how I imagine Nikolajev-Jones must understand her own bodily awareness as a trained and virtuosic dancer. My experience of my mutable state in my post-fertility years is also profoundly different from how I understood change when I was pregnant. Young notes the differences between her awareness of her body in pregnancy and in other acute states:*

> *In attending to my pregnant body in such circumstances, I do not feel myself alienated from it, as in illness. I merely notice its borders and rumblings with interest, sometimes with pleasure, and this aesthetic interest does not divert me from my business.* (2005, p. 52)

Nikolajev-Jones uses a series of exercises to engage with 'creativity and imagination' (Nikolajev-Jones with Underwood-Lee 2020, p. 6) *in order to develop an awareness of the dancer's 'authentic body'; here she is using 'authentic body' to indicate an internal understanding of the body that is always transitional rather than a particular fixed bodily state, an understanding that reminds me of Young's equation of the observation of her pregnant body with an aesthetic experience. Nikolajev-Jones tells me that instead of falling into the trap of exploring her own pregnancy as a time of heaviness, she wished to open up this new sense of gravitational pull and celebrate the artistic opportunities that this presented her with* (Fig. 3.2).

In conversation, Nikolajev-Jones' has termed her choreography as 'a weighted waiting' and 'a brilliant unknowing'. Her dancers dance between states, between time and corporeality, embodying Kristeva's assertion that the maternal can move beyond 'not avoiding the embarrassing and inevitable issue of the law but instead bringing to the law flesh, language, and jouissance' (1985, p. 151). *It is particularly appealing for me, as someone who will not be pregnant again, that Nikolajev-Jones opens up the possibility that this unique moment, when pregnancy offers us the opportunity to inhabit both the Real and the Symbolic and to question and enliven both, can be accessed through memories of being pregnant or 'empathy with the pregnant'. Nikolajev-Jones evokes this state by employing particular body exercises and techniques that she has developed; I wonder if we might also be able to come close to this through the privileged opportunities to consider pregnancy that are opened up by those practitioners who manage to bring pregnant embodiment to the realm of representation via performance.*

Lena on Quarantine's *Spring*.

In Croatian, pregnancy is described as 'u drugom stanju' (literally, in other state). There is a kind of otherness about it, something 'otherwise' which pregnancy invites us towards. Is that a kind of poetry, something sublime in its representation? Does not the language and subsequently culture fall into the old trap of idealizing the pregnant body, putting it on a pedestal? I realize I am stuck in the idealization of the pregnant body myself, in this desire for the sublime in pregnancy, in the desire for otherness in its performance representation too. I too am wanting some kind of 'pregnant poetry', something almost transcendental, something 'otherwise'. How to hold the critical and political together with the poetic in maternal performance?

Fig. 3.2 Tanja Raman and Lara Ward in Gravida, *Pregnant Tango* (2015) (Image by Iwan Brioc)

I saw Spring. *as a part of the quartet of performances in the spring of 2016 at Old Granada Studios in Manchester, UK.* Spring. *sees a stage full of pregnant women, a chorus of them. The piece was also performed at Noorderzon Performing Arts Festival in Groningen, the Netherlands, and at Norfolk & Norwich Festival, UK in 2017. I am remembering the Manchester version now for this writing. I notice that Quarantine's website describes it as: 'Fuelled by incessant karaoke and a text built out of hundreds of awkward questions,* Spring. *asks about absence and presence and what it means to be hopeful'* (Quarantine 2016–2017).

The piece projects us into the future, all the pregnant bodies, together. I remember questions. I remember hope and uncertainty. What I do not remember at all in the piece is the karaoke singing. Was there pregnant poetry on stage? I remember Leentje Van de Cruys as one of the co-devisors/performers leading a group of pregnant women, kind of managing them. Van de Cruys was not pregnant, or at least she did not seem to be. It felt as if she was the master performer, and all other, pregnant women were just ordinary people. Quarantine theatre company works with ordinary people, volunteers. This immediately raises questions of labour and payments. Are the performers/volunteers paid? Do they get their expenses covered? What do they get out of this? I remember thinking that the pregnant women on stage form a kind of antenatal group, lucky to be put together through the process of making a performance. Pregnant women on stage were a new community emerging.

Summer.Autumn.Winter.Spring. *was a whole day of performance experiences.* Spring. *was the end. It was hopeful; it was about the future; it was poetic. Did the women sing? I just remember them standing around the stage and asking, or being asked, all these questions about their future children. Questions like: 'What if you are obsessed with your looks? What if you don't care about anything at all? What will you care for? … Will you look after me one day?'* (Delgado-Garcia 2019, p. 158). *There were so many questions, no answers, no stops, no considerations. This was an endless cycle of production and reproduction. Children, more babies, more women, more pregnant bellies, more bodies. A kind of poetry, in motion, which refuses to stay still and be represented, frozen in understanding. However, there was something consuming about it, the crowd of all these women who are presented as strangers on stage but have created a community that also exists out of the limelight.*

In an interview conducted by Cristina Delgado-Garcia, Richard Gregory, the director of the piece, says that for Norwich the five Manchester women were brought in: 'They were like rock stars, a SWAT team of Quarantine performers... They'd become an incredibly close bunch of friends who supported each other during this year—some of them went to each other's babies' births' (Delgado-Garcia 2019, p. 156). *The pregnant women from the Manchester performance in 2016 had become friends and reunited for the Norwich piece in 2017, with their babies in tow. A community had been formed, and renewed.*

Looking at the old programme notes I have from the whole set of performances in 2016, and my own handwritten comments, I wondered about its managed experience, with ushers who were all wearing Summer.Autumn.Winter.Spring. *T-shirts. In my fragmented writing I complained that it felt urban and cool, and that the ticket was £25. Do I not belong to the cool and urban crowd who is happy to pay £25 for a whole afternoon and evening in the theatre? I worried if all the performers were paid or not. I speculated whether they could be reconfigured as a new community who cares; however, I did not want to assume on behalf of the involved mothers-to-be. I held in my mind the same old questions of agency and money. During one of the breaks I met one of the fathers-to-be, whose girlfriend was in* Spring. *He told me that his ticket was only £10 and that they got silver balloons and nice photos. He told me his girlfriend was happy to be involved. Having found a note of his email address, I tried to get in touch with him and with the then pregnant performer. I wondered what her recollection of the event is now. They never got back to me. Maybe the email was no longer in use; maybe they split up. My final question in my handwritten notes was: 'What kind of society allows for these kinds of labour relations in performance?' Now I am also wondering if pregnant women on stage are a commodity, a fetish, a luxury product with an expiry date. I am pulled back to thinking about the precarity of maternal time, and particularly pregnant time. This temporal precarity informs and confirms my critical thoughts around perception and the use of pregnant women in performance as precious objects, who cannot seem to hold their own representation.*

Am I too critical? I held similar views about mothers with their babies and toddlers performing at the opening of the PSi conference in Zagreb in 2009 (Šimić 2018). *Do pregnant women, do small children, when placed on display, evoke feelings of public scrutiny, open judgment? Do we dare be much more vocal about our opinions upon seeing them revealed in public, disclosed from their private sphere where they 'rightfully belong'? Was this performance too much poetry in motion, and no apparent agency? Does the pregnant body on stage have to remain unresolved, a puzzle, a frustration almost?*

Presenting the Uncontainable

As we discussed early on in this chapter, Hannah Ballou gives a unique example of both the practical and philosophical difficulty of making a show while pregnant. Ballou clearly articulates this when she states in her performance *goo:ga:*

> A very interesting thing about making a show with a body that is just radically changing out from underneath you is that some decisions can become problematic, and a great example of that is that this bikini fit so much better a month ago. (Ballou 2016)

Ballou's show is all about the state of being pregnant: she dances with her belly on show, asks the audience to rub oil into her belly, wears a variety of costumes that highlight her pregnancy, and actively invites us to explore both the comic and problematic moments she has encountered while pregnant throughout this work; and yet, in this statement she is humorously showcasing just how difficult it is to articulate her pregnancy through the medium of performance. Her body has changed in a month and it means that, even at the accelerated pace at which she has made this work, her costume choices have become 'problematic'. Despite this, by articulating the artistic problems presented by her pregnancy, she is able to claim agency in and through performance and represent the essential uncontainability and unruliness of the pregnant body on stage. Young notes that, through attending to the pregnant body, the pregnant woman can experience her weighted embodiment as joyful. Much like the assertions that Nikolajev-Jones makes around pregnancy as a period of weighted waiting that can be celebrated in dance, Young states: 'Pregnancy roots me to the earth, makes me conscious of the physicality of my body not as an object, but as the material weight that I am in movement' (2005 [1990], p. 52). This attention to pregnant embodiment, and the agency that it can give us, is manifest in Ballou's performance, where she is presenting and making public her embodied experience of pregnancy through performance. Ballou's performance is markedly different from *Gravida* and *Spring.*, in that she is both author and executor of her work, while Nikolajev-Jones and Quarantine employ pregnant performers to enact the choreographic/directorial vision. Ballou also manages to achieve this by fixing on one very specific moment of pregnancy, the moment at which the baby's sex is revealed, or to follow Ballou's own terminology when the parents find out 'what the baby's genitals look like' (Ballou 2016). The gender reveal that Ballou focuses our attention on might be read through a Kristevan lens as a freezing of pregnancy: just as Kristeva proposes in 'Stabat Mater' that the mother must be fixed in order to be contained in representation, the baby must be fixed by the confirmation of their gender. In choosing this particular fixed, temporal point Ballou is able to make a representation of her experience of pregnancy that goes beyond this moment and embraces the constantly changing body while also reaching towards a static point.

Fanny Soderback argues for a reading of Kristeva's 'Stabat Mater' that enables us to think of the maternal as both temporal and corporeal and states: 'the maternal body *qua generative* brings our attention to the continuity between time and matter' (2010, p. 10, original emphasis). If, following Soderback's reading of Kristeva, maternal bodies can bring together an understanding of both temporality and corporeality, then perhaps we are offered a third option for presenting the maternal body on stage that takes us beyond our previously asserted dual choice of fixity or unrepresentability. Perhaps it is this very unrepresentability that we are able to represent when we place the pregnant body on stage, and which Ballou opens up in *goo:ga*.

Notes

1. See https://performanceandthematernal.com/ for more details of our Performance and the Maternal project.
2. See https://foundlingmuseum.org.uk/wp-content/uploads/2015/07/Portraying-Pregnancy-press-release.pdf, https://www.richardsaltoun.com/exhibitions/79-part-1-matrescence/overview/, https://www.richardsaltoun.com/exhibitions/80-part-2-maternality/overview/, https://www.richardsaltoun.com/artists/301/.
3. In terms of further visual representations of pregnancy it is also worth noting Rosemary Betterton's *Maternal Bodies in the Visual Arts* (2014) and Birth Rites Collection. See http://birthritescollection.org.uk/.
4. We are mindful here that many literary critics, often drawing from Barthes' essay 'The Death of the Author' (1977), would argue that the literary text is never stable; however, it is our contention that at least some aspects of the text become fixed through the process of writing in a way that is never possible with live performance.

We could also say that live musical performance has these qualities; however, Kristeva is concerned in her article with musical compositions which become fixed as sheet music or recordings rather than instances of the performance of music.

5. For a discussion of Demi Moore's iconic image see Tyler (2001).

References

Arts Council of Wales. n.d. Small and Large Grants. Arts Council of Wales. https://arts.wales/small-and-large-grants-individuals. Accessed 2 Feb 2020.

Ballou, Hannah. n.d. *Hannah Ballou*. http://www.hannahballou.com/home.html. Accessed 15 Oct 2020.

Barthes, Roland. 1977. *Image, Music, Text*. London: Fontana.

Betterton, Rosemary. 2014. *Maternal Bodies in the Visual Arts*. Manchester: Manchester University Press.

Delgado-Garcia, Cristina. 2019. An Interview with Simon Banham, Richard Gregory and Renny O'Shea, Part Five. In *Summer. Autumn. Winter. Spring. Staging Life and Death by Quarantine*, ed. S. Banham, S. Hunter, M. Brady, and R. O'Shea. Manchester: Manchester University Press.

Grover, Natalie. 2020. Plans to Record Pregnant Women's Alcohol Consumption in England Criticised. *The Guardian*, 16 September. https://www.theguardian.com/lifeandstyle/2020/sep/16/plans-to-record-pregnant-womens-alcohol-consumption-in-england-criticised. Accessed 2 Feb 2021.

Kristeva, Julia. 1985. Stabat Mater. *Poetics Today* 6 (1/2): 133–152.

March, Polly. 2013. New Work Celebrates the Movement of Pregnant Women. *BBC*, 24 May. https://www.bbc.co.uk/blogs/wales/entries/504bd131-f5f3-308d-af8e-64de2f4379ea. Accessed 2 Feb 2021.

Nikolajev-Jones, Aleksandra with Emily Underwood-Lee. 2020. Interview with Aleksandra Nikolajev-Jones. Performance and the Maternal. https://performanceandthematernal.files.wordpress.com/2020/10/aleksandra-nikolajev-jones.pdf. Accessed 15 Oct 2020.

Šimić, Lena. 2018. Encountering Performing (M)Others: Feminist Maternal Practice in Contemporary Performance. *Contemporary Theatre Review* 28 (3): 401–412.

Soderback, Fanny. 2010. Motherhood: A Site of Repression of Liberation? Kristeva and Butler on the Maternal Body. *Studies in the Maternal* 2 (1).

Tyler, Imogen. 2001. Skin-Tight: Celebrity, Pregnancy and Subjectivity. In *Thinking through the Skin*, ed. S. Ahmed, and J. Stacey. London: Routledge.

Vincent Dance Theatre. 2009. *Pregnancy and Parenthood: The Dancer's Perspective.* https://www.vincentdt.com/wp-content/uploads/2008/12/Pregnancy Report.pdf. Accessed 15 Oct 2020.

Westwater, Carrie, and Aleksandra Jones. 2019. Gravida: Case study. *WAHWN*. https://wahwn.cymru/uploads/resources/Gravida%20Case%20S tudy%20(002).docx. Accessed 16 Jan 2020.

Young, Iris Marion. 2005 [1990]. *On Female Body Experience: Throwing Like a Girl and Other Essays*. Oxford: Oxford University Press.

Performances and Artworks Cited

Ballou, Hannah. 2015. *hoo:ha* [performance].

Ballou, Hannah. 2016. *goo:ga* [performance].

Justesen, Kirsten. 1973. *Circumstances* [photography series].

Leibovitz, Annie. 1991, August. More Demi Moore. *Vanity Fair* [cover photograph].

Nikolajev-Jones, Aleksandra. 2012–2020. *Gravida* [performance series].

Pennington, Liv. 2002–2010. *Private View* [mixed media].

Quarantine. 2016–2017. *Summer.Autumn.Winter.Spring.* [performance].

Richard Saltoun Gallery. 2019. Part 1: Matrescence, 15 November–21 December. London [exhibition].

Richard Saltoun Gallery. 2020. Part 2 Maternality, 10 January–15 February. London [exhibition].

Šimić, Lena. 2004. *Medea Mothers' Clothes* [performance].

Šimić, Lena. 2005. *Joan Trial* [performance].

Šimić, Lena. 2007–2008. *Contemplation Time* [mixed media].

Šimić, Lena. 2013. *1994* [performance].

Šimić, Lena. 2014. *Friday Records* [mixed media].

The Foundling Museum. 2020. 'Portraying Pregnancy: From Holbein to Social Media', 25 January–26 April. London [exhibition].

The Photographers' Gallery and the Foundling Museum. 'Home Truths: Photography and Motherhood', 11 October 2013–5 January 2014. London. [exhibition].

Underwood-Lee, Emily. 2007. *Ode to Morten Harket* [performance].

Underwood-Lee, Emily. 2010. *Titillation* [performance].

CHAPTER 4

Birth (4 Months)

Emily: I didn't sleep last night. I spent the time trying to remember my twenty-nine-hour labour, trying to find the feelings again in my body. I pressed my belly, I tried to think into my uterus, I looked for the scar from my episiotomy at five in the morning. I could not find the memory of the sensations, just as I could not find the physical marks. I remember this birth so clearly but also I remember nothing. Surely birthing my daughter, something that was so profound for me, should be traceable on or in my body? (5 February 2020, on my daughter's eighth birthday)

Lena: The contractions were very strong. It was as if someone was ripping me from inside, stretching me out. The midwife kept saying I will have my baby really soon. ... The crowning is a familiar pain; it's ripping you open. It's bearable because it's familiar. Tear, cut. His head came out at 4.11 a.m. I remember being at the bed and wanting to stand up tall from my 'on all fours' position. Instead I had to lie down and they spread out my legs. I had to push. Another shoulder dystocia. He got stuck for 4 minutes. We pushed/pulled him out at 4.15 a.m. There was no panic. He was placed on my tummy. ('Birth Story' written over four days, 10–13 January 2014)

As we began our work on this chapter concerning birth in February 2020, Emily's youngest daughter turned eight years old.[1] On her daughter's birthday Emily wondered, why is it always the child who was born

L. Šimić and E. Underwood-Lee, *Maternal Performance*, Contemporary Performance InterActions,
https://doi.org/10.1007/978-3-030-80226-4_4

who celebrates the birthday—surely this is also a day about the woman who gave birth? Perhaps this is a rather selfish sentiment; it goes against that popularly perpetuated myth of the mother as all sacrificing, denying her own needs in order to service the general happiness of her child. To acknowledge the mother on the child's birthday might take something away from the child's putatively *special day*. Emily's grandmother always said that the mother should get a present on her children's birthdays as it is the mother who did all the work. Those mothers who birth a child from their uterus, and then witness that child's birthdays, have both given birth—the labour of labour—as well as laboured to ensure the child survives well enough to celebrate each passing year. Emily's grandmother's proclamation annoyed the young Emily as she felt like her grandmother was trying to spoil or co-opt the event. Now we get what she meant.

The instance of birth is difficult to remember for the birthing mother and impossible to remember for the child. Our memory of birth is fragile, uncertain, disjointed. With the birth of her fourth child Lena learnt the importance of recording the birth story, and narrated her experience in written form, juxtaposing the reality of taking care of the newborn to the very recent memory of giving birth. This particular 'Birth Story' (Šimić 2014) was composed over four days, between 10 January, the birthdate of her youngest son, and 13 January, which marked two years since her miscarriage.

Narrating Birth

In *Relating Narratives: Storytelling and Selfhood* (2000) Adriana Cavarero asks us to consider the importance of birth stories as told to us by others. Cavarero uses the Oedipus myth to explore how birth is both the moment at which we become an independent subject and the point at which our subjectivity is defined in relation to another. Cavarero highlights how Oedipus confronts the sphinx without knowledge of his birth and therefore without knowledge of who he truly is (2000, p. 10). Equally, Iocasta is both herself and not herself, both wife and mother of Oedipus but ignorant of her dual status. Neither Oedipus nor Iocasta can know their own identity without understanding the story of the moment at which mother and son were both birthed into their subjectivities. Cavarero further argues that it is through our understanding of the stories that are told about our birth that we can come to understand our intersubjective identity. She draws on author Karen Blixen's childhood recollection to show that one can never understand the story of one's life at the moment it is lived; instead it is through looking back at the footprints that are left behind that the path taken and the completeness of the image becomes clear, and further, that generally, it is only after one's own death that the totality of the story is revealed and so the looking back always has to be done by another (p. 3). Following Cavarero's argument we can see that our identity (if we can consider one understanding of identity to be the story of our lives) is formed both at our birth and after the moment of our death. Yet these are the two positions we will never be able to recount for ourselves, because they are both beyond our independent memory and story; thus our identity is always multiple and relational, or as Cavarero states: 'two unrepeatable uniquenesses, who distinguish themselves by mutually appearing together' (p. 111). Further, our births and deaths take us beyond the Symbolic and into the Lacanian Real, as we have explored in our Loss chapter. In Loss we explored our closeness to the Real in moments of grief; here we discuss the Real that we enter through the experience of giving birth.

When discussing *This Imaginary Woman* (2003) we have followed Lacan in arguing that grief takes us close to the Real; similarly, at birth we are at a stage before the point at which we can articulate ourselves as subjects or enter the realm of the Symbolic, or, as Lacan states, the human child is in a pre-linguistic and pre-subjective state 'before language restores to it, in the universal, its function as subject' (Lacan 1999 [1970], p. 76). Lacanian psychoanalysis insists that the mother enables us to pass through this pre-Symbolic stage and enter the realm of language. The necessity Lacan places on the child passing through this pre-Symbolic stage enables society to apportion blame to the mother who does not 'successfully' negotiate this stage for her child. What is neglected in this Lacanian analysis is the experience of the birthing mother, who, we argue here, is also thrust into the Real through her experience of bringing the child into the world through her body.

The intensity of the extreme bodily experience and heightened emotional state induced in the experience of birth, which lingers for months, as we shall explore in the following chapter, Aftermath, marks the mother's identity. Birth is bodily in nature in the extreme, unnerving, and emotional. Dazed and let into the streams of the Real at the moment of birth, the new mother must look back in order to enter the process of memorizing and reflecting on the birth. With reflection and consideration, the mother is able to reconstruct the birth story, sharing the origins of how both mother and child were birthed into their new co-dependent subjectivities. Cavarero's mythically influenced analysis places the mother at the heart of our intersubjectivity; our mothers can narrate our births to us, can tell us the stories that constitute the beginning of our lives and the beginning of the formation of our identity. The mother must also recount this story for herself in order to understand her new maternal status. In this chapter we will explore how these stories have been told through the performance and installation *The Birth of Baby X* by Marni Kotak (2011), the performance *Partus* by Third Angel (2015), and in the ongoing performance and story work of Tracy Breathnach-Evans, in particular *Cord* (2016b).[2]

Birth is the transitional moment at which not only a child but also a mother are born together into their new subjectivities and yet we cannot observe or narrate our experience of being born for ourselves. Similarly, our closeness to the Real while in the act of birthing might be said to prevent us from being able to narrate our story of giving birth, and thus our own birth into our new maternal subjectivity eludes us. It is at this crucial point of being born, both as a child and into our identity as a mother, that we are dependent on the other. The identities of both mother and child are intrinsically linked through dependence on the other; our identities are co-produced. At the same time the visceral sensations at the moment of giving birth take us beyond intellectual understanding, and our very newness prevents us from comprehending that we are being born. Following this logic, it might be argued that birth stories will always elude us and be limited to a simulacrum, representing and yet never fully able to capture the whole of the story.

The history of philosophical thought has often either ignored the moment of birth altogether or focussed on the moment of being born as a child-subject, obfuscating the experience of the birthing mother. In his 1929 psychoanalytic treatise on birth trauma Otto Rank notes that 'the whole psychical development of man' is framed by the trauma of birth and 'the continually recurring attempts to overcome it [this birth trauma]' (1993, p. xxiv). Here Rank marks birth as the primary consideration for understanding what it is to be human, but his consideration is only from the perspective of the person being born rather than that of the birthing mother. Yet again, the mother in this configuration is only there to enable the subjectivity of the child; her own experience in relation to her own maternal subjectivity is entirely missing from the discussion. And yet the mother matters, not only in terms of her own experience and her own subjectivity, but also in relation to the new subject who is being born. The mother holds their story, however fragile, disjointed, and visceral that memory is. It is the mother who narrates each one of our existences; we are dependent on them telling us our individual stories, as Cavarero powerfully articulates.

To Begin Anew

Hannah Arendt made an important intervention towards bringing birth into the frame of critical thinking when she subverted the Freudian death drive and asked us to consider natality, and birth itself, as the human capacity for beginning. Arendt writes:

> men [*sic*] are equipped for the logically paradoxical task of making a new beginning because they themselves are new beginnings and hence beginners, that the very capacity for beginning is rooted in natality, in the fact that human beings appear in the world by virtue of birth. (1990 [1963], p. 112)

To align birth and the notion of natality with the human capacity to begin in the world, again and again, anew each time, is extraordinary, a leap of faith in our understanding of what thinking through natality, rather than mortality and the death drive, opens up in understanding of the human condition and experience of life. This human capacity to begin anew is, according to Arendt, linked with 'action', which alongside labour and work, Arendt places as one of the primary conditions that make us human. In Arendt's configuration, 'labour' is linked with the biological and reproductive, maintaining functions, and 'work' with durable outputs. In contrast, 'action' takes us into the realm of the *polis* and is the means by which we mark and distinguish each other in the world.

It is worth quoting Arendt at length here to fully pay attention to the forcefulness of her argument for natality, as most strongly connected to action, as the basis of the human condition:

> Labor and work, as well as action, are also rooted in natality in so far as they have the task to provide and preserve the world for, to foresee

> and reckon with, the constant influx of newcomers who are born into the world as strangers. However, of the three, action has the closest connection with the human condition of natality; the new beginning inherent in birth can make itself felt in the world only because the newcomer possesses the capacity of beginning something anew, that is, of acting. In this sense of initiative, an element of action, and therefore of natality, is inherent in all human activities. (1958, p. 9)

Arendt foregrounds that the act of being born locates us within the realm of beginnings and action. Through action we find agency, where we are able to take political action and where we become full subjects. Arendt states that action is '*the* condition ... of all political life' (1958, p. 7, original emphasis) and clearly locates the production of individual subjectivity and capacity for action in the public sphere. For Arendt, the biological, and therefore the act of giving birth, is situated with the category of labour, which is perceived as if of lesser value than action and which confines the birthing subject to the domestic.[3] Just as we explored through Simone de Beauvoir in our Beginnings chapter, for Arendt the mother, the birthing subject, is not a part of the public sphere; she labours behind closed doors. As for the new subject, the inability to articulate the experience of birth means that for Arendt, birth itself can never be part of the realm of action (1958, p. 63). In Arendt's formulation of natality, we must move beyond the biological moment of birth and think of birth as a point of potential, newness, and beginning rather than a physical event in which a mother's body labours to bring a new child into the world. Natality is thus conceptually aligned with a potential, with the capacity for beginning and newness.

As Imogen Tyler notes, in Arendt's conception natality is linked to social reproduction and not to the act of birthing and we are yet again without a birthing maternal body (Tyler 2009, p. 1). It is almost as if the mother is only there to serve a new individual who will eventually be born into the public sphere with their capacity for action, their new beginnings. Tyler makes a compelling case for a re-evaluation of birth that considers the birthing maternal subject and the need for her to be made visible as an essential project of feminist thinking (p. 6). Tyler calls for a reinsertion of birth into the frame of critical thinking and feminist action, and traces a history not only of the unwillingness of Western philosophical thought to give any consideration to birth but also of the structural and material conditions that disadvantage women. She argues that a considered, intergenerational, and interdisciplinary understanding of birth is central if we are to remove discrimination against bodies that birth or have the potential to birth. While Tyler may critique much of Arendt's removal of birth itself from the frame of the public sphere, she demonstrates that the issues that Arendt was addressing in the middle of the twentieth century are still just as pressing more than half a century later (2009, p. 6).

Through our discussion of maternal performances which consider birth, we centralize the mother with her birthing body and the birth stories she tells as they are gifted to the child, just as Tyler, Arendt, and Cavarero incite us to do. We ought to celebrate the act of birth as her action in the public sphere, action which takes on affective, intellectual, and aesthetic dimensions. Mothers hold the stories of the child and there is and must be relatedness to the mother with each new beginning, with each new subject entering the world with their capacity for newness and action. Cavarero, whose whole philosophical project is influenced by Arendt, can help us here.[4] We must consider the stories the mother holds and how she tells them. The staged performance of personal stories is always an act of bringing the private into the public sphere. When a performance centralizes the experience of the birthing mother it brings together a foregrounding of birth and natality as told by the mother who recounts both her own story and the story of the child as both emerge into their new subjectivities.

Birth in Performance

The 'making visible' of birth stories might be effectively and affectively done when we consider birth within the framework of live art and performance. The performance space is inherently public; therefore, by elevating birth to the status of a subject worthy of dramatic consideration, we literally push the birthing body of the mother and her subjectivity into the limelight. The performances we consider in this chapter ask us to not only reflect on the intellectual aspects of birth but also the aesthetics of birth as presented through performance, which is an artistic representation in the public sphere. The performances that we discuss in this chapter, through giving intellectual and aesthetic dimensions to the experience of birth, move birth from the realm of labour to that of action, to use an Arendtian formulation. Furthermore, it is through art and performance that the body and its senses are awoken, yet again. The focus on the visual spectacle of birth, and inevitably its representation, is not only present in performance. The event of birth has received considerable popular attention through TV programmes such as *One Born Every Minute* (2010–2018) as well as YouTube birthing stories and other social media platforms where mums-to-be play out their new identities.[5] These 'real-life' birth presentations differ significantly from the performances we consider in that they attempt to present birth as dramatic but do not necessarily foreground the aesthetic. We are, ironically, expected to see birth 'as it happens' in these highly sanitized, mediated, and sentimentalized representations, rather than a reflection of birth, which can be offered to us in art and performance, or through stories told about birth as Cavarero notes.

Artistic representations of birth in both contemporary theatre and the visual arts are also on the rise.[6] All these birth performances have, in their very different ways and in various contexts including live art and theatre, supported this cultural and artistic rise of the topic of birth. It is within this proliferation of portrayals of birth that the *Birth of Baby X*, *Partus*, and *Cord*, the principal performances that we consider here, emerge. These performances do the important work of bringing birth into the public sphere intimately and enabling us to discuss it carefully, prompting a reflection of birth from the perspective of the birthing subject.

On Marni Kotak's *The Birth of Baby X*

Before turning to our individual considerations of *Partus* and *Cord*, we explore the literal conflation of birth and performance that occurred in *The Birth of Baby X* (2011) by Marni Kotak, shown at the Microscope Gallery in Brooklyn. Kotak describes the piece on her website as 'a durational performance that Kotak conducted from October 8 through November 7 … culminating in the live birth of her baby boy Ajax, on October 25, 2011' (Kotak, n.d.). Although in the title of the piece the baby was nameless, i.e. Baby X, in the retrospective description Kotak names her child 'Ajax'. It is often at the point of birth that we are given a name and thus entered to a partial degree into the Symbolic realm. Kotak's own description of her work and her change from using 'Baby X' to 'Ajax' marks this transition for the emerging child-subject; however, the work is primarily concerned with Kotak's experience of birth rather than focussing on the child. Not only did Kotak exhibit her birthing body but she also created an installation in the gallery space of her imagined ideal birthing space. In *The Birth of Baby X* the birth event, environment, and the birthing body of the mother become a spectacle for public consumption; we might think about spectacle here in relation to the spectacular and also the speculum used for exploring the intimacies of the biological body and reproductive organs, both taking their origin from the Latin *specio* meaning 'to look'. We are invited to look closely at the environment and expectations of birth. The performative nature and classic dramatic arc of birth are highlighted in *The Birth of Baby X* through marking the birth itself as a performance for a small, invited audience.

Kotak's performance and exhibition take us to a point beyond representation which could reinstate the birth as purely 'labour-some'. Kotak treads the fine line between being an artist, in charge of her representation, and a birthing human, in the act of giving birth. Kotak moves past the point at which she is representing birth and into an artistic presentation framed within a gallery setting. Her birthing body is not being narrated back to her through representation but is live in the space; this is not the retelling that Cavarero highlights, because in some sense we are before the point at which the story is told. The mother is not telling her story but developing it live in front of and with the audience. A complete story only becomes known through the documentation of the live birth event, which exists extensively on Kotak's website and in press accounts. Of course, the story can, in some senses, never be complete and the various protagonists will all bring different perspectives to their memory and interpretation. Kotak acknowledges this incomplete narrative as she continues to make work with and about her parenting of her son, Ajax; including *Ajax's Disco Dinosaur Halloween 8th Birthday Party* (2019) and *Love Masks* (2020). Despite the impossibility of ever finishing a maternal story, by curating the press coverage and documentation of *The Birth of Baby X* Kotak presents us with a birth story told from her own subjective position as birthing subject and as artist in control of her representation. Interestingly, none of the press coverage of *The Birth of Baby X* focusses on the particularity of the birth but instead tells a somewhat sensational story of how a birth took place in a gallery, which might mark the limits of our control of our birth stories once we place them in the public domain through artworks.

Arendt is clear that putting bodily activity in the public domain is not enough to transform it into action, instead she states that this can never be more than 'private activities displayed in the open' (1958, p. 134).

This somewhat biting argument from Arendt might be countered by much contemporary performance art, and is challenged in our reading of Kotak's *The Birth of Baby X*, where it is the constructed environment, in the form of an idealized birth environment displayed as a gallery exhibition, that moves the bodily process of delivering a baby into the public sphere. The birthing body remains mostly absent for the general public while in the event of giving birth, yet the documentation remains, again raising the artistic endeavour to the sphere of action. Kotak's actual birthing experience may have moved beyond representation into labour, to use Arendt's term, but the environment the artist created in the gallery focusses on an anticipated birth. This anticipation of birth returns us to the notion of a perfect birth as rehearsed in the birth plan. The exhibition in which the performance occurred opened on 8 October and Ajax was born on 25 October (Kotak n.d.). During the seventeen-day period before Ajax's birth the installation existed as a site for birth, rather than the site of birth. In constructing this site Kotak creates a public display and moves birth from Arendt's categories of labour and work into that of action, making an artwork that will endure and mark her own public engagement with the world. The public nature of the exhibition of a birth space rehearses, re-creates, and repeats birth as a performance event (Fig. 4.1).

The live birth that presented the culmination of *The Birth of Baby X* was made visible to only a very few members of a selected audience; what endures is the story told about the birth, both through the space created beforehand and the documentation of that space on Kotak's website and beyond in the significant press coverage that the piece received in the *New York Times*, *Wall Street Journal*, *The Times*, and many more media outlets (Kotak, n.d.). Kotak's performance happens somewhere between the private realm of labour and the public realm of action. Action here functions through the artist's decision to make the piece and present it live, in the public sphere. However, the birth event itself is not an open public event and ultimately becomes invisible, which prompts us to ask if it is ever possible to align live birth with action, or is it always doomed to slip back into Arendt's category of 'labour'? It is only through the stories that are told about Kotak's birth experience by the artist and reviewers that we are able to understand the subjectivity of the birthing mother

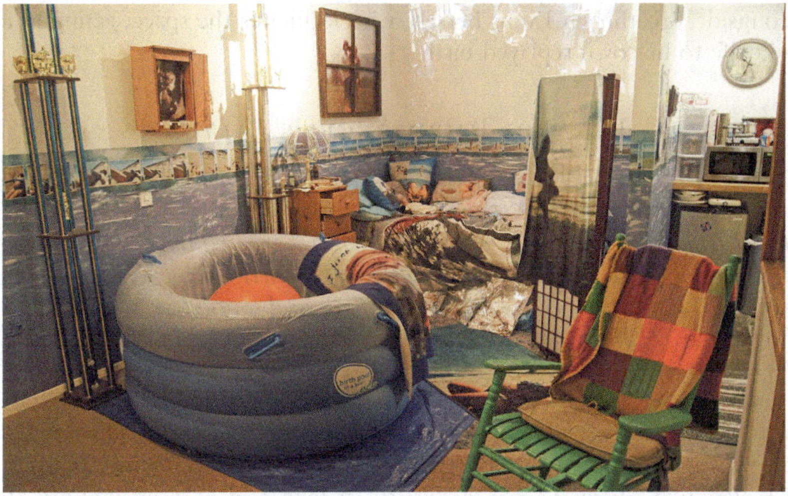

Fig. 4.1 Marni Kotąk, *The Birth of Baby X* (2011) (Image courtesy of the artist and Microscope Gallery)

and her move from labour to action, asserting herself as subject within the public sphere.

To further uncover the potential for moving birth into the realm of action we will consider two performances that explore the failed idea of 'the perfect birth', something which socially and culturally most new mothers are encouraged to aspire towards and which generally disappoints. Lena will reflect on *Partus* (2015), Third Angel's performance of birth stories, and Emily on Tracy Breathnach-Evans' performance installation *Cord* (2016b). We focus on these works in particular as they both, to some degree, rehearse a 'perfect' birth through the use of repetition in performance. In *Partus* a number of women tell us their birth plans and recount their experiences of birth, noting, rather didactically, how the reality of their experience of birth differed from the birth plans they had created for themselves. The politics, disappointments, and stereotypes of birth are writ large in this performance. *Cord* is a much quieter work where we are invited to share a recollection of a birth and to bear witness to this moment of transition again and again without judgement. In *Cord* a group of women are invited to enter an environment where they can listen to a recording of the final stage of Breathnach-Evans' labour alongside Breathnach-Evans herself, who facilitates the space, acting as a midwife to her own replayed birth.

Lena on Third Angel's *Partus*

Partus *was a part of a bigger research project, concerned with the presentation of birth through arts practice and mutual recovery. According to the Third Angel website* Partus *'was commissioned by the University of Derby as part of The Birth Project, a two year research project looking at how various art forms can explore the experiences of birth and mutual recovery'* (Third Angel, n.d.).[7] *Third Angel are a theatre company, based in Sheffield, UK. In January 2016, at the Studio, Crucible Theatre in Sheffield they presented* Partus. *I wrote my response to the show soon after seeing it; there is an immediacy in my response to the live event, a kind of proclamation of somewhat disjointed thoughts on the piece as well as the further questions it posed. I realize that the show's own aesthetics, its loud and assertive manner, its jolliness through songs and the collectiveness of a theatre ensemble, encourage my own somewhat declamatory writing voice.*

There is this empty sensation in me having listened to so many birth stories, so many beginnings, complaints, tears of pain, exhaustion, and joy. What is it that this theatre encounter presenting births wants? Why do I leave feeling deflated, empty, and quietly disappointed? What were my expectations in relation to each pregnant woman's birth plan? No, it didn't go to plan. Oh, theatre, the artform that demands too much, and yet its direct address and the immediacy often lower the experience to the most common entertainment. This is often my fear when in the theatre space; a fear that we shall all connect through laughter and humour and easy understanding. We shall have to all agree, we shall not be too deep about any of it, we might want to think more critically about it after the event, alone. In the theatre space, we sing and dance about it all; we understand it all, we consume it, together. We are this awkward audience that gathers for one hour and forty minutes (with a tea break included) to listen, to participate, to feel embarrassed, to be touched too much.

What kind of sensibility is possible here? What kind of careful performance aesthetics would do at all? Birth is the moment of a beginning, of ambivalence, of complexity, of contradictions, of the Real. Birth is impossible. Yes, it can be funny too. Yes, it can be considered collectively, with mutual understandings. But with birth words fail me—this is primarily a bodily experience. I long to be touched and propelled elsewhere. I don't want everything that I understand through language. I don't want it all explained. I want to be surprised and moved and affected and perplexed. I want a transformation, a new sensibility, a new life. So, what kind of representation is allowed or even possible here in the theatre depicting birth? Is birth too much to be held in representation? Can anyone give it an appropriate form? Does birth need a new aesthetic form altogether?

As an audience member, and a mother myself, of course I demand too much. My expectations are too high. And, yet, am I really entitled to these expectations any more than to that perfect birth plan? Should I feel so empowered to demand a transformative art encounter when I know too well that the reality of a birth plan disappointed as well? After all, I know that the birth plan never delivers.

Yet, there is something available here—there is a relation. The performers on stage move me. In theatre, there is someone on stage who can charm you, someone you can fall in love with, someone you can even care for. That is theatre's secret weapon, regardless of the knowledge that seduction and theatre are deeply entwined. That seductive charm of immediacy and encounter with the performers remains somehow authentic, at least for the duration of the performance. There is an agreement, a play between performers and audience members, a kind of coaxing. I'm with you, my dear performer. We are in relation. Once the show has established me as a passive spectator who sits in her chair and waits to be courted, the performer's charm becomes all I have. I put my trust in the performer and their delivery. We are all reliant on their skill and there is an enjoyment in that asymmetrical relation: I am in the performers' hands, reliant on their skill, as the birthing woman often gives herself over to the midwives and medical professionals. Maybe it is fine to be cared for, to relax into someone else's presence. Maybe it is about allowing others to hold us, to tell our stories, our narratives, as Cavarero (2000) *describes. In this particular case* Partus' *performers carry biographical stories of women who birthed, just like our mothers carry our own birth story.*

The theme of birth is great, it is immense and overwhelming, grand and furious, powerful. What do others think? My academic colleagues Adele Senior and Paula McCloskey, who were also in the audience? We didn't talk much afterwards, in person, nor by email. What did they expect? Was it enough? Were they satisfied? Since a new life is born, I demand a new world, I demand brand-new aesthetics! However, and as it stands, this particular performance language including songs, togetherness, and laughter is somehow insufficient for such a transformative life event. It is never good enough. It can never be good enough. Birth is aligned to the Real; it is not easily transferable and explained. By narrating it in performance (which demands a certain kind of collectivity and rhythm) it is possible to lessen it. I wonder if the collectivity of this encounter is so important after all. Do we need to have a public discussion at any cost? A reiteration: Why is it important for birth to enter the public sphere in this particular ensemble way?

What's affective about this performance, what moves, what enters? What stays after the event? I was expecting too much. I was too demanding. Just like most expectant mothers. No, it didn't go to plan.

I'm thinking about Helena Walsh's violent imagery in M.O.M. Marks of Motherlands (2007) *and* In Pursuit of Pleasure (2012) *that shocks and seduces into difficulty, repulsion, and a new understanding. This was something brutal and beautiful. I am also recalling Marni Kotak's spectacular birth in the gallery,* The Birth of Baby X (2011)*: there we concluded that the live birthing act itself lacked a sense of 'action'; the artist became a birthing subject and slipped into labour. And here, it feels the opposite—too much representation.*

Yet Partus *was sweet and righteous, good and important. What moves? What gives? What parts? What works in* Partus *are those moments in the individual birth stories, those moments with the specificities of each story. Stacey's story, which is presented at the opening of the performance details birth trauma and repetition and that unavoidable desire of wanting to go over it again and again. I held her close to me at that point. The biographical story spoke… and then moved on, somewhere else. Maybe Stacey's story could have been compulsively repeated itself, right there and then with us all in audience, all over again, and again, made us feel uncomfortable, exhausted us.*

Intermission, from the Collective to the Particular

When we read Lena's reflections on *Partus* we are reminded of Tracy Breathnach-Evans' *20 Minutes* (2012), her arrival at trauma, at the understanding she had undergone a traumatic experience due to an emergency caesarean, during the making of the birth story video piece. Breathnach-Evans reflects on the process of making the piece, as well as her realization of her incapacity to articulate what actually happened:

> What had stayed with me most was the twenty minutes of being unconscious when he was born – when he came into the world, and I was not there to see that or be there with him. … So, where was I during the birth? … What I discovered when I looked back at the film shocked me because there were so many pauses. It looked like I had paused the film because I was totally frozen. Yet in my experience of articulating those moments, I was not frozen. In these pauses, however, there was still a huge energy present, a very intense charge going on because what I realised was that I was remembering, but on the inside. That's when I realised for the first time that this experience of being unconscious was actually a trauma, and that these freezes in the 'now' were me performing the trauma in my body of the 'then'. So that was it. That was the beginning of the whole search for me. (Breathnach-Evans with Šimić and Underwood-Lee 2018, p. 5)

What follows for Breathnach-Evans is a strong body of performance work inspired by the search to know and narrate a particular birth story. Tracy Breathnach-Evans is an Irish performance artist based in South Wales in the UK. *Cord* follows on from her trilogy of birth performances that includes *Caesura* (2013), *Rehearsals for a Birth Story* (2015), and *After-Birth* (2016a). *Cord* is created and performed by Breathnach-Evans and includes design by Francesc Serra Vila. It was funded by the Arts Council of Wales and to date has been performed only once for an invited audience of five women at Carnegie House in Bridgend, Wales, on 13 September 2016. Breathnach-Evans herself describes the piece thus: 'A mother listens to herself, in the presence of others. A baby is born. Again. Again. The woman becomes mother. Again' (Breathnach-Evans, n.d.). Breathnach-Evans' choice to make small-scale, intimate performance events which tour only minimally, if at all, means there is little critical consideration of her work. Just as with Kotak's *The Birth of Baby X*, Breathnach-Evans chooses carefully who she will invite to sit alongside her to witness her birth through documentation. The small-scale nature of Breathnach-Evans' work also makes questionable our assertion that *Cord* brings birth into the public sphere. It is a challenging choice for many reasons to only show publicly funded work to an invited audience of five, and yet this piece was funded as research and development and has been part of Breathnach-Evans' development of her storytelling Birth Café, which we will consider later in this chapter. It is sufficient to say here that Breathnach-Evans' repeated gestures to enable herself and others to tell the story of birth from the perspective of the one birthing are a sustained project of considering birth intellectually, aesthetically, and publicly through story, and *Cord* can be viewed as one aspect of this wider project to bring birth to action as formulated by Arendt. As in Lena's reflections on *Partus*, Emily wrote this piece shortly after witnessing *Cord* and shares an immediate reaction to the work and the questions it provokes.

Emily on Tracy Breathnach-Evans' *Cord*

It is a rainy Tuesday morning in a post-industrial town in South Wales. I get lost finding the car park and then get lost walking from the car park to the venue. I have not dressed for the weather and am wet and shivering slightly. I arrive in a dark entrance hall in the faded elegance of a building that I guess was formerly a Carnegie Library: the history is hinted at not only in the name, Carnegie House, but also in the imposing Victorian architecture.[8] *I find myself among a group of women I do not know. Occasionally Breathnach-Evans, the initiator and performance artist behind today's event, enters the hall and invites one of us to go with her through a large door. I know the performer and her familiarity makes this wait seem less foreboding. I am not the first to be chosen. I am cold and feeling a little sullen. When it is my turn, Breathnach-Evans takes me through the door into a light-filled room. It has a general air of emptiness about it. In front of me is a table set out with a beautiful selection of colourful blankets and neatly ordered pairs of clean white socks. I am invited to sit in a chair, my shoes are removed (I can't remember if Breathnach-Evans does this or if I do this myself), and then she places a pair of white socks on my feet, wraps a soft, wool blanket around my shoulders and invites me to follow her into the space. I don't remember any words being spoken but I suppose they must have been. I feel overwhelmed by comfort; I feel cared for. The hall we have entered feels light, open, and silent. Although I know I am not, I feel completely alone and I don't notice anyone other than the performer in the room. Tucked around a corner but dominating the space is a large white glowing ball surrounded by cushions, one of which I am directed to sit upon. Nothing happens.*

In these opening moments I am transported from one reality to another. I move from a dark, damp, slightly claustrophobic space where I feel ill at ease and exposed to the gaze of strangers to an open, light, safe space where I feel protected and looked after. This movement is a kind of birth, a passage from one state of being to another. Birth is on my mind, and I know what I am coming to see. Maybe I am reading too much of the content into the form. This movement in the introduction to Cord *of course echoes the content, which is framed around the opportunity for an audience to share with Breathnach-Evans the repetition of the birth of her second child.*

All participants are seated now and Breathnach-Evans joins us at the periphery of the circle. She picks up a tube which connects her to the mound in the centre, a tube reminiscent of the umbilical cord and also of the plastic tubes that abound in the medicalized birth experience. I think of the thirteen cannulas that were placed in my body over the course of my second labour, the epidural tube in my spine. I mourn the 'natural' birth I never had.

I cannot see clearly what the performer is doing. I sit next to the glowing orb in what feels like silence. This white, shining object is fecund and it reminds me of the fullness of the pregnant belly, so stretched it feels ready to burst. I think of all the fluid I carried within me when my own children inhabited my uterus and the way my body distended and changed through my pregnancies. After a long time (perhaps twenty minutes, perhaps five—it is difficult to follow linear paths now, all I know is it feels like I am attempting an act of endurance) I start to notice that sound is emanating from the shape in the centre of the circle of women. The sound is difficult to make out and I have to move nearer and turn my head to hear clearly. I listen deeply and realize that this is the sound of a woman in labour—there are sighs, occasional words. There are words that seem to come from the birthing mother and words that seem to come from others who are with her—encouragement and support, mantras being repeated. The birthing act here creates a community. The quiet presence of the birth audio somehow makes the room feel all the more still and soundless. I shut my eyes to listen better (Fig. 4.2).

When I open my eyes again, I notice the globe has started to deflate. I didn't realize it was full of air but it must be. My attention is drawn away from the recorded birth and into this room, this time, with these women around me. The decrease in size of the orb means I can see the women sitting in a circle listening with me and I can see Breathnach-Evans, as she slowly opens and closes the plastic tube with her fingers, this discreet action performed by a living, present body must be controlling the flow of air and deflation of the maternal body evoked in the glowing mound. After some time, the globe is deflated completely and we hear the sound of the final moments of birth, the mother and child united and meeting for the first time after being together for so long. It is only now I notice that I am crying, thinking not of the births of my children, as I might have expected to, but

Fig. 4.2 Tracy Breathnach, *Cord* (2016b) (Image by Peter Morgan)

of the child I miscarried and the births of the children I will never have due to my unwanted salpingo-oophorectomy. As the performer's body came into focus, I also began to notice the bodily presence of the other women in the room and my own corporeal reaction to the piece in the tears that flowed down my cheeks. I reflect on my own birth experiences through the gentle, and yet so visceral, experience of listening to a birth. The form, aesthetics, content, and community created in this piece allow me to sit with birth. To consider it over time. To understand it more deeply. By bringing birth to an audience in the very public space of Carnegie House, Breathnach-Evans has made birth a subject that is important, that is for public debate and discussion. This piece adds to the history of the venue as a local council owned building with its past as a library. Cord*'s state funding by the Arts Council further marks it as a public event in the world.* Cord *does not assert itself, it does not make any overt statements, Breathnach-Evans simply invites us to be with her as she frames and makes manifest her own birth story as artistic representation. Breathnach-Evans is both the birthing subject and* *one who can narrate that story back to the birthing mother who was too far into the Real to be able to articulate her own experience at the time of giving birth. Just by existing here and now with this small group of women in this most gentle of performances,* Cord *assertively makes the narratives retold by the birthing mother part of a public debate and transforms birth into 'action'.*

Birth Stories as Action

Breathnach-Evans brings birth into the public space of performance and asks us to witness the active birthing body of the mother as evoked in sound, and the caring others that facilitate that birth who we hear recorded and who we witness in Breathnach-Evans' own movements within this performance space. We are also enabled to reflect on our own bodily experience of birth and the times we may or may not have birthed children. Breathnach-Evans' desire to present her own birthing body through repeated performance, and the birth stories of the mothers in *Partus* by Third Angel, might be seen as enacting the feminist desire to make visible the bodies doing the labour of birthing as outlined by Tyler. In a sense, if we are to return to Arendt's terms, birth moves from the dimension of labour to action through considered, aesthetic, maternal performances in the public sphere. These performances also bring in a presentation of reciprocal care. In *Cord* Breathnach-Evans' performance is that of a facilitator. She delivers us into the space, makes us comfortable, takes care of us, and facilitates our transition from one space to another. In *Partus* we are in the hands of the skilled performers and we allow them to carry us through the piece. We are offered a cup of tea, we are looked after, it is uncomfortable and participatory. We must take part, we must get on with the act, collectively. Birth stories are delivered with a cup of tea, and a biscuit or two, making it easier, more digestible. *Partus* is an attempt to care. *Cord* makes visible the performance of care within the live birth but achieves this without forcing participation—instead we act as quiet witnesses.

Cord is careful, intimate, and particular. It has developed its very own aesthetics, its very own birth story. *Partus* in some sense cannot get away from the expected, from the collective desire to have a perfect birth story, and if not a perfect birth story, then at least a successful, effective theatre performance, containing women's stories, relying on humour and musical numbers, telling it as it is, 'in all its bloody glory' as the programme notes state. However, birth is the ultimate experience, the greatest drama even when so common and therefore unremarkable. It is the event we have somehow forgotten, both as children, as well as society, and which can only be narrated back to us carefully and intimately in the stories told by those who were present at the scene—mothers, fathers, companions, midwives. We are keen to emphasize the mothers, given their unique position and bodily experience. It is up to those who remain with the memories, the mothers, to keep at it, to keep telling the story, in private, and in public, through performance and otherwise. Mothers build relationships through their laboursome work to bring their birth stories to action, as Tyler and Cavarero so compellingly argue is the feminist goal at the heart of the act of listening to birth stories. Performance elevates birth into the public sphere; the aesthetic and intellectual dimensions at play in a constructed performance ensure that these birth stories can be shared through representation and repeated not just within the mother/child dyad but in the public realm, even when that birth is not the perfect birth we may imagine or plan for.

Breathnach-Evans' desire to make performances focussing on birth was first explored in relation to a traumatic experience during the birth of her first son, where it was necessary that she be given a general anaesthetic in order that her first child be born by emergency caesarean section. Following on from the video piece *20 Minutes* (2012), Breathnach-Evans has made a series of performances that re-perform the lost moment of birth *Caesura* (2013), *Rehearsals for a Birth Story* (2015), *AfterBirth* (2016a), and *Cord* (2016b), repeatedly trying to lay claim to and reconcile the absence of her conscious self at the moment she was born as a mother. More recently, Breathnach-Evans has created an ongoing series of Birth Cafés with PeopleSpeakUp, a social arts and well-being enterprise led by Eleanor Shaw in Llanelli. Birth Cafés, which are spaces for women to share their birth stories, are an invitation to speak otherwise, as if speaking for the first time, allowing the body to speak, to tell the story in a different way, and to address trauma. In a way the Birth Café is an attempt to find one's narrative. This, of course, is markedly different from the artist's body in a public, collective space as exhibited in the birth performances we have discussed. Despite the difference, the Birth Café is still notably a public space that works to use performance techniques to make a collective public consideration of birth. While they do not have a passive audience that listen to the stories, the participants create a collective public that can generate stories together. The process is described in

Breathnach-Evans' TEDx talk, 'Birth Cafe: A transformational approach to birth storytelling' (Breathnach-Evans 2020).

Susan Hogan, David Sheffield, and Amelia Woodward note that current guidelines from the National Institute for Clinical Excellence (NICE) neglect to recommend that new mothers are given an opportunity to discuss a traumatic birth as a matter of routine; in response to the problems they have identified in the approach taken by NICE, Hogan et al. identify arts practice as one possible way of working with mothers following trauma in order to address their mental health and well-being needs (Hogan et al. 2017, p. 179). *Partus* was created, alongside a series of workshops for mothers, in response to this need. *Partus* allows for a public, aesthetic, and collective consideration of some birth stories. Breathnach-Evans' work also emerges from a desire to heal trauma through performance; however, what is more interesting for us, rather than the healing potential of performance, is the ability of performance to place birth stories in the public sphere. *Cord* enables the audience to sit with the birthing body of the mother and to imaginatively repeat their own birth experiences. *Partus* emphasizes the collective potential of experiences of birth. These shows bring the stories of the birthing woman to the fore and offer an opportunity to reflect on birth not from the perspective of the moment a child comes into being but as a repeated moment when our maternal subjectivity and corporeal experience are renegotiated.

The Birth Café extends Breathnach-Evans' methods and makes the performance of birth available to many women. A Birth Café does not make a particular performance of a singular birth story. Instead, it inserts birth into the public sphere by the performativity of the event itself. A public space is created where women can discuss birth stories together, collectively foregrounding the stories of many birthing bodies. The aesthetic and intellectual aspects are carefully considered by Breathnach-Evans and PeopleSpeakUp in their Birth Café events. While considering the private and public spheres, Arendt argues:

> Although the distinction between private and public coincides with the opposition of necessity and freedom, of futility and permanence, and, finally, of shame and honor, it is by no means true that only the necessary, the futile, and the shameful have their proper place in the private realm. The most elementary meaning of the two realms indicates that there are things that need to be hidden and others that need to be displayed publicly if they are to exist at all. (1958, p. 74)

In the Birth Café, the private, ephemeral, and sometimes shameful stories of birth are brought into the public realm in order that they might be witnessed. Breathnach-Evans' sustained efforts to frame birth stories as worthy of consideration bring together Arendt's assertion that natality is the foundation of human action with Cavarero's call for relational stories and, as such, are an important intervention in maternal performance. Through maternal performance we have moved from labour to action and birth has left the confines of the domestic and become elevated to the realm of the public and the political.

Notes

1. A version of this chapter was first presented as Šimić, L. and Underwood-Lee, E. 'Birth in Contemporary Performance Practice: *Cord* by Tracy Evans and *Partus* by Third Angel' at *Birth, The Body and Performance*, Brunel University London, Uxbridge, 5 June 2018.
2. At the time of making *Cord* Tracy was known as Tracy Evans; she has since changed her name to Tracy Breathnach-Evans. We use Breathnach-Evans throughout the book.
3. The simplicity of our argument that action in the Arendtian sense is of a higher value than labour or work is complicated by her assertion that without work we would find ourselves in a state of depressing indolence (Arendt 1958, p. 5), an assertion that is usefully explored by Roger Berkowitz (2018, p. 345). For the purposes of this chapter, we will follow Arendt's proposal that there is a human aspiration to move beyond labour and work, even if, in reality, that might leave us without direction or function.
4. For a detailed analysis of how Cavarero extends Arendt's propositions see Fanny Soderback (2018).
5. See Tyler and Baraitser (2013) and Baraitser (2017) for an analysis of birth as portrayed in *One Born Every Minute* and on YouTube.
6. For example, the 'Birth' festival at the Royal Exchange, Manchester in 2016; the Birth Rites collection at King's College London; Áine Phillips *Sex, Birth and Death* (2003) and the documentary play *Birth* (2008) by Karen Brody, which turned into the BOLD movement with various performances across the USA. See also 'The Mums and Babies Ensemble' workshops and performances that included a birth stories section at 'Gateshead International Festival

of Theatre', 'All Change Festival', Lyric Hammersmith Theatre, London, Bubble Theatre Company and Camden People's Theatre in 2014 and 2015 (Radosavljević et al. 2015).

7. For more information please see The Birth Project at https://www.derby.ac.uk/media/derbyacuk/assets/departments/business-services/documents/65835-The-Birth-Project.pdf (Hogan 2018).
8. The evoking of the Carnegie Library movement here emphasizes the placing of birth within the public sphere in *Cord*. The Carnegie Library movement, founded by American industrialist and philanthropist Andrew Carnegie, was a movement to build free to access public libraries. Carnegie House is owned by Bridgend Council and was built with money from the Carnegie Trust (Carnegie House n.d.).

References

Arendt, Hannah. 1958. *The Human Condition*. Chicago: The University of Chicago Press.

Arendt, Hannah. 1990 [1963]. *On Revolution*. New York: Penguin Books.

Baraitser, Lisa. 2017. YouTube Birth and the Primal Scene. *Performance Research* 22 (4): 7–17.

Berkowitz, Roger. 2018. The Singularity and the Human Condition. *Philosophy Today* 62 (2): 337–355.

Breathnach-Evans, Tracy. 2020. Birth Cafe: A Transformational Approach to Birth Storytelling. *TEDxNantymoel*, February 13. https://youtu.be/w94saeRC_Sk. Accessed 20 Oct 2020.

Breathnach-Evans, Tracy. n.d. *Cord*. http://cord-performance.weebly.com/. Accessed 2 Feb 2021.

Breathnach-Evans, Tracy with Lena Šimić and EmilyUnderwood-Lee. 2018. Interview with Tracy Breathnach-Evans. *Performance and the Maternal*. https://performanceandthematernal.files.wordpress.com/2020/10/tracy-breathnach-evans-1.pdf. Accessed 28 Oct 2020.

Cavarero, Adriana. 2000. *Relating Narratives: Storytelling and Selfhood*. London: Routledge.

Hogan, Susan. 2018. *The Birth Project: Using the Arts to Explore Birth*. https://www.derby.ac.uk/media/derbyacuk/assets/departments/business-services/documents/65835-The-Birth-Project.pdf. Accessed 25 Feb 2020.

Hogan, Susan, David Sheffield, and Amelia Woodward. 2017. The Value of Art Therapy in Antenatal and Postnatal Care: A Brief Literature Review with

Recommendations for Future Research. *International Journal of Art Therapy* 22 (4): 169–179.
Kotak, Marni. n.d. *Marni Kotak*. http://www.marnikotak.com/. Accessed 27 Oct 2020.
Lacan, Jacques. 1999 [1970]. *Ecrits*, trans. Bruce Fink. London: W. W. Norton.
Radosavljević, Duška, Annie Rigby, and Lena Šimić. 2015. *The Mums and Babies Ensemble: A Manual*. Liverpool: The Institute of Art and Practice of Dissent at Home.
Rank, Otto. 1993 [1929]. *The Trauma of Birth*. New York: Dover Publications.
Šimić, Lena. 2014. Birth Story. *Performance Research* 19 (4): 24–30.
Soderback, Fanny. 2018. Natality or Birth? Arendt and Cavarero on the Human Condition of Being Born. *Hypatia* 33 (2): 273–288.
Third Angel. n.d. Partus. *Third Angel*. https://thirdangel.co.uk/shows-projects/partus. Accessed 27 Oct 2020.
Tyler, Imogen. 2009. Introduction: Birth. *Feminist Review* 93: 1–7.
Tyler, Imogen, and Lisa Baraitser. 2013. Private View, Public Birth: Making Feminist Sense of the New Visual Culture of Childbirth. *Studies in the Maternal* 5 (2): 1–27.

Performances and Artworks Cited

Birth Rites Collection. n.d. [art collection].
Breathnach-Evans, Tracy. 2012. *20 Minutes* [film].
Breathnach-Evans, Tracy. 2013. *Caesura* [performance].
Breathnach-Evans, Tracy. 2015. *Rehearsals for a Birth Story* [performance].
Breathnach-Evans, Tracy. 2016a. *AfterBirth* [performance].
Breathnach-Evans, Tracy. 2016b. *Cord* [performance].
Brody, Karen. 2008. *Birth*. Authorhouse [performance].
Kotak, Marni. 2011. *The Birth of Baby X* [performance and installation].
Kotak, Marni. 2019. *Ajax's Disco Dinosaur Halloween 8th Birthday Party* [performance].
Kotak, Marni. 2020. *Love Masks* [performance].
Phillips, Áine. 2003. *Sex, Birth and Death* [performance].
Royal Exchange Theatr. 2016, October 19–October 22. *Birth—A Global Festival of Theatre and Debate*. Manchester [festival].
Third Angel. 2015. *Partus* [performance].
Walsh, Helena. 2007. *M.O.M. Marks of Motherlands* [performance].
Walsh, Helena. 2012. *In Pursuit of Pleasure* [performance].

CHAPTER 5

Aftermath (5 Months)

Maternal Jouissance

In this chapter we explore artworks by Lenka Clayton, Lizzie Philps, Grace Surman, and Megan Wynne that have been made during the early days after the birth of a baby, when mother and child are coming to know one another as separate but linked individuals. We examine artworks through the lens of jouissance as first proposed by Jacques Lacan and developed by feminist scholars including Julia Kristeva and Luce Irigaray, who build on Lacan's theory of feminine jouissance.

In our writing in this chapter we take two different approaches. Reflecting on her own performance making during her maternity leave periods with her children, Lena is drawn to work that explores the repetitive nature of the early days with one's baby, while Emily turns to work that celebrates the playfulness of the experience of first coming to know one's child and one's own maternal subjectivity.

Following the Birth, there is the Aftermath. It is like an emergent land, after the earthquake. An abyss opens for some, serenity for others, and then everything changes, again, and again. Mood swings, baby blues, and post-natal depression might occur, as well as a kind of deeper understanding of the absurdity and fragility of one's condition and life. As we explored in our chapters on Loss and Birth, together with death, birth is

L. Šimić and E. Underwood-Lee, *Maternal Performance*, Contemporary Performance InterActions, https://doi.org/10.1007/978-3-030-80226-4_5

close to the Real; birth forces us to encounter that unspeakable, unsayable experience of one's sense of fractured self and fragmented reality. Through the act of birth, the illusion of composure is dissolved. One becomes two and two become many. Worlds split and open, terrifying but also full of possibility and joy. What formulates this period of aftermath when we must rebuild ourselves, ready for the maintenance we will later come to, both in the next stage of our parenting and in the next chapter of this book?

This chapter is about play and about repetition, about pleasure and pain, and primarily about jouissance, which comes following the birth of a child and during the mother's early experiences of her bodily split from the child carried in the womb. Lacan established his concept of feminine jouissance most significantly within his Seminar XX *Encore*. This seminar was developed between 1972 and 1973 and marks a turning point in Lacan's theorizing of feminine sexuality. Lacan proposes the notion of a feminine jouissance. This is distinct from his earlier model of phallic jouissance, which he uses to refer to the realm that the child inhabits before they enter the Symbolic. In regard of feminine jouissance, Lacan writes:

> There is a *jouissance* proper to her, to this 'her' which does not exist and which signified nothing. There is a *jouissance* proper to her and of which she herself may know nothing, except that she experiences it – that much she does know. She knows it of course when it happens. (1985, p. 145)

Lacan's propositions prompt us to ask two questions: What does the mother/artist know? What is her knowledge? Lacan notes that jouissance functions as supplementary to the phallic, or Symbolic, as lack that women encounter. In Lacan's argument woman is always excluded from and yet invested in the phallic; this inherent split means that woman is always in excess. The divine pleasure that Lacan sees in this position of excess is what he terms 'jouissance' (1985, pp. 144–145).

In his earlier works Lacan had positioned the feminine as the absolute other, in opposition to the phallus, which signifies the whole and the Symbolic and which the woman must in some respect become or take on (2001 [1977], p. 321).[1] In Seminar XX Lacan moves beyond this statement, acknowledging that woman can neither be the other nor possess the other and so the notion of a fixed or complete subject position is a myth (1985, p. 141). In the central lecture 'God and the *Jouissance* of ~~The~~ Woman' Lacan proposes:

> There is no such thing as *The* woman, where the definite article stands for the universal. There is no such thing as *The* woman since of her essence – having already risked the term, why think twice about it? – of her essence she is not all. (p. 144, original emphasis)

Her subjectivity is divided and moreover, ~~the~~ woman can be understood as *Encore*: she has access to something more, something beyond the Symbolic, beyond the law. In their introduction to the publication of this lecture, Jacqueline Rose and Juliet Mitchell note that jouissance is always 'in excess' (Lacan 1985, p. 137). The feminine jouissance identified by Lacan is always transgressive and uncontainable, since it is outside of the rule of the law. Lacan states that it 'serves no purpose' (1985, p. 149) other than joy since it is beyond signification. As we have stated in our previous chapters Loss and Birth, death and birth bring us close to the Real. Death and birth are also both critically linked to the post-partum period; however, it is in this moment of aftermath, after the sudden shock of being thrust into the Real during birth, that the mother has a chance to understand her divided subjectivity and thus moves from shock into potential jouissance.

Following Lacan, Kristeva examines jouissance and its location in the realm of the feminine (1981b, p. 27). She asserts that the maternal condition is one of a split self: 'A mother is a permanent sharing out, a division in flesh itself' (Kristeva cited in Jones 1984, p. 62). Those that were united are separated at the moment that a baby is born and yet their subjectivity is always both together and divided. Mother and child are united during pregnancy, sharing one body, blood stream, and identity. Upon giving birth the mother finds that which was part of her is removed from her body and the child begins their journey towards independent subjectivity. In the early stage of her bodily split from her child, the mother inhabits a liminal state where she still has the possibility of experiencing herself as both one with her child and separate from them. Andrea Liss theorizes the post-partum period as a phase of surprise where the mother and child find 'a new kind of connection' that is 'intimate, fresh, full of wonder and fear' (2009, p. 23). Elsewhere she has termed this time as the 'surprise of the Real' (2013, p. 1). We struggled to decide on the title of the chapter exploring this post-partum time and settled on the Aftermath, which implies fear and destruction and picking up the pieces. Even when the birth has not been a catastrophic event, we need to pick up the pieces of ourselves after it. The aftermath is a time of repair and rebuilding, and also of forging something new when we shape ourselves into our new maternal identities. This is also a time of great discoveries, as well as potential and joyful transcendence.

Ildikó Rippel and Rosie Garton propose that jouissance has an equivalence with performance, and in particular with performance that engages with babies and other untrained performers, where the performer can be 'off script, … beyond words, beneath the symbolic, dangling dangerously close over the flames of the Real' (2017, p. 43). In the following pages we explore how different artworks have used art making and performance to make sense of and represent the post-partum period, offering us an opportunity to come to an understanding of these new maternal subjectivities and a 'maternal jouissance'.

Lena on Lenka Clayton's *An Artist Residency in Motherhood* and Lizzie Philps' *Maternity Leaves*

Upon giving birth to my first child, at one point I realized that I actually had to take this baby home with me, and take care of him, this fragile little infant. This other. Who was I to be entrusted to care for such a new entity, a creature of this universe, in his own right? And moreover, who was there to take care of me, while taking care of this new life?

In those early hours, days, and weeks, emotions can throw a new mother in various directions; she has inhabited a new land of motherhood, which can appear highly idealized, and mothering, a very specific yet relentless practice, both offering a world transformed; she's no longer whole—she's wounded, injured, different. I remember experiencing a kind of outer bodily projection of my life, and, at the same time, being so bodily aware, through the experience of unsuccessful, painful breastfeeding, uterus contractions, lochia bleeding, blood clots, brownish discharge, difficulty passing stools, sagginess of flesh… I was no longer myself. Who was I with this new slow-moving and painful body, open wide, bleeding, porous, with tender breasts leaking breast milk? I remember feeling happiest in the shower, alone, with water running over my battered skin, my tired body. This was my time, and yet this was also stolen time from everyone else. Giving birth felt like a battle, and there was I, a soldier returning home, and not recognizing myself, and feeling that home is also a foreign country, a new geography. And then there is the crying, needy infant as well, always by my side. Little other.

Time, which we both inhabited, took on a new dimension, divided into chunks of sleep-deprived zones, in between baby's feeds, formula smells, and soiled nappy changes. Night-time sleep got lost, and beds were made up everywhere around the house. I became a shift worker. One of the things that struck me as quite absurd was that the name of this fractured time and space was 'maternity leave', implying I was on a kind of a break from reality. And that exhausting 'maternity leave' was paid badly—I wasn't entitled to much. Was I appreciated for all the labour I was providing to society, to my own family unit? In my attempt to make sense of this messy disorganized time, to recognize it (and at this point I was already with my third baby) I renamed 'maternity leave' as Contemplation Time (2007–2008) *and presented it, to myself and the wider public, as a kind of art project of maternity leave.*

In such a state of disarray, I realized art could become a structuring device, a method through which one could organize one's life, regain some sense of self in this new crisis mode. Personally, I only came to 'maternity leave art making' with the births of my third and fourth children. However, my artwork does not stand isolated, far from it. Its main predecessor is the seminal Post-Partum Document *(1973–1979) by Mary Kelly. And nowadays since the 2010s it is possible to claim that there is a kind of genre of such maternity leave art, considering and enacting the time of the aftermath. Inevitably such maternity leave artwork is performative or tends towards a performance genre, engrossed as it is in the repetitive actions of everyday life, reframing them as art.*

The period following the birth of a child has been well-documented in art practice. Mary Kelly's Post-Partum Document *five-year-long art endeavour (1973–1979) paved the way and what might be viewed as a genre of post-partum artwork has since emerged. The work of Elena Marchevska's* Valid Until… (2009–2011), *Natalie Loveless under the title 'Maternal Ecologies'* (2010–2013), *Lenka Clayton's* An Artist Residency in Motherhood (2012–2014), *Lizzie Philps'* Maternity Leaves (2013), *Helen Sargeant's* M(other) Stories (2015–2016), *albeit recording the life of herself as the mother with an older child of nursery age, as well as my own art projects* Contemplation Time (2007–2008) *and* Friday Records (2014) *created explicitly during maternity leaves, can all fit into such a genre of post-partum artwork, consisting of repetitive daily durational maternal performances. In all of these examples, the artists reframe and reconfigure their everyday life with babies, toddlers, and small children as art making practice. In most of these works, mothers are invisible in the documentation and some of the motifs that appear are images of prams, in shadows or left behind, and plastic objects associated with children: dummies, toys, baby bottles… While mothers are mostly absent from the images, the art is used to negotiate, understand, and express their newly found maternal subjectivity as well as the relationship to their child/ren. I question the developing aesthetics of the post-partum artwork genre, its relationship to maternal time and space, as well as its jouissance.*

As I have already indicated there is an attempt from all the above-mentioned artists to reconfigure and frame their time with the infant, give the messy maternity days some structure, tame the content into a form. However, Lenka Clayton formalized the post-partum artwork genre further in An Artist Residency in Motherhood (2016–ongoing) *artist residency programme. As a part of her artist's statement, when starting her own* An Artist Residency in Motherhood *Clayton writes, 'In common with all new parents, the birth of my first child in April 2011 changed many things in my life. One of those changes has been the way I and others think about my career as an artist'* (Clayton 2012–2014).[2] *As a result of this, following the creation of the artist residency in motherhood for herself, Clayton subsequently opened this option to others through an open-source artist residency programme.* An Artist Residency in Motherhood, *where an artist grants themselves the opportunity to spend time making work while with their baby and considering their time with the baby an essential part of their arts practice, has to date been taken up by over 1000 artists in sixty-nine countries* (Artist Residency in Motherhood, n.d.). *While this approach of replicating the model of the artist residency in motherhood has proved strong in terms of the creation of maternal communities and the sense of mother/artist agency, as many testimonials on Clayton's website indicate, I am somewhat troubled about the potential loss of a more authentic arrival at one's maternal aesthetics. I am aware I might be idealizing this connection between the 'surprise of the Real' and aesthetics* (Liss 2013), *seduced as I am by the question of how jouissance can be represented in art. I am seeking that jouissance which is, as Lacan proposed, 'proper to her'. The step between knowing jouissance, 'when it happens', when it is experienced, and a decision to frame it (possibly even formalize it by such framing) in an aesthetic form is a delicate one. This is a crucial part of the artistic process, which is about emerging, about finding one's form, about uncertainty, about the specificity of each mother/artist, and a certain point in her creation: an inevitable fusion of art with life, and the decision that certain aspects of life can be framed as art. It is because the decision-making process of framing has been taken away from the artist herself that I find the collective model of* An Artist Residency in Motherhood, *which has emerged from a very specific singular arts practice, somewhat problematic, although the project works beautifully on many different levels, particularly in relation to maternal solidarity.*

In the aftermath of the birth, the mother/artist rebuilds her world, and through it comes to surprise herself in her discovery of new aesthetic forms. As I reflected in the 'Desperate Artwives' podcast:

> *In* Contemplation Time, *I was searching for a form, an appropriate way to record my experience of being on maternity leave. In some ways* Contemplation Time *is raw and testing – there's an uneasiness in it, a quest for the form. In the end the artwork became a series of journal entries and photographs taken during my visits with baby Sid to the local park, in particular, it later on became clear, to one specific bench in Sefton Park in Liverpool. (Woman Up! Podcast [Lena Simic]* 2019)

This active unpolished search for the artform gave the project its breath, its originality. On reflection it was a transformation from jouissance, if not always in its experiential sense, then definitely from its messy time-based pre-Oedipal frame, to an artistic form. The search was a part of the artwork. In my case, some of the maternal aesthetics I employed included working with interruptive and negotiated time, engaging in public spaces, playing with proximity and distance, and at the same time actively seeking the artform.

In Friday Records (2014), *my maternity leave with my fourth child, I engaged in the artform with more expertise in maternal art making and on the Wordpress blog, and for that, the work is not as testing. Yet,* Friday Records *works more clearly with the concept of interrupted maternal time, especially as it developed from online journal to live performance, which was created only on Fridays, when I was at the same time looking after my little boy, then a toddler. I was purposefully giving myself a challenge in the art making by putting myself in the position of both artworking and looking after my child. Initially* Friday Records *was a blog, which was not advertised to my friends and colleagues during my maternity leave. This blog was a place where I could be secretive but also somewhat public about my maternal experience. That was an important phase of the artwork, tethering between the private and the public, figuring out what is happening, to me as a mother/artist, to my existence with a newborn. Later on* Friday

Records *became a performance for Dublin Live Art Festival in 2016. At this stage, I was able to critically reflect on the artwork and its process, and publicly showcase and as such defend my explorations. In a sense Clayton's* An Artist Residency in Motherhood *artist residency programme provides, immediately, upon signing up, that security, a frame, a stamp of approval. And yet it is actually the struggle which is probably the most engaging in the artistic process and outcome, being the closest to jouissance. Considering my two maternity leave artworks now, in comparison with* Contemplation Time, Friday Records *is a neater, more ordered art project with clearer aesthetics; there is a certain arrival at the knowledge of the form in it. In a way, the project also has a certain security, a predetermined frame.*

I have decided to reflect on my own two maternity leave projects through this reflexive stance in order to better understand emerging post-partum aesthetics, this new artwork genre and its potential for the exposure of jouissance not only in the mother/infant dyad but beyond it in representational maternal aesthetics. For example, while Contemplation Time *was framed through the time of my maternity leave between 5 July 2007 and 27 April 2008, it was one particular bench and the place of Sefton Park in Liverpool, UK as evidenced in photographs, that became the central feature of the work; the emphasis was on place as much as it was on time. With* Friday Records, *the emphasis was on time and its interruptive qualities.*

Both of my projects became meticulously gathered daily documents of the everyday in the form of photographs, diary entries, sound files, and finally live performances after the completion of maternity leaves. These live performances were Sid Jonah Anderson by Lena Šimić *as a part of MAP live event at the Source Café in Carlisle in 2008, and* Friday Records Live Art Event *at MART Gallery for Dublin Live Art Festival in 2016. Both of these performances comprised live action on stage (performing a bedtime routine with a baby in the first, diary writing being soaked in salty water and destroyed to be left hanging on stage on a washing line in the second) including some video projection in the background, which comprised the images and footage gathered during maternity leaves. In effect both performances were multi-media pieces that attempted to encompass and yet order the messiness of the post-partum experience. The* Friday Records *promotional material contains a kind of warning about the piece, describing:*

> *Lena, who is fighting with amplified noise in her head, insistence, never-ending, relentless, Lena, who is fighting for some writing time, in between interruptions, intense bouts of love and kissing, squeezing, tantrums, hugs, screaming, demanding, hopping, shouting, let go, let go, enough, enough.* (Šimić, n.d.)

There is a clear desire and need to order the messiness of the post-partum into the artform, an impossible attempt to tame, understand, and know jouissance.

I now turn to Clayton's An Artist Residency in Motherhood (2012–2014) *as first developed by herself and Philps'* Maternity Leaves (2013) *precisely for the reasons that they both also deal explicitly with 'maternity leave' time, the infantile pre-Oedipal experience of life. In Kristeva's terms this disposition is called semiotic, with its maternal bodily drives and before the infant's signification into language, a time and space of poetic language and heterogeneous meaning which is in relation to the Symbolic, disrupting it, and yet reliant on and therefore impossible without it. Kristeva explains this particular condition:*

> *We shall call this disposition semiotic (*le sémiotique*), meaning, according to the etymology of the Greek* sémeion *(σημεῖον), a distinctive mark, trace, index, the premonitory sign, the proof, engraved mark, imprint – in short, a* distinctiveness *admitting of an uncertain and indeterminate articulation because it does not yet refer (for younger children) or no longer refers (in psychotic discourse) to a signified object for a thetic consciousness (this side of, or through, both object and consciousness).* (Kristeva 1981a, p. 133, original emphasis)

What kind of mark, an imprint, is possible for mother/artists experiencing maternity leave, a time which is tender, chaotic, and contemplative? How do their aesthetic practices come to matter?

According to Kristeva poetic language is linked with the maternal body, and the time before the entrance into the Symbolic. She further explores maternity, bodily drives, and semiotic processes:

> *The semiotic activity, which introduces wandering or fuzziness into language and, a fortiori, into poetic language is, from a synchronic point of view, a mark of the workings of drives (appropriation/rejection, orality/anality, love/hate, life/death) and, from a diachronic point of view, stems from the archaisms of the semiotic body. Before recognizing itself as identical in a*

> *mirror and consequently, as signifying, this body is dependent vis-à-vis mother. At the same time instinctual and maternal, semiotic processes prepare the future speaker for entrance into meaning and signification (the symbolic).* (p. 136)

It is difficult to disentangle the maternal from the instinctual. For example, de Beauvoir disengages with the idea of maternal instincts and proposes they are culturally constructed, a fiction, which has been indoctrinated within girls from childhood through play and behaviour (1988 [1949], pp. 295–351). *Therefore, motherhood should be understood as an institution and not a natural instinctual certainty. What I am attempting to argue for here, through Kristeva, is not necessarily the instinctual, biological view of motherhood, even when the presence of the maternal body in all its excessiveness and expansiveness, desires, leaks, cries, demands is not to be overlooked, but a drive and desire for a kind of art production which allows for intuitive slips into daily maternal performance making during this messy maternity leave time. It might be that the maternal art production during this time of the aftermath is instinctive and reflective. It is curious that we can now chart a kind of genre of maternity leave art.*

Returning to Mitchell and Rose's assertion that jouissance is that moment in sexuality which is 'always in excess', I am interested to move the discussion to art and aesthetics. Lacan is clearly intrigued with the mystical (and criticized for aligning it with the feminine), as his allusion to Gian Lorenzo Bernini's sculpture of St. Teresa indicates (1985, p. 147). *Moreover, Lacan is dismayed at 'an attempt to reduce the mystical to questions of fucking'* (p. 147), *therefore a fertile connection between feminine sexuality, maternity, and aesthetic forms might not be amiss. How does excess appear in the contemporary artworks mentioned?*

In the artworks discussed here excess can be measured and limited by the conceptual frame itself which marks and details formally as well as in the timeframe of project making. Just as the Symbolic and the semiotic interact, and produce one another, the conceptual artistic frame contains an excess; the frame is overfilled with content. One of Clayton's poignant images from An Artist Residency in Motherhood *is called* 63 Objects from My Son's Mouth (Clayton 2013a), *a photograph of various stuff that ended up in the mouth of her boy between the ages of eight and fifteen months, from cigarette butts to Christmas decorations. It is important to note that* An Artist Residency in Motherhood *functions primarily as a framing device, an artist's statement which describes it as a 'self-imposed artist residency' through which Clayton, as stated in her artist's statement, will 'fully experience and explore the fragmented focus, nap-length studio time, limited movement and resources and general upheaval that parenthood brings and allow it to shape the direction of my work, rather than try to work "despite it"'* (Clayton 2012–2014).

The residency as such contains a number of projects in different media, including a series of video works entitled The Distance I Can Be From My Son (Clayton 2013b). *What is intriguing about these videos, which take place in various locations, such as a supermarket, a park, and a back alley, is the artist's exploration of distance and its limits. These short videos all feature a toddler who walks away from the camera/mother, and disappears out of the frame. As the child is no longer in the frame, there is a tension and finally a release, at which point we see the mother running towards him, leaving the camera stand. The final images of all of these videos are measurements of the distance the mother was away from the child, for example for the back alley it's 45.9 yards/43 metres. Yet, the most arresting moment in the videos is just before the final measurements are revealed, when the mother decides to run after the toddler, when the mother enters the frame, sometimes watched by onlookers. The piece is about pushing oneself as a mother/artist to one's own limits, as both the mother and the artist. The mother plays with the idea of being a bad mother for the sake of art: the mother tests and exhibits the distance she can be away from the child for the sake of art, her artist self. There is a portrayal of excess in the work, the limit, the distance that the mother/artist can be away from her child, can push herself inside and outside the video frame. It is a performance of good/bad motherhood that Clayton undoes for the camera. The mother/artist is instructing the infant towards the Symbolic, putting them back into the frame, holding their space of freedom. Could it be that the maternal performance works as a kind of measuring device between jouissance and the Symbolic, chaos and order?*

Lizzie Philps' series of documentation photographs entitled Maternity Leaves *are also about excessive distance, named in 'paces'. Describing the project on her website, Philps writes: 'Witnessed by unwitting suburbanites, and documented on a phone camera,* Maternity Leaves *documents a series of short performative walks within a mile radius of my home, exploring the time and space of motherhood'* (Philps n.d.).[3] *Philps names the genre of her work 'short performative walks', therefore expanding our understanding of maternal performance. And again, we witness a mother/artist who dares, who plays with the im/permissible limits. Framing the project through the idea of 'Resistance' Philps acknowledges this provocation:*

> *Creating the distance needed for the photos became an invisible performance, witnessed by an unwitting audience of imaginary social workers posing as passing dog walkers. What began as a personal dare to take a few more steps away from the buggy than was comfortable became an intentional act of provocation; the difference between 'ah, look, a mother photographing her baby' and 'what the hell is she doing?!' is only a few paces. Though the titles, detailing the number of steps taken, are a plaintiff acknowledgement of responsibility, through this momentary transgression I wanted to trouble definitions of 'good' mothering and to challenge the viewers' right to assess my own.* (Philps 2016, p. 30)

This mother/artist left the baby in the pram, which is evident in a series of photographs. One photo caption reads 'Forty-one paces and a gate'; the pram is next to a church, at the doorstep of it. Another documentary photograph sees the pram at the bus stop, across the road, the caption says 'Eighteen paces (traffic dependent)'. While these photographs never reveal the mother in the ecstasy of jouissance, there appears to be something playful and sinister in the framing of the seemingly unattended infant in the pram, the excess again, although quite different than the portrayal of St. Teresa (Fig. 5.1).

The mystical that Lacan was referring to in his lecture 'God and the Jouissance *of ~~The~~ Woman'* (1985, pp. 138–148), *when discussing feminine jouissance and alluding to St. Teresa as portrayed by Bernini in 'The Ecstasy of St Teresa' statue, holds attractive, seductive, and divine qualities. One of its appeals might lie precisely in the lack of knowledge and recognition of one's state, in the surprise, in the fractures. In this case it is Gian Lorenzo Bernini, the male sculptor from the seventeenth century, who frames St. Teresa, aided by an angel, and Teresa's own description of the experience. In her own words:*

> *In his hands I saw a great golden spear, and at the iron tip there appeared to be a point of fire. This he plunged it into my heart several times so that it penetrated to my entrails. When he pulled it out, I felt that he took them with it, and left me utterly consumed by the great love of God.* (Teresa of Avila 2004, p. 210)

Is jouissance experienced by St. Teresa, in the form of religious rapture, and Bernini, in the act of art making? There is a clear relationship between the artist and his artwork, the model, the object. It is St. Teresa, the sculpture, which undergoes rapture. It is through artwork that we discuss feminine jouissance. Art, of course, of any form or kind, obliges in its form, its appeal to public recognition. Can art, and moreover, maternal performance which

Fig. 5.1 Lizzie Philps, *Eighteen Paces (traffic dependent)* (2013) (Image courtesy of the artist)

is authored and performed by a mother/artist, this double figure, hold jouissance? Can the mother/artist, who is with an infant, be her own subject and object at the same time, the subject/object close to jouissance? Can she transfer it to an aesthetic form in the way Bernini's sculpture might appear to do? Do Clayton's quick runs towards the child, Philps' almost sinister frames, and, as Emily will describe, Surman's playful encounters and Wynne's assertions of identity, show us a different kind of feminine jouissance, not the one aligned to the mystical, but to the inner limits of mothering practice, the mundane moments of the everyday, explored and revealed through maternal performance?

Emily on Grace Surman's *I Love My Baby and My Baby Loves Me* and Megan Wynne's *Affirmation (I Am a Professional Artist)* and *My Puppet*

A week after the birth of my first child, prematurely at thirty-two weeks by an 'elective' caesarean that I did not elect, I began chemotherapy. My experience of the post-partum period was somewhat unusual; however, there is something perfect about the timing—if you are going to have chemotherapy, with all the sickness, tiredness, mood swings, despair, pain, and fear that it brings, you might as well do it when your life is suspended. I left the normal, everyday routines—leaving to enter my maternity 'leave'. Chemotherapy and the post-partum period were conflated for me. I was ill, very ill, life threateningly so. In an immune compromised state I had several critical stays in isolation in solitary hospital rooms. My mastitis made me feel like I was dying. My c-section meant my body was wounded and cut open, mirroring the cut on my breast from my first lumpectomy. I did not make art because I was too ill to begin. I placed my hands on my baby's tiny body in her incubator and, when I was able to, I held her too small form against my chest. During this time, I wrote letters to my daughter. With hindsight I realized these letters were too raw to ever give to her and I have destroyed them—but before I got rid of the letters I rewrote them as the basis for my performance piece Patience (2008). *I have written about* Patience *elsewhere* (Šimić and Underwood-Lee 2020) *and do not want to explore it extensively here; instead I simply offer my brief reflection on my post-partum period in this short paragraph as a starting point for my own exploration of work by Grace Surman and Megan Wynne below.*

The view of the aftermath period I see in the works by Surman and Wynne is not what I had, but what I wanted. Through looking at work that celebrates the exploration of time spent as mother and infant together, negotiating new identities through play and art making, I seek a representation of jouissance in art. Despite my illness, I felt pleasure at being with my child, physical wholeness when I held her and when I gazed at her tiny body in her tiny crib. Although each period of aftermath will be different, and as noted my own experience of the aftermath period is different in its particularities from the ones I see depicted in works by Surman and Wynne, through watching their works, I can see my own joy, exploration, and come to new understandings of my maternal subjectivity, both as it was and as I desired it to be.

Grace Surman is a UK-based artist. Her practice has included dance, film, and performance works. She describes herself as 'an artist who dallies around the terms performance (art), live art, theatre and choreography' (Surman, n.d.). *She works as a solo artist as well as with her family, which includes her two children, Merrick and Hope, and her partner Gary Winters* (Youngs 2019). *In her 2010 film piece* I Love My Baby and My Baby Loves Me *we see the artist in her kitchen with her one-year-old son.*[4] *The fixed position camera frames a stylish domestic interior that has all the hallmarks of a typical middle-class home. There are tastefully hanging kitchen implements, clean surfaces, and patio doors leading out to a garden. To the side of the frame is what appears to be a pantry door and stairs off to the rest of the house. At the centre of the frame is a kitchen island. Daylight streams in, illuminating the comfortable, familiar scene. This is the kind of home-scape the viewer might recognize from soap operas and sitcoms about family life or from the pages of aspirational life-style magazines. The space is devoid of people but a few seconds into the film we hear the sound of a baby from off camera. Surman enters the space wearing a pretty, grey summer dress and carrying her baby boy at her hip. She does not acknowledge the camera and sets the baby on the floor to one side of the island. She then runs around and 'hides' on the other side, lying on the floor with her feet raised against the island and waits for her baby to find her. A game of hide and seek ensues where Surman sets either herself or a series of household objects on the floor and allows her baby to encounter and explore them. The baby crawls around the island and finds the object or his mother; when he finds Surman he pulls at her face, when he finds raw flour he spreads it around the floor, and when he finds an apple he bites and throws it. Each time the baby begins to bore of an item, Surman picks up the child, tends to his immediate needs by giving him a drink or wiping his face, and then resets the scene ready for another surprise encounter around the island. The film lasts for twelve minutes and forty-five seconds, during which Surman gives her child encounters with various objects and the artist herself in three different poses including one where her face is covered by a sheet.*

Surman separates herself from her child. In this film I am allowed to revel in her divided subjectivity and her play at being physically absent from the child but, more than this, her enabling of her child's autonomy as he chooses how and when to engage with each object and directs the action. I see the baby's emerging psychic independence from his mother. Surman hides herself; she allows her baby to explore his own separateness from her and then to be reunited. The baby shows obvious joy at finding his mother again and crawls over her, laughs, pulls at her hair, and grabs her face. Child and mother are reunited and the threat of separation is mitigated, for both mother and child, by the return to the mother. The child, not the mother, is ostensibly in control of when he will return—he sets the timing and crawls to her when he is ready. In one instance the child chooses to crawl away from his mother to explore some water that has been split from his drink, exercising the small amount of independence that he has been granted. This pleasure in enacting disappearance and return for the child was noted by Sigmund Freud in his 1955 work Beyond the Pleasure Principle, *the text from which Lacan developed his thesis on jouissance. In Freud's much-cited reflection on a game he termed 'fort-da', for which 'gone away-there it is!' would be an approximate translation, he notes that the child threw a wooden reel with string wrapped around it and then pulled it back. Freud reads the play of separation and return as a metaphor for the child's awareness of his mother's departures and returns. Freud noted that this game created a safe environment in which the child could explore their own subjectivity as separate from their mother* (1955, p. 15). *Lacan developed this notion of separation from the child but from the perspective of the mother, and it is from here that he starts his thinking on jouissance, which includes not only the mother's separation from the child but also the mother's separation from her own self, as Jacqueline Rose notes in her introduction to her collection of Lacan's essays on feminine sexuality* (Lacan 1985, p. 34).

Moving on from Lacan, I return to Surman's artwork and consider this separation in response to the divided mother and child. Surman uses her choreographic practice to formalize this play with separation for the child into a series of choreographed encounters within a space. The rules of the game are firmly established as a series of performative actions that create a safe environment in which the child can experience his separation from the mother but also be certain of her return or his own capacity to return to her. This safety is also extended to me as a viewer and I am reassured by the visual, formal, and cultural signifiers in the film, as well as the reference to maternal love in the title of the work, that this is a 'good mother' I am watching who will take care of her child and ensure he is okay. Surman's bodily and domestic signifiers mark her out as the 'right' kind of mother. As described above, her home is clean, well-kept, and stylish. Surman's appearance bestows her with a huge level of cultural capital as a white, young (but not too young), able-bodied, neatly dressed, arts professional. Her actions also reassure me that this is a safe environment in which the baby can play—when the child has eaten raw flour she gives him a drink, when he strays too far from the designated play areas she picks him up and returns him to the frame, when she is lying on the floor, ostensibly passive, her eyes continuously dart to check where her baby is and what he is doing. All this serves to signify to me that I can relax and enjoy these moments of play with Surman and her child rather than having to be concerned about any actual jeopardy. The jeopardy in this work is presented in the form of the realization that this time is fleeting. The mother experiencing jouissance can revel in her excess, and in her divided and united subjectivity with her child, and yet she also knows that the child will grow and 'successful' mothering is about enabling the child to move away from the other and form their own independent subjectivity. Despite the pathos in the realization of the fleeting nature of the period of aftermath, Surman's work allows me to revel in the maternal jouissance that she demonstrates as mother. Through this artwork Surman reflects maternal jouissance and the pleasure of the mother's own divided subjectivity through this playful and performative separation and unity with the child.

Luce Irigaray poetically articulates the experience of the child who is exploring their separation from the mother in 'And the One Doesn't Stir without the Other' (1981). *This piece talks of both the momentary split as the infant and mother separate and the more decisive division between mother and child as the child grows and becomes independent of the mother. Initially, the child in Irigaray's writing is overwhelmed by her mother and yet there is joy for both mother and child at the moment when they are able to play with their identity as one but not one:*

> *I have a home inside me, another outside, and I take myself from one to the other, from the one into the other. And I no longer need your belly, your arms, your eyes or your words to return or to leave. I am still so close to you and already so far away. It's morning, my first morning. Hello. You're there. I'm here. Between us so much air, light, space to share with each other.* (p. 61)

However, while the daughter in Irigaray's text is able to delight in this separation, this play is dangerous for the mother—her separateness from her child will expel her from the realm of jouissance and she will become '[a] self separated from another self. A self missing some other self. Two dead selves distanced from each other, with no ties binding them' (p. 64). *Of course, the child will be expelled too but the child does not yet have knowledge of what is at stake. The mother senses these moments of sensual unity with her child as the fleeting thing that they are. In* I Love My Baby and My Baby

Loves Me, *I see the capturing of these moments of jouissance. By watching Surman at play with her child, I am prompted to consider my own moments with my children and to keep hold of these fleeting memories, trying to hold on to a feeling of jouissance. Through Surman's depiction of her unity with her child, and the ever-present threat of separation, I am reminded that once I and my baby were one, united in our pleasure and intermingled subjectivity.*

Megan Wynne's Affirmation (I Am A Professional Artist) (2018) *also delights in moments of unity and the possibility of creating work together with her child. Wynne is a US-based artist who works in what she describes as 'the often-converging mediums of performance, photography, video, and the discipline of mothering'* (Wynne, n.d.). *Her work has been widely exhibited in the US since 2002 and has gained currency within the fields of maternal studies and feminist art making* (Chambers 2017; deSouza 2018; Greer 2018). Affirmation (I Am A Professional Artist) *is a forty-two-second film work by Wynne, made with her baby son. In the opening shot of* Affirmation *we see a close-up frame of a table with a blank piece of paper and pen on it. Wynne's hand grasps the pen, which her baby is trying to catch hold of. During the film Wynne attempts to write the words 'I am a professional artist' while also trying to hold her baby, who is distorting her words through his snatches at the pen and paper* (Fig. 5.2).

Like I Love My Baby and My Baby Loves Me, Affirmation *is a single-shot video made in a domestic environment. Although I cannot see anything but the table surface, paper, pen, and the hands of mother and child, I am able to read the visual clues that demarcate this as a home environment rather than an art studio—the pen is a disposable biro and the paper looks to have been ripped from a notebook more suited to writing shopping lists. As the baby turns the paper over, I see that the artist is working on the back of the paper and on the other side it is lined writing paper.*

As Wynne's baby grabs at the paper and pen, her writing becomes shakier and the words cease to be properly formed. Wynne's artistic identity is mutated by her maternal identity. She reaches towards an assertion of herself as an artist but is compromised by the child in her lap and is unable to ever achieve her goal of writing a simple sentence and stating an uncomplicated role. And yet it is more nuanced than this; Wynne's public identity, as portrayed in her website and texts about her work, is as an artist who makes work about her maternal body in collaboration with her children. Her identity as an artist is dependent on and complexly interlaced with

Fig. 5.2 Megan Wynne, *Affirmation (I Am A Professional Artist)* (2018) (Image courtesy of the artist)

her identity as a mother. Without the intervention of her child, Affirmation *would not make sense as an artwork. It is within the complicated split subjectivities of the mother and child who are making themselves together that this artwork is able to exist, a testament to the generative possibilities of jouissance. The mother and child are playing together—this is a way to do something with her child and so serves a practical purpose in finding a way to bridge the two roles that Wynne inhabits, much like the validation of the maternity leave as part of the art practice that is found in Clayton's* An Artist Residency in Motherhood *examined by Lena above. And yet this is more than simply a negotiation of two identities that allows Wynne to be both artist and mother; the child and mother are co-creating the artwork together and the affirmation would make no sense without the intervention of the child. This artwork simply could not exist without the play between mother and child as both united and divided subjects.*

Wynne also makes artworks with her older children. As Wynne's children grow they are able to complete more sophisticated actions and act as agents to direct certain aspects of the work, as in Wynne's series of still photographic images where her daughters faces are pressed against the inside of Wynne's clothes, making them appear as growths rising out of her body (Belly 2016a; Impregnated 2015; Postpartum Nightgown 2016c), *or in the film works* Mask of Motherhood (2016b) *and* Futility (2019), *where her children draw on or stick things to Wynne's face. These images show the hallmarks of professional production, printed large for exhibition, and the films are carefully edited; they are sophisticated both formally and in terms of their content. These works are still created by Wynne working together with her children, but bear the marks of pieces made by individuals with their own agency in conversation with their mother, rather than as part of an intermingling of subjectivities as occurs* in Affirmation. *The children and their mother do not have authorial parity, and this is acknowledged as the works are credited as Wynne's; furthermore, Wynne is a trained artist with years of experience and a sophisticated visual language that her children cannot possibly yet have developed. The pieces made with her older children demonstrate that these children have a degree of autonomy and play with this power dynamic—it is from the incongruence of placing the growing child in the foetal position that these works gain their uncanny resonance. Wynne herself states that the artworks she makes with her children are about transgressing the good/bad mother divide, asserting that 'each piece is an investigation of maternal anxiety, ambivalence, the shifting powers dynamic of the mother–child relationship, and prevailing notions of being a "good" mother'* (Wynne, n.d.). *Something very different is at play in Wynne's work with her babies, who cannot conceive of themselves as participants in an artwork. This work is all about the mother; it is her excessive subjectivity that is at play here.*

Wynne demonstrates the potentially overbearing and disconcerting nature of the maternal identity that is projected onto the child when she speaks for her baby in her 2013 work My Puppet, *a video piece where she moves the mouth of her sleeping baby and voices an apology to the mother from the child for being 'sooo selfish'* (Wynne 2013). *Wynne's thumb manipulates the baby's mouth so that it appears as if the sleeping child speaks and lists all the ways in which she does not consider or understand the needs of her mother. Wynne articulates her uncomfortable relationship with the piece, which viscerally brings to the fore her complex rebuilding of herself during the aftermath period with her first child and how she has come to an understanding of her divided maternal subjectivity:*

> *This piece was really important to me in terms of realising my voice and the strange dynamic of interconnectivity that I had with her as a baby. My second child was very young then, she was three or four days old. … I can hardly watch the piece myself because I find it so disturbing. But that was*

> *intentional. I went about it with this idea of being a character, while at the same time speaking this kind of exaggerated underlying true feeling.* (Wynne with Šimić and Underwood-Lee 2020, pp. 14–15)

My Puppet *draws its power from the excessive and disconcerting unity and separation at play here. The newness of the child, and thus her passivity, makes this unity manifestly different from that displayed in* Affirmation. *Both pieces, of course, rely on the baby being present with the mother but* My Puppet *is essentially different from* Affirmation *as the baby does not exert agency in the piece. This moment is perhaps a more uncomplicated jouissance, when the melancholy of the baby's departure has not yet come to the fore, and yet Wynne demonstrates that departure that is to come by giving the child a pretence of autonomy and agency. The child cannot have agency in this piece and her actions, were she to make any, would mean that the artwork could not function. In* My Puppet, *the separation of mother and child is essential to the work, and the disquieting humour of the piece arises from demonstrating the control that the mother has over her child, whereas* Affirmation *can only function if mother and child both exert their own will, pulling in different directions.* Affirmation *does not simply subvert or question the power dynamics in the parent–child relationship but moves beyond those dynamics through a unity of mother and child into one divided subject in an embrace of maternal jouissance.*[5]

Surman and Wynne, in these pieces, are able to move away from the mother directing the child and to create together with their children. As Adele Senior has suggested, the power relations in Grace Surman's work with her children are shifted away from the usual parent–child interaction (2018, p. 32). *Wynne's* Affirmation *and Surman's* I Love My Baby and My Baby Loves Me *are dependent on collaboration and an interlaced mother/child subjectivity. Both Surman and Wynne had an established arts practice before becoming mothers and Surman continues to make solo works without her children alongside her family-based practice. There is a danger in limiting Surman and Wynne to mother/artists, a title which, as we have explored in Beginnings, may limit or marginalize their practice. Wynne herself reflects on her ambivalence in relation to the term mother/artist:*

> *That title has so much baggage, and I want to fight it. So part of me wants to say 'no' but part of me also wants to rebel against the negative associations I have with that word. I'm kind of conflicted about it. It's a really hard question to answer but in my answer you are going to get an idea of how I*

> *feel about that word and its associations with not being a full artist, instead being like a niche artist, making niche work that's not for everyone. I resent that. I resent making work with the pressure of needing to 'be appropriate' in some way, like appropriate for children to see, puritan constraints on motherhood that I believe are put on that term.* (Wynne with Šimić and Underwood-Lee 2020, p. 1)

Despite the reservations that Wynne expresses about the confinement of her work to the category of maternal art, in the particular works I am concerned with here, the connected subjectivity of mother and child is critical and this results in artworks that I read as complicated, challenging, and compelling explorations of maternal jouissance. In 'And the One Doesn't Stir Without the Other' Irigaray's daughter is cruel, her rejection of her mother metaphorically killing them both, and yet she returns, eventually, to the ultimate and inescapable interdependence of mother and child. With knowledge she begins to understand that she and her mother are the same, the fate of her mother awaits her also, and they will always be united by their sameness—for one to have a completeness so must the other: 'And what I wanted from you, Mother, was this: that in giving me life, you still remain alive' (Irigaray 1981, p. 67). *In* Affirmation *and* I Love My Baby and My Baby Loves Me *the artists remain alive. Wynne captures her playfulness with her child but asserts her identity in the words she writes—she is an artist and a mother and the one state enhances, rather than detracts from, the other. Surman, in playing with her child, makes art. She dances with her child, asserting herself as artist and mother. Both these works delight in the maternal jouissance of the post-partum period and remind us of the artistic potential of a split maternal subjectivity in the aftermath.*

Maternal Knowledge

Prompted by our reading of Lacan, we opened this chapter with two questions 'What does the mother/artist know?' and 'What is her knowledge?' To us, it seems that Clayton, Philps, Surman, and Wynne know something of their maternal jouissance and allow us to know that too through their artworks. Lacan highlights feminine jouissance as always unknowable except in the moment of its experience, and yet these maternal performances allow us to sense jouissance, albeit often beyond the frame of direct experience. The split self and sharing out that Kristeva highlights as the early stage of maternal subjectivity is made manifest as Clayton, Philps,

Surman, and Wynne experiment with separating from and reuniting with their infant children. We are able to see the terrifying threat of separation from the child and to reflect on our own divided subjectivity as mothers in the midst of the aftermath; and yet, we also see the generative potential and transcendent possibilities this opens up in terms of reclaiming new mothering identities. In the maternal performance practice that we have examined here, the divided subjectivity that underpins jouissance is at play not only in the mother as divided from her child, or as neither the phallic object nor the possessor of the phallic object, but also in the split identity between ourselves as mother *or* artist. These works show artists making sense of their new maternal identities and their artistic identities, not as separate but as inextricably linked to both their babies and their various personal and professional identities. Perhaps these artworks allow us to glimpse the whole unified mother/artist in the moment of aftermath: excessive and more than she was before. Clayton Philps, Wynne, and Surman do not present themselves as divided subjects but complete as artists, mothers, and babies come together in moments created, framed, documented, and offered to others through maternal performances.

Notes

1. It is important to note that Lacan makes a valuable contribution to moving beyond the biological categories of man and woman by exploring feminine and masculine tendencies, which he argues are social constructs rather than sexed positions, as is outlined in Juliet Mitchell's introduction to her co-edited edition of Lacan's *Feminine Sexuality* (Mitchell, p. 6 in Lacan 1985).
2. For the full artist's statement which started Lenka Clayton's *An Artist Residency in Motherhood* see http://www.lenkaclayton.com/work#/man-boy-man-etc/.
3. For more information about Lizzie Philps' *Maternity Leaves* see https://lizziephilps.com/?page_id=8.
4. The piece is also known as *I Love My Baby and My Baby Loves…* In this writing I have used the title that Surman uses on her own online documentation of the piece at https://vimeo.com/71245322.
5. See *Performance Research* (2018) 23 (1) 'On Children' edited by Adele Senior and the Institute for the Arts and Practice of Dissent at Home for a nuanced exploration of the ethics of representing children in and through performance.

References

Artist Residency in Motherhood. n.d. *An Artist Residency in Motherhood*. http://www.artistresidencyinmotherhood.com/. Accessed 10 Feb 2021.

Chambers, Paula. 2017. The Nightdress I Wore to Give Birth In: Performative Materialities and Maternal Intersubjectivities. *Performance Research* 22 (4): 18–27.

Clayton, Lenka. n.d. An Artist Residency in Motherhood. *Lenka Clayton*. http://www.lenkaclayton.com/work#/man-boy-man-etc/. Accessed 10 Feb 2021.

de Beauvoir, Simone. 1988 [1949]. *The Second Sex*, trans. H.M. Parshley. London: Picador.

deSouza, Allan. 2018. *How Art Can Be Thought: A Handbook for Change*. Durham, NC: Duke University Press.

Freud, Sigmund. 1955. Beyond the Pleasure Principle. In *The Standard Edition of the Complete Psychological Works of Sigmund Freud, Vol. XVIII*, ed. J. Strachey. London: Hogarth Press.

Greer, Anna. 2018. 24 Women Artists Challenge Breastfeeding Stigma in This New Exhibit. *Bust Magazine*. https://bust.com/arts/194292-brooklyn-breastfeeding-art-exhibit-reception.html. Accessed 20 Mar 2020.

Irigaray, Luce. 1981. And the One Doesn't Stir Without the Other, trans. Hélène Vivienne Wenzel. *Signs* 7 (1): 60–67.

Jones, Ann Rosalind. 1984. Julia Kristeva on Femininity: The Limits of a Semiotic Politics. *Feminist Review* 18: 56–73.

Kristeva, Julia. 1981a. *Desire in Language: A Semiotic Approach to Literature and Art*, trans. Thomas Gorz, Alice Jardin, and Leon S. Roudiez. Oxford: Basil Blackwell.

Kristeva, Julia. 1981b. Women's Time. *Signs* 7 (1): 13–35.

Lacan, Jacques. 1985. *Feminine Sexuality*, ed. Juliet Mitchell and Jacqueline Rose, trans. Jacqueline Rose. New York and London: W. W. Norton.

Lacan, Jacques. 2001 [1977]. *Ecrits: A Selection*, trans. Alan Sheridan. London: Tavistock.

Liss, Andrea. 2009. *Feminist Art and the Maternal*. Minneapolis: University of Minnesota Press.

Liss, Andrea. 2013. Maternal Aesthetics: The Surprise of the Real. *Studies in the Maternal* 5 (1): 1.

Philps, Lizzie. n.d. Maternity Leaves. *Lizzie Philps*. https://lizziephilps.com/?page_id=8. Accessed 2 Feb 2021.

Philps, Lizzie. 2016. Resistance. In *Live Art and Motherhood: Study Room Guide on Live Art and the Maternal*, ed. Lena Šimić and Emily Underwood-Lee. London: Live Art Development Agency.

Rippel, Ildikó, and Rosie Garton. 2017. Maternal Ruptures/Raptures. *Performance Research* 22 (4): 36–43.

Senior, Adele. 2018. "Age Transvestism" in Contemporary Performance and Live Art with Children. *Performance Research* 23 (1): 26–36.

Senior, Adele, and the Institute for the Art and Practice of Dissent at Home (eds.). 2018. *Performance Research* 23 (1): 1–5.

Šimić, Lena. n.d. Friday Records. *Lena Šimić*. https://lenasimic.art/artsprojects/maternal-matters/friday-records/. Accessed 2 Feb 2021.

Šimić, Lena, and Emily Underwood-Lee. 2020. Returning to Ourselves: Medea/Mothers' Clothes and Patience One Decade On. In *Maternal in Creative Work: Intergenerational Discussions on Motherhood and Art*, ed. E. Marchevska and V. Walkerdine. London and New York: Routledge.

Surman, Grace. n.d. *Grace Surman*. https://gracesurman.wordpress.com/. Accessed 2 Feb 2021.

Teresa of Avila. 2004. *The Life of St. Teresa of Avila by Herself*, trans. J.M. Cohen. London: Penguin.

Woman Up! Podcast (Lena Simic). 2019. *Episode 9: Lena Simic* [audio podcast], September 15. https://www.desperateartwives.co.uk/woman-up-podcast-episode-9-dr-lena-simic/?mbuilder=true. Accessed 23 Oct 2020.

Wynne, Megan. n.d. *Megan Wynne*. http://meganwynne.net/. Accessed 2 Feb 2021.

Wynne, Megan with Lena Šimić, and Emily Underwood-Lee. 2020. An Interview with Megan Wynne. *Performance and the Maternal*. https://performanceandthematernal.files.wordpress.com/2020/12/megan-wynne-1.pdf. Accessed 24 Dec 2020.

Youngs, Ian. 2019. We Are a Family—And an Art Collective. *BBC News*, July 14. https://www.bbc.co.uk/news/entertainment-arts-48723612. Accessed 29 Oct 2020.

Performances and Artworks Cited

Clayton, Lenka. 2012–2014. *An Artist Residency in Motherhood* [art project].

Clayton, Lenka. 2013a. *63 Objects Taken from My Son's Mouth* [photographic series].

Clayton, Lenka. 2013b. *The Distance I Can Be From My Son* [film series].

Clayton, Lenka. 2016–ongoing. *An Artist Residency in Motherhood* [artist residency programme].

Loveless, Natalie. 2010–2013. 'Maternal Ecologies' [exhibition].

Marchevska, Elena. 2009–2011. *Valid Until…* [photography series].

Philps, Lizzie. 2013. *Maternity Leaves* [photography series].

Sargeant, Helen. 2015–2016. *M(other) Stories* [blog].

Šimić, Lena. 2007–2008. *Contemplation Time* [mixed media].

Šimić, Lena. 2014. *Friday Records* [mixed media].

Surman, Grace. 2010. *I Love My Baby and My Baby Loves Me* [film].

Underwood-Lee, Emily. 2008. *Patience* [performance].
Wynne, Megan. 2013. *My Puppet* [film].
Wynne, Megan. 2015. *Impregnated* [performance for camera].
Wynne, Megan. 2016a. *Belly* [performance for camera].
Wynne, Megan. 2016b. *Mask of Motherhood* [film].
Wynne, Megan. 2016c. *Postpartum Nightgown* [performance for camera].
Wynne, Megan. 2018. *Affirmation (I Am a Professional Artist)* [film].
Wynne, Megan. 2019. *Futility* [performance for camera].

CHAPTER 6

Maintenance (6 Months)

The Maternal and Labour

For the last three chapters we have looked at the early stages of biological motherhood, immersing ourselves in pregnancy and birth and its aftermath. We have examined the need to find our new maternal subjectivity alongside the baby, the emerging other that once was part of us. Now we move into maintenance and care. We follow three particular strands of enquiry in relation to maintenance. In the following writing we turn to the work of Jessica Olah, an artist who created a durational performance about her own mother's maternal labour, working from the position of a daughter. We also examine the work of experienced mother/artists (Grace Surman and Liz Clarke) who have continued addressing the theme of the maternal beyond the early years of mothering. Firstly, we explore how to empathize with the ongoing labour involved in daily mothering, which we examine through the lens of Jessica Olah's *2 340 Peanut Butter and Jelly Sandwiches* (2016). We then move into an examination of the changing role and relationships of the mother as our children grow, as shown in Grace Surman's *Performance with Hope* (2017). Our final section explores the way that Liz Clarke has practised care for her audience and her art practice with particular reference to her show *Cannonballista* (2017–2018). We are keen to think about maintenance as both a topic for performances, as will be seen from the standpoint of a daughter

L. Šimić and E. Underwood-Lee, *Maternal Performance*, Contemporary Performance InterActions,
https://doi.org/10.1007/978-3-030-80226-4_6

in Olah's case, and also the very arduous acts of maintenance that it takes to sustain an artistic career, as Surman and Clarke demonstrate. We examine the practices of mother/artists who integrate performance making with maternal care. We find solidarity and affirmation in the work of Surman and Clarke and recognize our own situation in the works they present. This is the maternal stage we both find ourselves in—caring for our children over the long term.

Olah's durational performance *2 340 Peanut Butter and Jelly Sandwiches* (2016) is, in the artist's own words, 'an exercise in empathy with mother' (Olah with Šimić and Underwood-Lee 2016). Olah set herself the massive task of making 2340 peanut butter and jelly lunch sandwiches—2340 representing the number of days she was in school and the thousands of packed lunches prepared for Olah by her mother. This durational performance took place in Specials on C, 'a community bodega for creative expression', a former family deli turned community centre in the East Village neighbourhood, Manhattan, New York, in January 2016; the venue was a deliberate choice by Olah to bring to mind the care for the wider society for which the community art venue can act as a locus.[1]

Grace Surman's *Performance with Hope* (2017) and Liz Clarke's *Cannonballista* (2017–2018) present us with another model of taking care and maintaining. Both artists' work can be understood as a part of their larger opus; Surman and Clarke are self-reflexive in their mothering and their performance works: they comment on themselves and the way they sustain their practice as they move through the stages of their careers. Surman's piece is a play on the responsibilities between herself and her daughter, a game made of an exchange of roles between a child and a parent. *Cannonballista* presents us with a maternal act of care that supports both performer and audience. Clarke maintains the difficult position of artist and keeps herself going. She also adheres to the idea of presenting the often-unheard stories of women, which she identifies as a political act.

The concept of 'maintenance art' has been developed by Mierle Laderman Ukeles and her seminal Maintenance Art works, which were first conceptually outlined in the *Manifesto for Maintenance Art, 1969!* (1969) consisting of 'Ideas' and 'A Proposal for Maintenance Art Exhibition "Care"'. Ukeles' art practice has seen her occupy the position of official artist in residence of the New York City Department of Sanitation since 1978 (Steinhauer 2017). Maintenance is about care, the repetitive labour of caring. It seems fitting that we are writing about keeping going, the endless maintenance work, as we reach the middle of our book. We must keep going, keep writing and researching even though we may be getting a little tired. This is the sixth month of writing. The novelty of starting this project has gone; we move out of the period of beginnings and into the period of maturity, which brings with it its own joys and frustrations. We have reached our middle age. The artists we explore in this chapter make work considering this middle age. Surman and Clarke do this as artists who are in their forties, in this intermediate stage of the maternal journey with their biological children, and who have moved from the sphere of 'emerging artists' to that of 'established artists'. Olah is younger, both in terms of the amount of years since her birth and in professional terms; however, she reflects on the maintenance work of her own mother through the stages of mother with a child in kindergarten to mother of a high school child and thus Olah also reflects on the middle age of the maternal journey from the viewpoint of a daughter.

The Maternal and Care

We started this chapter during the Coronavirus lockdown in the spring of 2020, a time when we were working from home, home schooling our children, confined to our houses in Liverpool and Cardiff, and only allowed out for 'essential activities'.[2] We were maintaining our families, doing what we could to keep things going, keep everyone fed, educated, and safe. So much energy had to go into reassuring the children, looking after their emotional needs, enabling them to understand their new reality of social isolation, changes in routine, and the ever-present threat of disease, which is felt acutely across society. The children are starting to confront issues of mortality and fragility and seeing that people in their community and family are vulnerable, perhaps for the first time. The vulnerability of the other is a fundamental aspect of the work of maternal maintenance, as we will explore in this chapter through the lens of Adriana Cavarero's 'maternal inclination' (2011) and Lisa Baraitser's 'maternal time' (2017).

We were trying to maintain some sense of normality against a background where everything, even walking in the streets around our houses, had become strange. As so many have acknowledged, the work of maintaining family life hit mothers hardest of all during the Coronavirus pandemic: women were disproportionately affected economically as businesses shut down (Butler 2020) and mothers took on the bulk of the home schooling. A study by Mike and Saheeda Thelwall examined tweets shared during the virus and found that women were significantly more likely to tweet about the impact of the virus on family life (2020). An analysis carried out by Public Health Wales, the government body responsible for bringing together all aspects of the National Health Service in Wales, found that the impact of COVID-19 is gendered, with women more anxious about both getting the virus and themselves and their friends and family succumbing to the virus (World Health Organization Collaborating Centre on Investment for Health and Wellbeing, Public Health Wales 2020).[3]

Simon Kelly and Adele Senior (2020) have reflected on their own experience as two full-time academics and parents during the COVID lockdown in the UK in Spring 2020, while taking care of two small children. They discuss the disproportionate difference in terms of workload and a suddenly apparent division among those colleagues who have and those who do not have caring responsibilities. Kelly and Senior call for a feminist parental ethics, which they situate between the maternal and the ecological, thus encompassing more-than-human relations too. Building on previous work by Seyla Benhabib (1992) and Mary Phillips (2017), they write:

> Here we suggest that it may be useful to consider parenting as existing at the *intersection* between the maternal and the ecological. To parent, to give birth, and to bring forth is an ongoing ecological interaction, but it also requires *shared mothering* that is oriented towards certain *concrete others* within these ecologies (Benhabib 1992; Phillips 2017). It is the parental act of mothering, of nurturing, protecting, and providing space for moral development that creates new (and hopefully responsible and respectful) biophysical members within an ecological community. This act of bringing forth (of *parire*) is an important difference that parenting represents. (Kelly and Senior 2020, pp. 14–15, original emphasis)

While this particular call makes an invaluable intervention in how to recognize care as an integral part and skill of our embodied human existence, particularly in the context of the workplace, and the authors are clear in their self-identification as 'parents', we continue to employ the terms 'mothering', 'maternal', and 'mothers', rather than 'parents', to emphasize the gendered maintenance work which is still prevalent in our Western societies. In the main, maintenance work is gendered work;

women are mothering, caring for their children, their extended biological or chosen families and their communities.[4]

Maintenance work remains maternal work. We do not here state that all maintenance work is carried out by biological mothers but are keen to use the term 'maternal' rather than 'parental' to acknowledge these gender differences in the labour of mothering, pregnancy, and birth (as we have explored in previous chapters). Family life has become about care and maintaining a status quo or keeping everything going in the face of what has come to be described in popular parlance as 'the new normal'. This pandemic is throwing a light on our mothering responsibilities, not only to our immediate families but also to our wider communities, as 750,000 people take up voluntary roles within the National Health Service in the UK, and many informal mutual aid community schemes are established (NHS 2020; Booth 2020). Although we seek to recognize the gendered nature of maternal work, we do this in order to move beyond this gendered binary thinking, where women are responsible for home-life and child-rearing, and confined to 'caring professions'. It is highly problematic to reinforce the thinking that care work is women's and mothers' work, as *The Care Manifesto* (The Care Collective 2020) authors have observed. They remind us that 'care has historically been undervalued because it has been associated with the "feminine" and with care-taking, which is understood to be women's work, tied in with the domestic sphere and women's centrality in reproduction' (p. 24). Building on Rozsika Parker's (1995) work on maternal ambivalence *The Care Manifesto* calls for an understanding of 'ambivalences of care' (pp. 27–28) and moreover encourages us to understand care as an 'organising principle on each and every scale of life' from 'a feminist, queer, anti-racist and eco-socialist perspective' (p. 22). We seek to move beyond the narrow, idealized reading of an essentialized maternal where women are understood in terms of a biological imperative to care and a maternal caring sensibility within the nuclear family. In this chapter we try to think deeper and more broadly in terms of a politics of care that builds kinships and communities. We pay attention to those around us, maintain them, and take care and this is something which artists help us achieve.

The Maternal and Time

Lisa Baraitser examines the temporal qualities of maintenance and care in her 2017 monograph *Enduring Time*. She notes that practices of maintenance and maternal care require that we stay with a situation and pay 'careful attention' (2017, p. 15), and that this changes our relationship to time. She articulates this as maternal time, which she defines as 'the time it takes to become attached to one another through repetitive, obdurate, mundane practices of maternal care' (p. 76). This maternal time is the time of staying with and paying attention, maintaining and enduring. This is time that Baraitser argues 'pools' rather than 'flows' (p. 5). This is not the time of rupture or shock that we encountered in the early stages of this book, when the body itself was experiencing drastic changes. We have moved out of the pregnancy, birth, and aftermath.

In *Manifesto for Maintenance Art* Ukeles asks 'after the revolution, who's going to pick up the garbage on Monday morning?' (1969), a quote we keep returning to, and which features in our Futures chapter as well. In this period of maintenance, we find ourselves having moved from the revolution of birth and its aftermath and living that enduring, repetitive Monday morning, picking up the pieces, again and again, having a routine. Of course, there lingers still our desire for newness, which makes us rebel against this eternal picking up of the mess.

> I'm such a sucker for the new. I run on energy that's raw and exciting. ... I can't stand rereading the same old picture books I read to Neal, who is now seventeen, to James, who is now four. I've had it with farm animals, and Alfie and Annie-Rose and Petra and other baa-baa, moo-moo, diggers, tractors, firemen, and fish! I can't slow down for James. I run with him and encourage his nuclear flow, his momentum, his mania in our household. I worry about it as well, but I've had enough of being this patient slow caring mother-creature. (Šimić in Epp Buller et al. 2019, p. 341)

The mother figure is one of rebellion too. We resist painting her as a sacrificial, all understanding and caring entity. Mothers can be conflicted and ambivalent, bored and frustrated. It takes patience and skill to live through maintenance time. This is a long learning process. Baraitser and Ukeles invite us to look again at this enduring maintenance and to see this not as time we must live through but as a time we can live with, and which develops relationships of maternal care allowing us the capacity to continually begin anew.

Adriana Cavarero expands our understanding of care, which she positions as an attitude of inclination towards a vulnerable other. Cavarero points out that to act with kindness towards the vulnerable other is a choice and we could equally incline towards our other with the intent to harm (2011, p. 202). In highlighting the choice to care as one possible, but crucially not the only, maternal position, she alerts us to the ongoing work of care and to the fact that the mother figure must continue to choose to sustain her other, who reaches towards her as she reaches back towards them. In Cavarero's analysis care is active; care is not the universal or natural state of the maternal but one facet of a maternal inclination which, when combined with Baraitser's assertion of the temporal aspects of maternal care, enables us to understand the ongoing work of maternal maintenance.

Maintenance involves a continual starting again of the repetitive and engenders a form of renewal as it allows everyday life to carry on again and again (Baraitser 2017, p. 50). Baraitser points out that to maintain has a dual meaning—both to keep someone or something going and to keep an idea afloat or to maintain a constant position (p. 52). This is doubly emphasized in relation to the lockdowns that were experienced globally in response to the Coronavirus pandemic. The future seems suspended, unrecognized; we are stuck in the present, in the drudgery of our everyday tasks, from childcare and housework to work emails, online teaching, and this writing. Is it possible to observe that the time of Coronavirus makes us imagine some sort of collective maternity leave but without the cute and cuddly babies? Maintenance weighs on us—our households hold both the domestic and the public. Ukeles pays attention to the ongoing acts that are required to keep a civic sanitation programme going or to maintain artworks in a gallery, asking us to see the cleaning, picking up, and disposing that we are all dependent upon. These tasks are never-ending: more dust will always settle, just as our care will always be required to keep a society going. The exceptional times of a global pandemic have acutely highlighted maintenance for many of us, whose privilege generally shields us from having to give thought to the systems that sustain us. We have started seeing society and its operations through the importance of key workers: healthcare professionals, doctors and nurses, support staff, care workers, teachers, delivery drivers, postal workers, shop assistants, shelf stackers, checkout workers, parents.

Baraitser writes of the 'cancellation of the future' that is engendered by poverty, disability, or climate chaos (2017, p. 8). This cancellation of the future is something we felt acutely during the lockdown as we were stuck at home and yet disaster was imminent and we experienced, to again borrow Baraitser's words, 'time that is both relentlessly driven yet refuses to flow' (p. 9). The cancellation of the future, the suspension of plans, has gripped many of us, on a global level, and for some the scale of the grief and rupture is more extreme in relation to the death of close ones because of Coronavirus. For those of us who experience not the sudden shock of grief, but the changed temporality caused by the pandemic, time is stuck in the now, in the maintenance work of today. And it is from this position and these particular circumstances that we turn to the work of those artists who have considered maternal care work in other 'normal' times.

On Jessica Olah's *2 340 Peanut Butter and Jelly Sandwiches*

On her website, Jessica Olah notes of her durational performance *2 340 Peanut Butter and Jelly Sandwiches* (2016):

> The PB&J is a quintessentially American symbol, stirring up childhood memories for many. During my own childhood, my mother made me this sandwich every day, from Kindergarten through twelfth grade. Unintentionally, it became a symbol of love, a tiny gesture to say, 'I want to provide you with nourishment.' As an adult, I have mixed feelings when I think about how many of these sugary sandwiches I ate while growing up, and find it interesting how often we feed each other not quite nourishing foods as a sign of love. This project was a durational art piece, intending to explore the different emotional effects that result from committing to making 2,340 sandwiches – attempting to physically empathize with what my mother had done for me. By being intentional about making a peanut butter and jelly sandwich, I hope to transform a seemingly mundane task into a significant experience. I created a PB&J sandwich to represent each day of school from Kindergarten to twelfth grade, over a period of 5, ten-hour work days. Surrounding me as I worked were photographs my mother took in the 1980's, documenting the step-by-step process of making a PB&J. At the end of each day, I donated the sandwiches to The Bowery Mission. (Olah 2016)

In an interview we conducted in 2016, Olah shared with us the process, preparation, and conceptual and reflective narration around her *2 340 Peanut Butter and Jelly Sandwiches* durational performance (Olah with Šimić and Underwood-Lee 2016). Olah described herself as a difficult child who would only want to eat carbs and sugar in her school years. She thought of the love and care her mother had shown through this repetitive labour of sandwich making, but also how the mother's love can prove unintentionally harmful. This piece was therefore also about ambivalence. As a child Olah had suffered from hyperglycaemia and would often faint in school. When working on the project, Olah had undergone certain changes in her eating habits and therefore made an attempt to redeem this 'desert sandwich' into something nourishing and healthy. Bread, peanut butter, and jelly were all carefully sourced, local, and organic, and the sandwiches were donated twice a day, in order to ensure freshness, to the Bowery Mission, a homeless shelter. Olah's labour was not only about repaying her mother for the act of love and care she had given her through the schooling years, but also about acknowledging her wider Lower East Side community and thus imagining and creating a new set of feminist relations. The labour of making the sandwiches propelled the artist to think beyond her own individual situation, and rather extend towards the others she is in relation to and in so doing assign the project with a participatory and social aspect.

Early on during the five-day-long performance, Olah changed her expectations for the project when she realized that rather than only focus on the labour itself as a solitary activity, she would need to engage in the community of audiences around her. She noted how much the artwork also had to do with the other actors involved: the farmers' market jam, the importance of the setting and the aims of the community centre she was hosted in, the peanut butter company's ethical credentials, the support she had received from her Brooklyn friends and volunteers who were checking in on her emails and arranging interviews with the press, holding the phone to enable her to talk while continuing with sandwich making. This artwork was about welcoming the others, sharing the labour, sharing food and time.

The project was inspired by a conversation with a co-worker while they were both kitchen assistants, remarking upon repetitive labour. It was through this conversation that Olah realized how special it was that her mother would make her sandwiches for lunch on a daily basis, how this maternal labour was not to be taken for granted. She had wanted to visualize the work of making 2340 sandwiches, to experience it, to find out its duration. While the performance came into being through generosity and support from others, via a fundraising page, peanut butter donations, and friends giving their time to help with the work, it was Olah herself who was the one making all the sandwiches, getting on with the task for five days, ten hours a day, completing the labour, keeping to the integrity of the artwork.

There is 'tediousness' to this work, to this durational artwork, and there's patience in it, an endurance. *2 340 Peanut Butter and Jelly Sandwiches* is about memory, and it is predominantly about documentation rather than the art object or product itself. The similarities with Ukeles' ambition to make visible the labour rather than to produce a fixed artwork are particularly striking. However, unlike Ukeles' extended projects which came after the production of *Manifesto for Maintenance Art, 1969!* this performance is about time condensed: the labour of thirteen years of parenting a school child reduced down to five symbolic days. Olah's performance is temporally dual: it is repetitive and dull, time stagnating in the endless task of making sandwiches, as well as accelerated and compressed into five days during which Olah had to ensure she finished all the work within the designated timeframe. It is actually Olah's mother who has engaged in maintenance art making over the long thirteen years, while it is Olah who has framed it as such, made us understand such maternal labour by giving it a fixed compressed time of five days. In this one-off durational performance, Olah embodies the notion of pooling time and the 'repetitive, obdurate, mundane' maternal time Baraitser has articulated (2017, p. 76).

Olah's mother was surprised and flattered by Olah's artwork, which she and Olah's father came to see on its closing day. Both parents kept handing their daughter the necessary bread and thus speeding up the performance's process. Olah's mother recounted that the performance made her think about her own mum, and how she had taken her to swimming practice every day, and how such maternal actions had always been taken for granted. It is through the act of re-performance that the acknowledgement of maternal labour becomes visible. While in the beginning Olah feared that her mother would not conceive of the artwork being about honouring her, it became clear throughout the process of making, and in Olah's mother's response to the artwork, that feelings of gentleness and softness appeared between the two. For both mother and daughter the artwork created a better understanding of the extreme labour of maternal maintenance as well as maternal compassion (Fig. 6.1).

The making of sandwiches for lunch boxes was suspended during the pandemic due to the closure of schools, yet everyday maternal acts of care continued throughout our virus-stricken days. Could this time in history see the emergence of care as an organizing principle of our societies and thus end what the Care Collective calls the reign of carelessness within neo-liberal capitalist logic (2020, p. 1)? Does the sudden emphasis and visibility of care open our capacity to turn towards more compassionate social and ecological relations? The Care Collective claims: 'Care is our individual and common ability to provide the political, social, material, and emotional conditions that allow the vast majority of people and living creatures on this planet to thrive – along with the planet itself' (p. 6). Do performances like Olah's help us align maternal acts of care to those of communal needs, to the idea of shared thriving on the planet? The nourishment of the family unit and wider community might still predominantly be a woman's task, even a mother's task, a mother's load. It is she who makes sure the sandwiches can be made, and yet, as Olah reminds us,

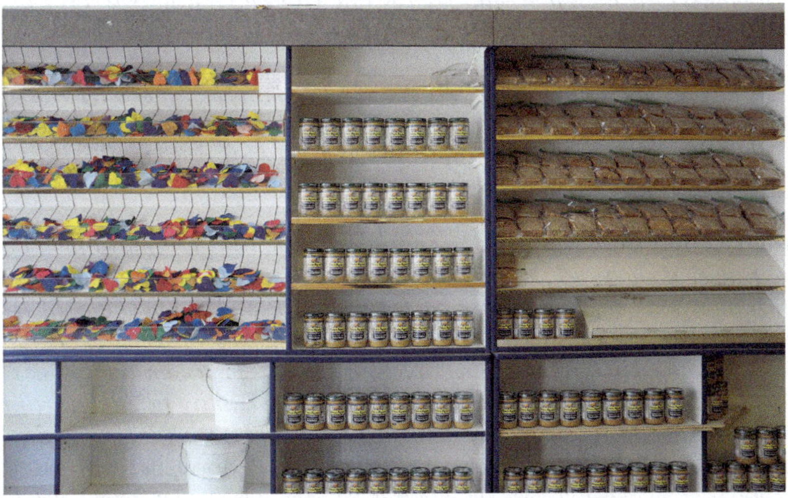

Fig. 6.1 Jessica Olah, *2 340 Peanut Butter and Jelly Sandwiches* (2016) (Image by Garrett Shore)

the old saying 'It takes a village to raise a child' rings true in both child-rearing and art making. We must rely on one another and engage in an ongoing and durational 'politics of interdependence' (The Care Collective 2020).

Lena on Grace Surman's *Performance with Hope*

In 2017 Grace Surman developed a tour under the title Mother Load, *which I saw in October at the Arts Centre, Edge Hill University, Ormskirk, UK.* Mother Load *consists of two performances*: Things Stuck Up *and* Performance with Hope.[5]

I am concerned to discuss Performance with Hope, *in which Surman performed with her then nine-year-old daughter, Hope. It is important to note that this piece is a part of an ongoing family art collective practice* (Youngs 2019). *In the previous chapter on Aftermath, Emily discussed Surman's work* I Love My Baby and My Baby Loves Me (2010), *which was made when Merrick, her son, was a baby. Clearly there is a continuation here in Surman's artistic career, a development of her maternal art practice throughout her life as a mother. Discussing the work of Roman Opalka, Tehching Hsieh and Janez Janša, Adrian Heathfield defines certain art practice as a 'lifework'. Heathfield writes:*

> *A lifework might be defined as art that involves the subjection of a life to a projected, sustained, and all consuming creative practice, where the body of the artist and their lived experiences become a formative content inseparable from the artwork.* (2014, p. 13)

While Performance with Hope *stands apart from lived everyday life as the content of the artwork, and is framed as a theatrical event of a certain duration, the long-term stance on family living and art making in the Surman-Winters household makes it fitting to discuss in terms of 'maintenance', marking it as one of many other art pieces the family have produced.*[6] *However, this piece also offers an opportunity to think further about the specificity of mother–daughter relationships, their frustrations and openings. The performance notes tell us that* Performance with Hope *captures a moment 'before she becomes an age where that might not be of interest to her'. The mother and daughter meet on stage, in a certain point of their 'development'. They reinvent their roles for the duration of the piece, which is similar to what Olah created in her durational work—the reversal of roles between mother and daughter, albeit without the mother's direct involvement. However, in Surman's case we are reminded that this performance must have taken time to develop and rehearse, together with her daughter, while Olah's is clearly a one-off durational performance work. Olah's work is removed from her everyday life: it is an occasion, an act of gratitude towards her mother. On the other hand, for Surman, performance making was a way of living for this particular mother, Grace, and daughter, Hope. While not a pure 'lifework', to borrow Heathfield's term again,* Performance with Hope *functions as an art practice which encourages a transference of the experience of mothering a daughter onto stage and thus reflecting on it, opening it up towards a new encounter between two subjects. This performance comments on and inevitably influences the way of raising one's child and living with them, at least for the duration of the time that the daughter was nine. In this analysis I will be addressing Surman by her first name, Grace, given that the title of the piece is* Performance with Hope, *which is her daughter's name. Through the title Surman plays with the name as well as the word meaning of Hope. The familiar first names Grace and Hope are more fitting to this analysis.*

The piece captures time, which is fleeting. The Greek divided time into chronos *(the chronological time, which is linear and sequential, measured by clocks) and* kairos *(the qualitative, opportune time, which has a capacity to interrupt the chronological)* (Baraitser 2017, p. 3). *In order to capture the fleeting time through which we understand and measure the child's growth, it might be that artist/mothers transform the* chronos *into* kairos *in the act of creating artworks; in this case Grace seeks the opportunity to capture but also experience these particular moments with Hope in performance, to quote her programme notes again, 'before she becomes an age where that might not be of interest to her'. Baraitser notes* kairos *as 'the transformational action of time that interrupts* chronos *with the new or unexpected'* (2017, p. 3). *It is via performance as an artform that this transformational action becomes possible, that the new and unexpected appear. The mother/artist creates a context for the transformation, for* kairos. *Inevitably* Performance with Hope *will age very quickly, as the child grows, and as sequential linear time marks us; yet the piece will become not only a part of a family album, but also a family art collective archive.*

Dressed in animal costumes—Grace in white, Hope in yellow, rabbit and lion—the mother and daughter engage in a number of choreographed scores. Choreography clearly indicates the flow of time. There is movement and action. They run around the stage in a highly set manner following the prescribed drawn-out circular lines. They showcase a number of physical exercises displaying and enacting support and dependency. They lean on each other. They embrace and carry one another; the performance sees them occupy each other's positions and exchange their prescribed parent/child roles, moreover specifically mother/daughter roles. There are passages in the performance where it is obvious that the daughter takes on the caring mothering role. Hope brushes and does Grace's hair.

The daughter also displays her physical skill, from cartwheels and hula hooping to the demonstration of the clap and cup routine in 'The Cup Song', originally created by Lulu and the Lampshades to A. P. Carter's 1931 'When I'm Gone' song, made popular through the film Pitch Perfect *(2012). At one point, Hope stands on Grace, with her hand up in the sky, possibly in triumph. This is one of the slightly unsettling choreographic sequences, unsettling just because of the knowledge that it is performed by a mother and daughter duo. The daughter is set to triumph over the mother; she is the one stealing all the thunder, younger and prettier, more graceful and playful, more able physically, the one who is to succeed. It is clear that Hope steals the show. But this is also clear to Grace: she knows and accepts this is the case. She comments on it through the choreographed actions. Hope jumps through hoops at the invitation of her mother, Grace. This is both literal and metaphorical. Hope is there to please Grace and the audiences; Hope does the artistic labour for the mother, and has fun in the process. Grace holds the space, the process, and invites criticism and praise upon their artwork. The ending lyrics of the show are a rendition of Ivor Cutler and Linda Hirst's song 'Women of the World'* (Cutler and Hirst 1983). *A female voice sings: 'Women of the world take over, because if you don't the world will come to an end…'. The mother and daughter become united under the term of 'women'. The competition, or rather their duality, becomes erased, if only for the moments of the song, as they hide together under the blanket and emerge again.*

I had a complex relationship to the show. While watching the performance I ended up siding with the daughter and 'blaming the mother'. Of course, I immediately felt guilty about it as well. Why did I prefer the daughter to the mother? Why is it that I am so easily charmed by a child on stage? Why do I fall for Hope's nonchalant and delightfully unintended, and yet almost Brechtian, distance from the act of performing? Hope runs on stage so effortlessly; she cares not. Hope fills the stage with her youthful energy, with carelessness. Hope appears in front of us, so easy, so sweet, so full of joy, almost beyond any negative judgement from the audience members. I was transfixed. In contrast, the mother, Grace, comes across as overwhelming—she cares too much. I saw in Grace an inevitable purpose of motherhood: its overbearingness, its overprotectiveness, its too-muchness, its claim, its defence, its being there, full on. Grace was the heavy maintenance. And yet, I knew that at the end of the day, this was her show, both in mothering and in performance making.

As I reflect on this particular performance, I wonder what prompts Grace's desire to be exposed in this way, as a mother/performer? And what makes me a disagreeable spectator to this mother's attempt? Why am I, even when (possibly especially as) a scholar and fellow mother/artist in maternal matters, often sceptical and critical? What I am in no doubt about is that Grace appears on stage as a mother/performer. Grace is the initiator, a ruler, an author who frames the piece; she creates the event; she manages our encounter. It is her role as the mother/performer and facilitator that brings this framing so sharply into focus. It appears that Grace knows this. However, and this is where I am having difficulty, Grace, the mother/performer, also asks me, as an audience member, to sympathize with her mother position, regardless of the fact that it is obviously a framed engagement. This call for sympathy unnerves me. It is clear that Grace only plays at the nonconformity within the parent–child relationships while on stage; Grace is not experiencing it really in the given space and time in front of us. This is not a durational performance or 'lifework' in which the life maintenance might actually be enacted and which therefore might allow for a better understanding of maternal sympathy; Grace is only representing her mothering in the piece, and there is a kind of pathos in it, mothering demand, almost a call for pity. At the same time Hope runs effortlessly on stage, and, it seems to me, has more of a chance at finding 'freedom' in this staged performance. This difference in the attitude which is developed between the positions of the mother and daughter jars somewhat, and makes me recognize the daughter, prefer her, be with her. As a feminist spectator, I run free with her, the daughter. I let the mother stay in her pity; I refuse a certain sympathy for her. I am bothered by my decision.

I am reminded of Alison Stone's writing in Feminism, Psychoanalysis, and Maternal Subjectivity (2012) *and her assertion, following on from Luce Irigaray's discussion of Antigone (and not the mother Jocasta), that we, as feminist creators, work from our own positions as daughters, rather than mothers* (pp. 58–61). *Stone writes: 'The feminist agent, psychically and symbolically if not always empirically, is the daughter'* (p. 60). *Stone elaborates on this point arguing that 'centring feminism upon daughterhood has certain ethical and political advantages' as not all women are mothers, but all are daughters* (p. 60). *The mother position is often seen as the one of care, obligation, passivity; it is from the daughter's position that feminist women are able to act and create. Feminism loves and enables its daughters. Now, as I return to Grace, who is 'performing the mother', I remember that she is also a creative daughter who writes her story. It is in the act of being an author, being an artist, that Grace enacts her freedom, her feminist daughter position which is enabling and affective. Grace's* Performance with Hope, *while dealing with maternal themes, strikes me through its authorial, feminist, daughterly voice. The mother position is only played at in this performance. Could it be that Grace writes her piece, and her mother/performer presence, from the position of a daughter? Is the same happening with my writing, right now? Where is this voice coming from? Is this writing voice not the one of an author, of an enabled daughter? What would it mean to move towards maternal writing and maternal critique?*

Performance with Hope *performs the difficulty of being a mother, of having a fixed role. The piece stages its mothering struggle. Throughout the performance the mother position remains fixed—Grace has entered the stage with a certain kind of knowledge. It is in the act of staging that the mother claims, stamps, and demands. This is her agency, her story. In the meantime, the child runs free in their tightly choreographed piece. I glimpse the nonchalance and unintentional distance, a certain kind of carelessness. As such, the child, and only in comparison with the mother/performer on stage, provides a place of not-knowing, and opening, something beyond agency and claim. Ultimately it remains that it is thanks to the mother/performer that the daughter moves towards this freedom of expression, this carelessness, which is catered for generously by her mother. The mother–daughter duo unsettles and provokes, delights and runs free, constrained within a theatrical frame of a performance,* Performance with Hope.

Emily on Liz Clarke's *Cannonballista*

Liz Clarke is a UK-based live artist and facilitator. Her work draws on queer, punk, and burlesque aesthetics to explore issues of gender and identity, and often considers her own evolving role as an artist and mother. Here I want to focus on one particular performance, Cannonballista, *which I watched twice, once in Newport, UK (Riverfront Theatre, 21 September 2017), and once in Cardiff, UK (Sherman Theatre, 8 March*

2018). Through this piece, and Clarke's practice more broadly, I am able to think through both Clarke's maintenance of her own artistic practice and also the intersection of maternal care and maternal maintenance in relation to both the form and subject matter of Cannonballista. *I read the performance through Adriana Cavarero's proposition that the mother figure is in relation to her other through inclination, rather than occupying a vertical posture, which Cavarero associates with individualism* (Cavarero 2011).

Cannonballista *charts Clarke's grief following the death of her sister, which is intercut with a cabaret romp led by Clarke's alter ego 'Betty Bruiser'. The central proposition is that at some point during the performance, Betty is going to fire herself from a cannon in one fantastic last act. Clarke, in character as herself, critiques Betty's frivolous actions and talks about the serious business of rebuilding herself after the death of her sister. Clarke does not shy away from difficult subject matter here; instead, she stays with the challenging area of grief. Clarke is able to take her audience with her as she examines and presents her grief because she performs acts of maintenance and maternal care in order to support their engagement with the work. While I will argue here that Clarke takes a maternal position in this work,* Cannonballista *does not deal explicitly with Clarke as a mother (a topic at the forefront of much of her other work including* I Tattooed My Baby [2013] *and* I'm Bitter About Glitter [2018]*) and there is only one mention of her children in the show.*[7] Cannonballista *is rich and powerful and many images and moments have stayed with me: the blue lamé-clad Betty escaping into a shed that billows smoke and sound across the stage; Sarah Moody's live cello playing throughout the show; Clarke's statement that she embraced 'happiness over security'* (Clarke 2018); *the images of previous performances that are shown on a screen at one point in the performance; the description of 'Zil'—Clarke's childhood alter ego; the move between live performance and recorded film. These are all complex elements of the work worthy of consideration; however, in this chapter I want to look at how this particular show reaches out maternally towards the audience.*

In the final scenes of Cannonballista, *Clarke, in character as her alter ego Betty Bruiser in a glittering blue lamé bikini and huge blue wig, asks four audience members to help her fire herself from a giant, glittering cannon. This attempt to 'shoot for the stars'* (Clarke 2018) *fails and Liz/Betty is left lying in the cannon, head towards the audience, very much earthbound as confetti and streamers drift to the ground. The character, who I call here Liz/Betty to denote the complex, intermingled performance of alternative selves that Betty Bruiser embodies, shows her disappointment—her face is fallen and the jubilant chorus of Europe's triumphant power pop song 'The Final Countdown' cuts to silence. Nonetheless, Liz/Betty picks herself up and brings me with her on a journey of recovery that parallels the show's deeper narrative of Clarke's own recovery after the death of her sister.*

Liz/Betty lies face towards us, recumbent in her cannon; this inclined position, and the less literal but equally prevalent inclination that is shown towards her audience throughout the performance, evoke Cavarero's attitude of inclination, or reaching towards in a maternal attitude of care (2011). *Cavarero employs a spatial metaphor to explore the move from the vertical position of the isolated individual to an inclined position of communion with others. She posits that when we think from a position of inclination, we become aware that we are constituted by our relationships to others, just as they are constituted in relation to us—not equal but interdependent. This, Cavarero argues, is a position where we are 'given over, exposed, offered, inclined to the other'; she continues, '[w]ithin feminist theory this unbalancing gesture nestles, more or less explicitly, in the imaginary ethics of care'* (p. 195). *This moves us from Cavarero's earlier understanding of the necessity of maternal narratives in order to constitute the self* (2000) *to an explicit understanding of the inequalities and power dynamics at the heart of our maternal relationships.*[8] *Just as is demonstrated in the work of Olah and Surman, it is the mother who cares for and maintains the child, yet equally the mother is able to reject this position of care and reach out in aggression or cause harm. Cavarero describes the maternal figure as leaning over or inclined towards a vulnerable other through an analysis of Leonardo da Vinci's image of the Madonna and child. She explores how maternal relationships are not based on equality but on a position of power where we can choose to incline towards the other with a caring or violent intention* (2011, p. 202). *While I am, of course, reading Cavarero rather literally in relation to Liz/Betty as she lies in the cannon, this metaphor of inclination gives me a compelling way to think about* Cannonballista *in terms of care and the maternal inclination that exists throughout the work, even when Liz/Betty is more figuratively inclined.*

At many points in Cannonballista *the audience are invited onto the stage to participate in the show. In one scene Clarke brings the audience onto the stage to wheel about her cannon; in order to do this she helps them learn how to do a 'burlesque knee bend'* (Clarke 2018); *she teaches them with care and consideration but not from a position of equality. As I reflect on this I am reminded of the issues of in/equality raised by Lena in relation to Surman's* Performance with Hope. *In* Cannonballista *it is made clear that Clarke is in control of the work and the 'expert' on stage, thus she occupies a parental position. Her control enables her to be 'in charge' of her audience in order to support them, rather than to expose their inadequacies. Here we see maternal maintenance work in action. Clarke's careful instruction to the audience members on where to position their legs enables the audience members to present themselves at their best and to celebrate their contribution; Clarke is the mother maintaining her child in order to allow them to shine. Too often we see audience participation that humiliates or causes discomfort; I am sure anyone who has attended even a small amount of live stand-up comedy, for example, will be familiar with the terror that comes from being singled out among the audience by the powerful presence on stage. When an audience sit in front of a performer, particularly when an audience member is singled out from the crowd by the performer, it is the performer who holds the power, we are exposed before them as is the naked Christ-child laid before his mother in Cavarero's example. The performer has status and power, they hold the microphone and direct the action, they know what is coming next and have marked out their territory.*[9] *In* Cannonballista *Clarke brings her audience onto the stage but is inclined towards the vulnerable other with care.*

Unlike much of the work that Clarke has previously created, where she co-creates with her participants, Cannonballista *is most definitely a one-woman show. The audience are invited onto the stage and they are there to serve Clarke's vision. That is not to say that the performance discounts the audience or utilizes them in an exploitative way; instead it is simply that meaning is located in Clarke's body, actions, and words as they are offered to the audience. There are often several people on the stage, including Sarah Moody, the cellist, who is there throughout, and* Cannonballista *was made in collaboration with director Holly Stoppit and producer Frances Bossom, but this performance is about one woman placing herself and her story centre stage rather than co-creating something together. In this sense this work aligns with Alphonso Lingis' useful definition of performance, which he positions as distinct from 'work' and 'ritual'. In Lingis' proposition work, ritual, and performance may all be comprised of the same series of actions but he argues that performance is an 'action that is turned to one or more witnesses … [that] … may acquire formal perfection… Performed with grace and style'* (Lingis 2018, p. 280). *I find this definition useful when I think about Clarke's work for two reasons: firstly, it invites me to think of her work as directed to another and, secondly, it recognizes that this direction towards another does not negate the possibility of virtuosity. This alignment of the virtuosic and turn to the other in performance, combined with Cavarero's notion of maternal inclination, makes for an interesting way of understanding maternal performance. I am drawn to these ways of identifying maternal performance as an active, skilful, and considered leaning or turning towards an other.*

In line with the maternal/performative lean towards that I have taken from Lingis and Cavarero, in Cannonballista *Clarke turns her action towards her audience with care. She invites the audience in and considers her responsibility towards them while they are there; in this way Clarke and her audience are always in relation and exchange. The relationship between Clarke and her audience is unbalanced, with roles clearly differentiated between performer and spectator, in what I propose is an ethical, caring inequality. The inequality in the performance is not just in relation to Clarke's authorship of the show or excellence as a performer, but it is also apparent in the way that Clarke takes responsibility for her audience.*

Cannonballista *is a performance that changes with its audience. The audience are asked to contribute and they are encouraged to whoop and cheer on Liz/Betty in her increasingly elaborate endeavours. Both audiences of which I was part responded differently to the invitations to participate and the show developed nuances and reshaped to accommodate them—Liz/Betty answered back, laughed, or encouraged the audience to new levels of daring. In an email exchange I had with Clarke she describes the script as 'organic', referring to its open and unfixed nature that allows her to work with the audience she has on the night. I found I was changed and shaped by the show in different ways depending on the context and atmosphere in which I encountered it. The performance I attended in Newport was quieter; the audience on that night seemed more in tune with the contemplative moments. The performance in Cardiff was loud and had something of the explosive and exuberant atmosphere of a raucous hen night. It is testament to the elasticity of the script, as well as the skill of the performer, that both these audience responses felt equally valid. On both occasions on which I sat in the audience, I experienced deep sadness, genuine laughter, and great joy—my joy not least engendered by the celebration of the latex-clad, cat-suited, body of a middle-aged woman with stars glittering out from her armpit hair. Although contradictory and alarmingly rapid in the speed with which we are asked to transition from one moment to another, none of this feels out of place and no position undermines the other. While not undermining, however, these fantastic visual spectacles and conflicting narratives do undercut, and I was never allowed to linger too long in any one emotional state. The show is pacey, driven on by Betty's relentless desire for novelty and excitement, which is contrasted with Liz's more contemplative passages. At one moment Liz will be scattering earth on the stage, lying on the floor performing a careful choreography of grief, and the next Betty emerges to pass comment on what she believes is Liz's unacceptable moping: 'She shouldn't be scattering Eaarrthtthththhhhh. She should be scattering … STAAAAAAAAAAAAAAAAAAAAAAAAAAAAAAR-RRRRRRRRRRRRSSSSSSSSSSS!' These moments, where one persona comments on the other, are comic and function as neat plot devices to move the performer from one character state to another. The transitional moments also serve another function in that they allow the audience to recover themselves after being made particularly vulnerable through their empathy with Clarke's performed grief and any personal reflection that might engender. Clarke's background as a community arts practitioner is apparent in* Cannonballista *and she uses skills honed through facilitating workshops throughout the show. As I watch, I feel utterly safe in Clarke's hands. I feel that my emotional engagement with the performance is being carefully considered and that Clarke attempts to ensure throughout that her whole audience is okay when we go to the dark places, are given time for reflection, are allowed relief, and are given resolution. This material is undoubtedly difficult—we are confronted with premature death, disease, and grief—and yet I am maintained and sustained throughout by Clarke's maternal inclination of care and her consideration of the audience experience. This engenders a feeling of safety and reassurance in me and I know that I will be recognized and sustained with responsibility by the performer. I have not attended a workshop led by Clarke, but I relish the thought of experiencing how these skills and attitudes might also function in a workshop context* (Fig. 6.2).

The attitude of maternal care is not surprising when considering Clarke's background as both a reflexive mother and community arts practitioner. She notes:

> *I only started making live art and performance as my full-time occupation when my son was born. With the birth of my son this became the work that I had to do. In order to fulfil his needs and happiness, I had to ensure that I was fulfilling my own needs and a desk job, I'm sorry, for me, was just not going to happen at that time.* (Clarke with Underwood-Lee 2018, p. 2)

Fig. 6.2 Liz Clarke, *Cannonballista* (2016) (Image by Vonalina Cake)

Self-care and maternal care are interdependent here; without one the other would not exist in Clarke's *practice. Maternal care is inextricably linked with maintaining and sustaining an art practice. Clarke's care in this respect extends beyond simply caring for herself and providing what she needs to make work and maintain a maternal life. Her considerations are also in regard of what maintains the aesthetics and integrity of her work. Clarke had made previous iterations of* Cannonballista *as a community workshop in which a number of women participated; this then resulted in a performance in which both Clarke and the workshop participants told the story. Clarke notes that this compromised both the workshop participants, due to the pressure to make a show, and also her own vision for how her story was told. Again, Clarke describes this process:*

> *In its previous showing a few years before, the show was an opportunity for ten womxn to do a three-day intensive with me and then devise work around the themes. Their stories were interwoven with my story… [We made] the decision to separate out the workshop and the performance so that in the final show this story was my story, it could be reclaimed and told.* (Clarke with Underwood-Lee 2018, pp. 2–3)

Clarke's process and decisions exemplify how maternal care for her participants, her work, and the practical requirements of sustaining an art practice and maternal life are indivisible in Cannonballista. *Clarke also notes that working as part of a collaborative team has been essential in order to ensure that she herself was cared for through the process of making and performing* Cannonballista:

> *I've been really well cared for and feel really privileged to have had that care, and also pleased I made the decisions to put that care in place, which feels really important. I'm recognising what care I need within my work, which feels like a really powerful place to be. I consider care for the material, and care for my history, and care for my process.* (Clarke with Underwood-Lee 2018, p. 3)

The supportive and maintaining roles of the producer and director are centralized by Clarke as essential structures for maintaining her work and described in maternal terms of care. Cavarero notes in her analysis of maternal inclination how each mother is supported by the mothers that have gone before them, which in turn allows each new mother to take on a maternal inclination (Cavarero 2011, p. 201). *Baraitser also notes the ongoing cycles of care offered by each generation anew, allowing us to feel part of our particular generation while repeating the acts of being mothered or mothering as those that came before us also did* (Baraitser 2017, p. 110). *Here we see Clarke supported and maintained by a team of women and thus enabled to undertake maternal care for her workshop participants, work,* audiences, *and herself*.

Prior to the maternal awareness that Clarke describes, her professional experience was in roles that require an ethics of care; she had been employed in various third sector roles including within the spheres of mental health, homelessness, and domestic abuse.[10] *Clarke's art practice has been one that has evolved out of participatory practice. In the 2018 version of* Cannonballista, *Clarke decided to separate out the workshops and final performance.*

This new iteration of Cannonballista *has the aesthetic rigour and conventions of a live art performance and yet is able to combine this with care that enables an engagement with audiences and workshop participants to coexist alongside Clarke's own artistic process and care for herself. Clarke states that part of her purpose in creating* Cannonballista *was to explore how to engage with groups in a more meaningful way without compromising the integrity of either the performance or the workshop and practise both care for her workshop participants and self-care as an artist. Clarke takes a political position, that as an artist she is able to find a space to enable many people to work through performance* (Clarke with Underwood-Lee 2018, p. 1). *However, this show gives voice without giving over the stage space. In the workshops Clarke is able to facilitate people to find their voice; in the show she is able to perform another function for the audience and continue her own artistic practice. Both of these positions are inclined towards another but are distinct and specific. The distinction between enabling the voices of others and ensuring the integrity of her artistic vision ensures that Clarke is able to maintain the distinct needs of her workshop participants, her audience, and her own artistic practice, as well as herself as a mother/artist.*

Cavarero's provocation on maternal inclination asks us to consider inclination as a position of dependence, as opposed to the interdependence more usually associated with discussions of care. It is this kind of care I feel in Cannonballista*—as an audience member I feel Clarke is in control, that she is taking care of me and my emotional response to her show but this is also a relinquishing of power to some degree. Cavarero's inclined subject holds power over the child who is dependent on her for their survival. We, as an audience, are dependent on the performer who brings this show to us, just as the Christ-child in Cavarero's analysis of painting of the Madonna and child is dependent on the mother. However, this dependence does not negate the mother's need for the child or performer's need for the audience in order to constitute their own subject position. A performance could theoretically exist without an audience, although this would mean it would not align with Lingis' above-discussed definition of performance as action turned towards witnesses* (2018, p. 280). *Any performance without an audience might be considered to be limited to a state of potential, particularly in work such as* Cannonballista *which is grounded in live audience interaction, just as a maternal inclination is always dependent on an inclination towards an other. In Cavarero's analysis the inclined mother leans towards the vulnerable child who she could equally care for or wound* (2011, p. 203). *When we enter the space of* Cannonballista *we are exposed as* *participants in the show and presented with the depths of Clarke's grief and so asked to consider our own instances of grief—certainly my own experiences of bereavement were made raw again when watching this show. Liz/Betty could leave us exposed, could inflict the psychological wound of our own grief or our inability to perform in front of an audience, instead Clarke inclines herself towards us in an attitude of care.* Cannonballista, *when read through the lens of Cavarero, gives us an example of a model of maternal performance that works towards an aesthetics of care and maintenance where the artist takes responsibility for the relationship they are creating with their audience, as well as their own needs as an artist, and considers their aesthetic endeavours from a maternal position.*

Renewal and Repetition

Olah, Surman, and Clarke demonstrate maternal maintenance in a variety of ways. Olah reminds us of the enduring, ongoing work of maintenance in the tradition of maintenance art first established by Mierle Laderman Ukeles. However, unlike Ukeles, Olah condenses this work to a duration of five days, developing a durational performance piece and paying homage to her mother's maintenance work rather than engaging in her own maintenance art work. She actively employs her position as a daughter doing her mother's work, which can be read as a feminist act of gratitude and acknowledgement of maternal labour. Surman reminds us of the lifework of a family art practice that evolves in consort with the evolution of the family, and Clarke explores the acts of maternal care that are necessary to maintain herself as a mother/artist and to maintain her audience as spectators of her work. These artists, from their various career positions as a young artist reflecting on the work of her mother or more established artists in the middle stages of their careers, enable us to think through performance about the ongoing, repetitive, and laborious acts of maintenance that are required to enable each generation to begin anew. Baraitser celebrates pooling maternal time that promotes an ethical encounter (2017, p. 74). The artists we have explored in this chapter also celebrate this maternal time, drawing our attention to it through their own careful, ethical, repetitive, and relational acts of performance. This ethical attitude, or, as Cavarero might put it, choosing to care rather than to harm, can give us another way of thinking about our maternal roles during times of crisis. COVID-19, as we explored in our introduction to this chapter, is trapping us in the now and is bringing our repetitive maternal labour for our families and our communities to the fore. This pandemic can be framed as a challenge to think of a 'new normal'—that is, to reconsider how we might want to live and the values that we might hold up as important. Maternal time links to a future through children but rejects constant growth and expansion; instead, the future is maintained through a constant state of renewal and repetition (Baraitser 2017, p. 83). Perhaps this maternal time is exactly what is required for our new normal; and perhaps artists who pay attention to their maternal relations can help us understand how to move towards that goal.

Notes

1. For more information about this 'Specials on C' community centre see http://www.specialsonc.com.
2. We are re-editing this chapter during the autumn of 2020, when England has just entered a new lockdown period and Wales has just completed a two-week 'firebreaker'. When we first wrote this chapter we did not anticipate the seismic shifts in the way we have needed to change our personal parenting or how the concept of care would evolve nationally and internationally in response to the global COVID-19 pandemic. Maintenance and endurance seem ever-more important topics for consideration given the extended duration of the pandemic.
3. The report also found that the impacts of the disease increased in line with deprivation and age (World Health Organization Collaborating Centre on Investment for Health and Wellbeing, Public Health Wales 2020).
4. A global study conducted between 2012 and 2019 DeRose et al. (2019) found that in all continents in families with children women undertook between 55 and 79 per cent of domestic labour. For an analysis of how queer and other non-heteronormative family configurations complicate this trend see Civettini (2016).
5. A short video of *Performance with Hope* (2017) is available on https://vimeo.com/217676283.
6. One of the further examples of Grace Surman and Gary Winter's practice with their children, Hope and Merrick, was a family residency at the border of Manchester and Salford in 2018, as a part of Quarantine's project 'Tenancy'. See https://qtine.com/work/tenancy/.

7. We have reflected on previous shows by Clarke in our *Live Art and Motherhood* (Šimić and Underwood-Lee 2016) with Clarke herself, and also in the conversations we had with Jodie Hawkes at one of our first Performance and the Maternal network meetings at Edge Hill in 2016.
8. For a fuller exploration of Cavarero's articulation of narrative see Chapter 4, Birth.
9. The power dynamics between audience and spectator in stand-up comedy and cabaret are complex and often complicated by heckling and other interactions where audience members interject without invitation. I am here limiting my comments to those moments where the audience are 'picked out' by the performer on stage. For an analysis of the role of heckling in stand-up comedy see Oliver Double *Getting the Joke* (2013, p. 346).
10. These caring roles within the public and third sector are being exposed as the critical carers of our time through the reliance upon 'key workers' within the COVID-19 pandemic, as we have described in our introduction to this chapter.

References

Baraitser, Lisa. 2017. *Enduring Time*. London: Bloomsbury.

Benhabib, Seyla. 1992. *Situating the Self: Gender, Community and Postmodernism in Contemporary Ethics*. Bloomington: Indiana University Press.

Booth, Robert. 2020. Community Aid Groups Set Up Across UK Amid Coronavirus Crisis. *The Guardian*, March 16.

Butler, Sarah. 2020. Coronavirus Lockdown to Hit Low-Paid, Young and Women Hardest, Warns IFS. *The Guardian*, April 6.

Cavarero, Adriana. 2000. *Relating Narratives: Storytelling and Selfhood*. London: Routledge.

Cavarero, Adriana. 2011. Inclining the Subject. In *Theory After 'Theory'*, ed. Jane Elliott and Derek Attridge. London and New York: Routledge.

Civettini, Nicole. 2016. Housework as Non-Normative Gender Display Among Lesbians and Gay Men. *Sex Roles* 74: 206–219.

Clarke, Liz, with Emily Underwood-Lee. 2018. Interview with Liz Clarke. *Performance and the Maternal*. https://performanceandthematernal.com/mother-artist-interviews/. Accessed 12 Feb 2021.

DeRose, Laurie F., Frances Goldscheider, Javiera R. Brito, et al. 2019. Are Children Barriers to the Gender Revolution? International Comparisons. *European Journal of Population* 35: 987–1021.

Double, Oliver. 2013. *Getting the Joke: The Inner Workings of Stand-Up Comedy*. London: Bloomsbury.

Epp Buller, Rachel, Lena Šimić, and Emily Underwood-Lee. 2019. The Body in Letters: Once Again, Through Time and Space. In *Inappropriate Bodies: Art, Design, and Maternity*, ed. Rachel Epp Buller and Charles Reeve. Bradford, CA: Demeter.

Heathfield, Adrian. 2014. Life Re-Encased. In *Janez Janša: Life II [in Progress]*, ed. Janez Janša. London: Maska Ljubljana and Live Art Development Agency.

Kelly, Simon, and Adele Senior. 2020. Towards a Feminist Parental Ethics. *Gender, Work and Organization*. https://doi.org/10.1111/gwao.12566. Accessed 3 Feb 2021.

Lingis, Alphonso. 2018. Irrevocable Loss. In *The Alphonso Lingis Reader*, ed. Tom Sparrow. Minneapolis: University of Minnesota Press.

NHS. 2020. *NHS Army of Volunteers to Start Protecting Vulnerable from Coronavirus in England*. https://www.england.nhs.uk/2020/04/nhs-volunteer-army-now-ready-to-support-even-more-people/. Accessed 7 Nov 2020.

Olah, Jessica with Lena Šimić and Emily Underwood-Lee. 2016. Interview with Jessica Olah. *Performance and the Maternal*. https://performanceandthematernal.files.wordpress.com/2020/12/jessica-olah.pdf. Accessed 24 Dec 2020.

Parker, Rozsika. 1995. *Torn in Two: The Experience of Maternal Ambivalence*. London: Virago.

Phillips, Mary. 2017. Embodied Care and Planet Earth: Ecofeminism, Maternalism and Postmaternalism. *Australian Feminist Studies* 31 (90): 468–485.

Šimić, Lena, and Emily Underwood-Lee, eds. 2016. *Live Art and Motherhood: Study Room Guide on Live Art and the Maternal*. London: Live Art Development Agency.

Steinhauer, Jillian. 2017. How Mierle Laderman Ukeles Turned Maintenance Work into Art. *Hyperallergic*. https://hyperallergic.com/355255/how-mierle-laderman-ukeles-turned-maintenance-work-into-art/. Accessed 18 Dec 2020.

Stone, Alison. 2012. *Feminism Psychoanalysis and Maternal Subjectivity*. London and New York: Routledge.

The Care Collective. 2020. *The Care Manifesto: The Politics of Interdependence*. London and New York: Verso.

Thelwall, Mike, and Saheeda Thelwall. 2020. *Covid-19 Tweeting in English: Gender Differences*. https://arxiv.org/abs/2003.11090v1. Accessed 24 Dec 2020.

Ukeles, Mierle Laderman. 1969. *Manifesto for Maintenance Art 1969!* Proposal for an Exhibition 'Care', Originally Published in Jack Burnham (1971) 'Problems of Criticism', *Artforum*, 41. http://www.queensmuseum.org/wp-content/uploads/2016/04/Ukeles_MANIFESTO.pdf. Accessed 19 Sept 2020.

World Health Organization Collaborating Centre on Investment for Health and Wellbeing, Public Health Wales. 2020. *How Are We Doing: Public Engagement Survey on Health and Wellbeing during Coronavirus Measures*. Cardiff: Public Health Wales.

Youngs, Ian. 2019. We Are a Family—And an Art Collective. *BBC News*, July 14. https://www.bbc.co.uk/news/entertainment-arts-48723612. Accessed 29 Oct 2020.

Performances and Artworks Cited

Clarke, Liz. 2013. *I Tattooed My Baby* [performance].

Clarke, Liz. 2017–2018. *Cannonballista* [performance].

Clarke, Liz. 2018. *I'm Bitter About Glitter* [performance].

Cutler, Ivor, and Linda Hirst. 1983. *Women of the World*. Single. Rough Trade Records [song].

Olah, Jessica. 2016. *2 340 Peanut Butter and Jelly Sandwiches* [performance].

Surman, Grace. 2010. *I Love My Baby and My Baby Loves Me* [film].

Surman, Grace. 2017. *Performance with Hope* [performance].

CHAPTER 7

Generations (7 Months)

Intergenerational Exchanges

The term 'generations' concurrently alludes to the ideas of sameness and difference. 'Generate' has its origins in the Latin *generatus*, which refers to the act of begetting or giving birth; to generate then is to create something new, but also to recognize the origins of that creation as rooted in another from whom we are birthed. 'Generations' invokes an exchange; one generation precedes the other. Here we ask: how can we think about maternal generations, feminist generations, and artistic ones? We examine how to look back to those who have produced us and forward to those that we will produce, biologically and culturally. We seek understanding through the work of feminist scholars and artists, particularly the North American artists Courtney Kessel and Peggy Shaw and UK dancer and choreographer Hannah Buckley.

Generations have, unsurprisingly, been at the heart of our maternal enquiries for some time. We have repeatedly turned to those who came before us, to our own generation of scholars and artists, and to the coming generations. In our introduction to this book, Beginnings, and in our *Live Art and Motherhood: Study Room Guide on Live Art and the Maternal*, we took care to acknowledge our feminist (grand) mothers. In our *Study Room Guide* we wrote:

L. Šimić and E. Underwood-Lee, *Maternal Performance*, Contemporary Performance InterActions,
https://doi.org/10.1007/978-3-030-80226-4_7

> As feminist artist/mothers we are standing beside our feminist (grand) mothers. The works of Mary Kelly, Lea Lublin, Mierle Laderman Ukeles, Laura Mulvey, Susan Hiller, the Mother Art Collective, the Magdalena Project network and Bobby Baker have been a source of inspiration, challenge and constant re-negotiations in our own work. (Šimić and Underwood-Lee 2016, p. 5)

We base our current artistic and scholarly practice in the acknowledgement of the feminist art that flourished in the decades before our own making. In the 'On the Maternal' edition of the journal *Performance Research* we gather 'a new generation of maternal thinkers, researchers and artists' naming 'maternal aesthetics, ethics, politics, labour, and care, as well as questions of national identity, queer mothering, reproductive rights, maternal activism and co-operation within the maternal' as the topics of concern for that new generation (Šimić and Underwood-Lee 2017, p. 3). Our hope is to contribute to a new generation of mother/artists/scholars, to advance the fields of both performance studies and maternal studies, embedding ourselves within a scholarly and artistic community which will be left to the generations that follow us. In turn, they may chart new territory, begin something again in the world, providing pathways and achievements that we might all benefit from together. By working together, raising up, both generations are enabled to ascend to new heights.[1]

We are not alone in our endeavour to think across generations. An extraordinary example of intergenerational thinking was shared at our 2020 online forum on 'Storytelling and Mothers'. Roiyah Saltus showed a story that she had made with her mother, Solange Saltus, where Solange Saltus reflects on 'making [her] way in the world' (Saltus and Saltus 2020). This story is built on work that Saltus has been doing recording the stories of older people of colour living in Wales as part of her 'Praisesongs: Honouring our elders in Wales' research project.[2] One of the stories that Saltus recorded was from her own mother. We invited Saltus to reflect on the process of recording her mother's story as part of our forum on 'Storytelling and Mothers'.[3] In response to our invitation, Saltus created a new story. The mother's story was immediately followed by a story by the daughter, Roiyah Saltus, in which she discusses her experience of being mothered. Roiyah Saltus notes what she was 'taught from the womb'. Together, these women explore the power that can be gained from an exchange across generations, with Roiyah Saltus saying of her experience of making and recording stories as part of a research process with her mother: 'with her, I remembered myself'. Saltus affectingly demonstrates how an intergenerational exchange and collaboration can add so much, amplifying and redoubling what we could ever do alone. A further example of thinking across generations can be found in a recent publication, *The Maternal in Creative Work: Intergenerational Discussions on Motherhood and Art* (2020). This collection, edited by Elena Marchevska and Valerie Walkerdine, is divided into three sections generationally and 'emphasises the need to reclaim and acknowledge intergenerational influence and to discuss these intergenerational art-encounters as modes of subjective transformation' (2020, p. 5). One of the most poignant intergenerational contributions in the book is a conversation between Natalie Loveless and Mary Kelly, who discuss the idea of 'unfinished business' (2020, p. 15). Kelly notes how her own early writings raised the question of gaps, and the future work that might be done within those gaps, as a deliberate invitation to others to follow on that which she began. Loveless acknowledges Kelly's influence on her own thinking and on her curatorial practice. This conversation between these two women of different generations, who are exploring their effects upon one another in a mutual exchange, is a moving example of the potential for feminist thinking across waves.

The *Studies in the Maternal* journal runs a special series, 'In Conversation', which is defined as 'intergenerational conversations between what are usually termed second-wave feminists and what could be referred to as the "daughters" of this generation' (Segal and Baraitser 2009, p. 1). These include exchanges between Lisa Baraitser with Lynne Segal (2009), Lisa Baraitser with Denise Riley (2016), Paula McCloskey with Mary Kelly (2012), and Griselda Pollock with Laura Mulvey (2010), among others. Generations thus open up to intergenerational dialogue in the form of free-flowing conversations, exchanges in maternal scholarship and experience. Interestingly, it is the political which keeps re-emerging as the pivotal concern. Segal and Baraitser's conversation from 2009 ends with Segal asserting that the maternal '*is* the crucial voice of politics ... the critical, feminist voice of politics' (Segal and Baraitser 2009, p. 18, original emphasis). A political agenda is placed high on the maternal list of concerns. Furthermore, looking at Baraitser's more recent writing, the maternal subject, specifically in the form of the mother/artist, is yet again interlinked with the political. Baraitser notes that 'a mother-artist pushes "the maternal" into a wide set of associations with technologies, bodies, care, labour, ethics, relationality, temporality, affect, psychosexuality' and reminds us that '[a] maternal subject, for instance, is never divorced from a political generation (both a political era and a part in the generation of the political)' (Baraitser 2020, p. xxii). Baraitser prompts us to reflect on our own generational situation as a political act.

Political Generations

We wonder what our political era is now in the 2020s. This new decade has started off with the COVID-19 epidemic in the spring of 2020 and is moreover linked with climate crisis and the fear of existential danger for our species in the near future, something we address in the penultimate chapter of this book. To what degree is it useful and political to name our time as 'maternal time'? Will this generation of mother/artists be acknowledged in the future? While we assess our current generational position, we also wonder what future generations might be raised up as well as looking back at our feminist pasts.

Aware that our own political generation might only be visible from afar, it is worth giving some thought to past feminist generations, their history, and narration. Clearly, there is a tendency and desire to think and feel generationally in feminist scholarships and art, to even clash one generation against the other. We speak of feminist waves.[4] It is not surprising that comparisons emerge between these feminist waves and the complexity of mother–daughter relationships. Yet, such translations between mother–daughter relationships and feminist art or scholarship histories can be difficult and tense. In her paper 'Feminist Histories: Conflict, coalitions and the maternal order' (2010) philosopher Gillian Howie discusses the maternal in relation to feminist histories and the problem of one feminist generation being placed in opposition to another, namely third wave feminists being posed as in resistance to second-wave feminists. Howie asserts that the third wave of feminism has a relationship of maternal lineage with the second wave beyond simply that of chronology; instead, she argues that we can chose to embrace, rebel against, or reclaim a genealogical inheritance across waves and generations (p. 3). Howie's consideration is particularly useful for our analysis of generations here because it considers generational exchange through the lens of Irigaray's 'maternal order' (Howie 2010, p. 5) and specifically aligns it with a mother–daughter exchange that is reciprocal and generous rather than antagonistic.

Howie writes: 'The mother-daughter trope accentuates intergenerational conflict between feminists and presents intellectual disagreement in terms of identification with, or breaking away from, symbolic, second-wave mothers' (p. 4). Through the lens of conflict outlined by Howie, each generation somehow needs to assert their difference against the former one, like a daughter who rejects her mother. Howie warns against 'psychodrama as the condition of the feminist historical narrative', which is premised on the attainment of political identity for young feminists being 'in conflict with and secured through the negation of a previous generation' (p. 3). The article alludes to the risks of confusing and collapsing 'political resistance with resistance understood in a straightforward psychoanalytic sense' (p. 3). For Howie, to be living in a certain time necessitates an awareness of the political moments of that time. We must remember to think about political generations and affiliations made through collective endeavours, rather than understand them in an individualized psychoanalytic sense.[5] While a certain kind of rejection might be necessary in psychoanalytic terms, Howie's article is an attempt to reconfigure the problematic relationship between generations of feminists through the idea of Luce Irigaray's maternal order, which refers to an ethical sensibility of acceptance of sexuate difference.

Drawing in particular on Irigaray's *I Love to You* (1996), as well as the idea of the placenta as the negotiator between the two evolving subjects, Howie suggests:

> the thought of the Maternal Order, so well expressed in *je, tu, nous*, offers a new hermeneutic of difference and a more developed sensibility; an image of the recognition by the mother of the other and her sensed responsibility towards the other; where the self and the other are continually renegotiated. It is the vulnerability of the other that commands. From this we can build a 'we': a being-with. (2010, p. 9)

The 'we' that Howie evokes is central to understanding the generational collaboration that we are keen to explore in this chapter. When thinking of generations as 'we', rather than thinking of one opposed to the other, we are returned to the affective, negotiated, and moving learning that we saw displayed in Saltus and Saltus' story and Loveless and Kelly's conversations as discussed above. Beyond simply evoking a community between generations, Howie employs Irigaray's critique of inheritance as something that is bestowed upon another and in order to invite us to think of 'antecedence … [as] … an ethical relationship' (Howie 2010, p. 8).

We see ethics in action when we examine our chosen performances in this chapter: an ethics of care for our other generations and an ethics of renegotiation for both the points of communion and the difference that intergenerational encounters provoke. The care and respect found in the works of Shaw, Buckley, and Kessel that we examine below enable an exchange between generations from which all can benefit and be raised up. Irigaray uses the placenta as a model of exchange that is both permeable and yet also works as a point of distinction between one and the other, which she terms 'a regulating third' (Irigaray et al. 2008, p. 5). For Howie, this enables a joining together of generations as an exchange in which both distinction and mutuality are enabled—'intersecting but not isomorphic' (2010, p. 9).

To truly recognize the other, rather than subsume or consume them within our own self, or even one's own generation, helps build a different kind of social order. To have patience with the constant negotiation of one another's vulnerabilities, to care for the other in order to carefully build towards a 'we' is the work of ethics. Such a maternal sensibility of ethics can enable a more productive and nourishing intergenerational exchange, among feminists and artists. We propose here that maternal performance and art can allow us to see a sensibility of ethics, to recognize and build a 'we' through being-with.

Opening this chapter with Howie, and her concern for feminist generations, to which we feel a specific political affiliation, allows us to think about maternal performance practice and art differently. The term 'generations' thus carries a few ideas with it, from the biological, which might be closely linked to the psychoanalytical, and therefore mother–daughter relationships, to the aesthetic, which can help us find, unlock, and understand a different meaning of the maternal beyond the home or the intimacies of biological relationships. The maternal here is possibly more explicitly linked with feminist aims and politics. To quote Howie again, 'The recognition of otherness, of alterity, while not the supreme goal of feminism, may well be the condition of historical narrative and woman-to-woman sociality, which is itself the condition for political intervention' (2010, p. 10). The performance works we explore in this chapter offer us a way to understand generations based on a shared development of ideas, a mutual renegotiation of selves, firstly from a grandmother considering her relationship to her grandson (Shaw), then from a granddaughter in collaboration with her grandmother (Buckley). Finally, we move to consider a mother bringing together a whole community of other mothers to pass on wisdom to her daughter (Kessel). Reading the work of Shaw, Buckley, and Kessel through the generational, ethical, and political lens offered by Howie, we attempt to map a specifically performance-based political intervention.

Emily on Peggy Shaw's *To My Chagrin*

Peggy Shaw is a co-founder of the renowned performance company Split Britches. Shaw founded the company along with Deb Margolin and Lois Weaver in 1981, after Weaver and Shaw met in 1977, and Split Britches has been the creative framework within which Shaw and Weaver have now been making work for over forty years (Harvie and Weaver 2015, p. 299).[6]

Queer, butch motherhood is a central concern in Shaw's work. Shaw states that she is a maternal person, she has birthed and raised a child, and has served as a performance grandmother to several generations of performers over her nearly half century long career, but Shaw does not identify as a 'mother/artist', a term about which she states 'I don't really care' (Shaw with Underwood-Lee 2020, p. 2). *This rejection of the maternal title is a demonstration of Shaw's refusal to be confined within her practice, which is intrinsically linked with her lived experience, queerness, and activism* (Shaw with Underwood-Lee 2020). *Despite Shaw's disengagement from the term 'mother/artist', I am turning to Shaw's work, and in particular her 2003 show* To My Chagrin, *as an example of maternal performance practice not only because it deals with her relationship with her grandson, but also because of the model of intergenerational compassion that this show offers.*

Despite Shaw's rejection of being defined by her maternal status in relation to her performance work, the maternal has been a significant theme throughout Shaw's career and her mothering and grandmothering of her daughter and grandson have always been linked with her life as an artist. Shaw opens her collected scripts, published under the title A Menopausal Gentleman, *with a dedication to her collaborator and partner, Lois Weaver, in which Shaw describes her own personal transformation over thirty-three years from 'brutal political smoking aggressive street criminal lesbian mother butch obvious cabaret performer' to 'subtle mature loving illogical polished anarchist lesbian grandmother'* (Shaw 2011). *Here Shaw places her interlinked maternal, lesbian, and activist identities front and centre. Jill Dolan also foregrounds the maternal aspect of Shaw's work in her introduction to the same anthology, which she opens with a quote from Shaw: 'Part of how I take care of people is that they don't have to be anything except how they are'* (Shaw in Dolan 2011). *In this statement Shaw foregrounds care; furthermore, she provokes me to think about what a maternal intergenerational conversation might look like through her role as a 'grand-butch-mother'* (Shaw 2011, p. 122) *to generations of genderqueer women exploring their own identities and to feminist performers finding a way to articulate their whole selves on stage. One of the principal ways in which Shaw has enabled performers to be 'how they are' is through modelling this herself. By bringing her lived experience and a heightened portrayal of herself to the stage, Shaw has become a role-model to generations of artists, who can see their queer identity represented and affirmed on stage and can use the example she sets to imagine and establish their own queer performance practice and communities. Alongside this lesbian, feminist, maternal relationship, biological generational inheritance has also been a prevalent concern in much of Shaw's work—most notably in her solo performances* You're Just Like My Father (1993) *in which she considers her relationship with her own parents, and* To My Chagrin (2003), *in which she passes on a certain version of masculinity, American-ness, and class to her then seven-year-old grandson Ian, while being prompted to reconsider her own whiteness by him. Shaw's maternal identity has also informed* Must—The Inside Story (2008), *where Shaw presents her recollections of various bodily experiences, including her birthing of her daughter, and* Retro-Perspective (2007) *in which Shaw and Weaver reflect on their four decades long creative and personal partnership. These markers of Shaw's caring, maternal role, and her transgression of socially ascribed notions of motherhood as aligned with a certain kind of femininity, along with the considerations of mothering, grandmothering, and being parented that are found throughout her work, are the foundation stones of my reading of Shaw as a maternal performer of huge significance for the field.*[7]

In line with Howie's identification of a matrilineal exchange that respects both unity and difference rather than an intergenerational conflict (2010, p. 9), *Shaw and Weaver work closely across generations. I am reminded of the advice that Peggy Shaw and Lois Weaver gave in the audience discussion that followed Shaw's keynote performance at the 'Storytelling for Health' conference in June 2019, where they pointed out the need for more mature feminists to take on young mentors, turning on its head the notion of the mentor as older and wiser, or of the one way sharing of knowledge implied by discussions of inheritance across generations that Howie and Irigaray also reject. Instead, Shaw and Weaver argued, a young mentor could teach much to their seniors and challenge stagnant thinking, while at the same time learning from those who preceded them. Shaw and Weaver shared the example of their own relationship with their then producer, Alex Legge, who is some four decades younger than Shaw and Weaver. Following this session at the 'Storytelling for Health' conference, I asked Shaw what I should do about a mentor in my awkward middle age (at the time of this conversation with Shaw I was forty-three); should I look for a younger or an older mentor? Shaw's typically insightful reply—I should probably have both. Shaw's words prompted me to think differently about these relationships and my own pedagogy, and to ask myself what I can give and learn from the various intergenerational relationships that I have. In the model of mentorship proposed by Shaw and Weaver there is an exchange of knowledge across generations rather than a one-directional flow, and, prompted by Shaw, I have come to value this exchange anew. Howie points us to a mutual exchange of ideas akin to the ebb and flow of ocean waves, receding and progressing along the shoreline in a dance that is never fixed. Howie asks us to consider generational exchange in terms of 'conversation'* (2010, p. 5), *which laps and undulates like water. Further, she argues that a maternal intergenerational conversation allows us to opt for radical collectivity over psychic individualism, or what Howie terms a 'being-with and being in it together'* (p. 9). *Shaw's work embraces this reciprocal exchange.*

While Shaw's whole career can be read through a maternal lens, in this writing I am particularly concerned with Shaw's ode to her grandson, To My Chagrin (2003). *In this work, Shaw explores a very personal intergenerational exchange with her grandson, Ian. She describes the show as 'a tender rock'n' roll lullaby from a cross-dressing grandma to her mixed-race grandson'* (Split Britches, n.d.). *Her grandson is the means through which Shaw considers her own 'grand-butch-motherhood', learning as much from him as he might from her. He is also the means through which she considers her whiteness in relation to her grandson, her 'dual-heritage, bi-racial, mixed-metaphor, well-bred, bye-bye, sweet island boy'* (Shaw 2011, p. 122). *Shaw is inspired to reconsider her own subjectivity and position in an act of reciprocal learning with the young Ian. Although Shaw certainly learns as much from Ian as she offers to teach him, the exchange is mutual but not identical; instead, Shaw learns from Ian as she offers him a perspective that she originates, authors, and controls and which he is free to take on or decline. Shaw recounts that Ian watched and enjoyed the work but was not involved in the authorship of the performance and found certain elements rather difficult to sit through, particularly the part where the image of Ian is projected onto Shaw's naked chest* (Shaw with Underwood-Lee 2020, pp. 5–6). *This is akin to the complex ethical consideration that Lena raises below, reading Courtney Kessel's work with her daughter and Hannah Buckley's work with her grandmother through the lens of Iris Marion Young's asymmetrical reciprocity* (1997). *Shaw and her grandson are not equal partners in the work. The show is clearly made by Shaw and offered to her grandson, and he is free to accept or reject the performance she gifts to him.*

I also find myself in a generous but differentiated exchange when I watch and read To My Chagrin. *Through this text I can explore what it means to 'be-with', as Howie would incite us to do, and I am pushed to reflect on my own experiences of learning with and from the various generations of my family. Shaw passes on lessons in masculinity, car-mechanics, and the history of blues music and makes clear the new ways she is learning to understand herself in relation to Ian and the vulnerability inherent in this relearning of self; Shaw states, 'through your eyes, my body felt, very feminine, very soft, and very naked'* (2011, p. 107). *Watching this exchange I am prompted to ask what I have learnt from my grandmother (tenacity, strength, how to be uncompromising, a love of dill in everything I cook, an understanding of what makes a dress well cut, and how to make chocolate truffles), what I might have taught my grandmother in return (I asked my grandmother this, she replied 'trying to be calm while children are screaming at each other, tolerance when my attention is demanded, calming the family when they are at loggerheads, making meals appear when there isn't enough in the house'), and what I might learn with the generations that follow me* (Fig. 7.1).

The exchange offered in Shaw's work is an act of community building and activism. Shaw states that she makes work because she 'must' and has always had to (Shaw with Underwood-Lee 2020, p. 9). *Performance making is an essential aspect of Shaw's desire to make change in the world. In a manifesto, co-authored by Shaw and Weaver, they state: 'We make public displays of policies by making public displays of ourselves … [towards] … making performance that makes change'* (Weaver and Shaw 2007, p. 174). *Here Shaw and Weaver highlight that their work is a conscious*

Fig. 7.1 Peggy Shaw, *To My Chagrin* (2003) (Image by Dona McAdams)

effort towards visibility and community building through performing their own identities. Split Britches highlight four guiding principles that run through all their work: 'Visibility', 'Communitas', 'Care', and 'Access' (Split Britches, n.d.). *The notion of performance practice as community building called to mind particularly by Split Britches' principles of 'Communitas' and 'Care', evokes for me Howie's notion of 'being with'* (2010, p. 9). *Shaw has had to fight for her rights as a lesbian mother and emphasizes the many prejudices she faced for bringing up her daughter in a queer performance community* (Shaw with Underwood-Lee 2020, p. 4). *While promoting 'Visibility' and 'Access' for Shaw personally, this fight also serves the needs of her whole queer community. In* To My Chagrin *Shaw highlights the ongoing fights she and her grandson will have to face together, particularly in relation to the tremendous challenge of raising/growing up as a young, Black boy in contemporary America.*

By presenting her maternal and grandmotherly self in performance, Shaw builds both visibility and understanding, making a queer maternal position possible and building strength in her community. Shaw encourages her audience to come together in exchange with her as a political act and it is through community that Shaw sees the potential for social change. Jaclyn Prior describes the experience of feeling part of the community of 'mixed-gendered grand-butch-children' that Shaw creates in her audiences (Prior 2014, p. 78). *Prior notes that Shaw made her feel as if all the audience were taken into Shaw's care, allowed to learn from her and allowed to bring their own queer experiences with them. I also experience care and community building as an audience member of Shaw's work. For me, this creation of a community stands as an example of Howie's 'being-with'. The community generated by Shaw, and in particular the 'we' that Shaw creates with both her grandson and her audience in* To My Chagrin, *returns me again to Howie and her assertion that a new maternal order enables us to move forward together as a collective of individuals across generations, each person forming part of the whole but with specific knowledge and experience.*

In To My Chagrin *Shaw refers to her grandchild as her 'grand-companion-son'* (2011, p. 106). *Companionship is a difficult word—it is often used in negative stereotyping of older age as a period of making do or a settling for what is available. In this view of companionship, older people are de-sexualized, de-radicalized, and passive; Shaw's companionship is diametrically opposed to this. Shaw's companionship with her grandson is about finding new ways to relate and to be active together. At one point in* To My Chagrin *Shaw unbuttons her shirt to show a film of her grandson, which is projected onto her bare breasts. Her grandson dances across her heart and the two bodies merge for a moment, differentiated by the regulating third (to return to Irigaray) of the film, which allows them to come together but without one ever being subsumed or secondary to the other. Shaw's body is made visible by the illuminating light of the image of her dancing grandson and the projected image of his body is made visible by the solidity of Shaw's flesh. In this moment Shaw's identity is entirely interdependent with Ian's. I find this a particularly moving point in the show. Shaw complicates her gender position and her grandmotherly relationship—she is passing on a version of butchness to her grandson and yet her body has carried a child in her uterus, which has enabled this young boy to come into existence. Shaw's breasts, exposed in this scene, remind us of the tender vulnerability of her maternal body and the generations which have been born from it. At another point in* To My Chagrin *Shaw again evokes the biological act of birth, and yet this time it is her grandson whom she imagines birthing her as she describes him digging her body out of the ground and comforting her: 'you wrapped me in blankets and held me tight like a new-born babe. … It's a butch! … It's a girl, a big butch girl'* (2011,

p. 125). *Through this imagined encounter Shaw articulates a moment when her grandson might take care of her as she cares for him. This is not the care that is commonly expressed in many intergenerational encounters within our particular historical and cultural moment, where care for the elderly is seen as a burden on state or family; instead Shaw is again reminding us of the two-way conversation and radical togetherness of the intergenerational exchange.*

It is hard for me to think of Shaw's work in relation to a conversation or two-way flow. Shaw is three decades my senior. I first encountered her work in 1996 as an undergraduate and I have been inspired by it ever since. Sue-Ellen Case notes that there is often a rather indistinguishable line between the position of the fan and the scholar in relation to Split Britches' work (2009, p. 8), *and I am most certainly a fan. There is a seductive charisma about Shaw in her performance and in person, and yet she is approachable and generous in her work, her interviews, and her teaching. There are many performance makers whose practice I admire and who I could have considered in relation to our chapter theme of generations (Jill Greenhalgh's* Daughter [2011], *Bobby Baker's* Drawing on a Grandmother's Experience [2015], *or Mimesis Heidi Dahlsveen's* Frigg Lost Her Son, So Did I [2016] *to name just a few). My choice to write about Shaw's work was certainly in part because of the fandom of which Case speaks. In no small part, however, I am drawn to Shaw's work because in engaging with her works I find myself experiencing a maternal, generational conversation. Key to Howie's exchange is perhaps a shared sense of purpose or goal—Howie is espousing an exchange between waves of feminism. Howie suggests that the second and third waves of feminism have, historically, been pitted against one another around arguments concerning essentialism and intersectionality; despite this, they have a shared purpose in promoting the position of women and in working towards a more equal society for all. This shared base is what enables my feeling of a conversational exchange with Shaw. It is not a grandmotherly exchange I have with her—the intimacy of my encounters with Shaw is something I feel in her performances but in actuality this is an illusion of intimacy as to Shaw I will be simply one face in the mass of the audience. Still, a generous generational exchange is possible through the maternal performance work that Shaw shares with the world. In Shaw's work I can feel immersed in a political, maternal exchange.*

Lena on Hannah Buckley's *Untitled (Elsie and Hannah)* and Courtney Kessel's *In Balance With* and *A Blessing, A Wish, A Spell for the Next Generation*

Foregrounding the political while thinking through intergenerational exchanges in maternal art, I consider the work of young dancer/choreographer Hannah Buckley. As a part of a bigger intergenerational project among women titled We Are Now, *Buckley, in collaboration with film maker Rowland Hill, created a short video film called* Untitled (Elsie and Hannah) (2015) *in which she and her grandmother perform a movement sequence based on Trisha Brown's* Accumulation (1971).[8] *I first came across Buckley and Rowland's short five-minute video film at 'The Lived Female Body in Performance' symposium organized by Anna Fenemore, Jenny Lawson, and Jacki Willson in April 2019 at the University of Leeds. This particular symposium was concerned to reassess the lived fleshy female body in the twenty-first century and gathered a group of predominantly women scholars and artists addressing excessive, in/fertile, ageing, oozing, leaking, natural/artificial, trans, racialized, abject, deviant, and impure bodies.*[9] *It is important to note that Buckley's work was presented within this particular context, which was affirmatively and carefully attuned to the reception and juxtaposition of her fairly young dancer's body and her grandmother's ageing frame* (Fig. 7.2).

For most of the film Untitled (Elsie and Hannah) *the grandmother and granddaughter duo, Elsie and Hannah, perform their repetitive actions in silence, seated on two chairs—a wheelchair and a stool—presumably watching Brown's movement on video and following it. The granddaughter is precise in her movement—she's a dancer/choreographer, her reactions are sharp, and, to the point, clear. The grandmother's movements are slower, but she's performing the given task, doing it to the best of her ability. There is seriousness in this work, in this artwork; there is a commitment to the movement sequence, to the choreography, as well as the grandmother's commitment to the granddaughter and her engagement with her project. The question arises as to whether the grandmother is doing the work only for the granddaughter. And, if so, is that acceptable? This question takes me back to the always prominent consideration of ethics which mothers as artists have to address when creating maternal performances with their children, as well as granddaughters and daughters when working with elderly and/or other family members. Prompted by Miffy Ryan, in 2017, the Institute for the*

Fig. 7.2 Hannah Buckley, Elsie Brown and Rowland Hill, *Untitled (Elsie and Hannah)* (2015) (Image courtesy of the artists)

Art and Practice of Dissent at Home engaged with such questions around the ethics of maternal performance making with children by hosting the research gathering 'Motherhood and Live Art 2: Are we screwing the kids up?' Ryan produced a report of the event, and one of the most prominent conclusions, which has guided my own artistic practice, has been an acknowledgement that each particular artwork, each performance, each situation always needs to be considered anew. 'Consent is actively sought in each new situation, process, or work between the mother and child' (Ryan 2017, p. 10).

Returning to Untitled (Elsie and Hannah), *the silent video is occasionally interrupted by snippets of conversation between the two about intergenerational living and young people's ideas. These are new ideas concerning how we ought to live, which carry political intent about how each generation can give and receive something else. The grandmother's voice is clear here. She says: 'I like to listen to young people, with their ideas.' This sentence is embraced by the silence around it. At one point the granddaughter is coaxing the grandmother into a conversation about intergenerational living; it seems this is her idea. The grandmother says that being in a nursing home just with old people would be very depressing. The sound of these snippets of conversations is roughly cut; it is in juxtaposition with the professionally slick work of the camera. The sound comes and goes; there is a sense of it being accidental, although the film is all intentional; there is no DIY style to it—it is smoothly edited and produced. The frame of the performance is tight, well considered. The grandmother and the granddaughter care for each other, and for the artistic work. The final scene is the two women smiling at the camera and then at one another. They exchange a smile, a gaze between them, a relief, a connection. The choreographic task has been completed. The grandmother's words voiced over the image: 'That's what I like, getting the old and the young together.' There is a quiet satisfaction at the end of the movement sequence, the completion of the task, the grandmother and the granddaughter united through the artwork, and yet, each separate in her own seat.*

In this instance, the intergenerational art project We Are Now *gives Buckley licence to connect with her grandmother in a new way. Art enables not only a new kind of relationship between grandmother and granddaughter, but also a new kind of intergenerational thinking. The granddaughter needs her grandmother for the film-making; the grandmother enjoys the company of her granddaughter, and she might enjoy accomplishing the movement task. The two women are bonded. A connection is made possible through an artwork, which enables a different kind of doing and sharing, a different kind of time spent, in choreography, in movement. And this becomes a particular way of desiring a new social order, a maternal order, which would integrate intergenerational co-living and thinking into our understanding and experience of living and dying. Political and ethical sensibilities are embedded in this artwork, although they are not explicit and direct. What is left at the end of the video is a feeling of care and love for one another, a smile, an accomplished movement task, which prompted important questions around intergenerational co-living and exchange. The grandmother and the granddaughter are working together, both in this video and in future thinking.*

I now turn my attention to two performances by Courtney Kessel, In Balance With (2012) *and* A Blessing, A Wish, A Spell for the Next Generation (2017), *both performed with her daughter Chloé. Courtney*

Kessel is an interdisciplinary artist based in Athens, Ohio, US. Kessel works in a variety of media, including performance. In her biography Kessel is unapologetic in describing herself as a mother/artist. On her website, underneath the photograph of herself with her young daughter, she states: 'Kessel's work strives to make visible the quiet, understated, and often unseen love and labor of motherhood' (Kessel, n.d.).

In Balance With (2012) *was a live thirty-minute performance between Courtney Kessel and her daughter, Chloé, sitting at opposite ends of a seesaw. While the very first performance of* In Balance With *took place in 2010 and the work continues throughout the years as the daughter is growing up, I am noting the one from 2012 here in this discussion.* In Balance With *is a series of evolving performances between mother and daughter. Presenting the work in the* Studies in the Maternal *journal*, Kessel (2013, p. 1) *notes that the seesaw holds representative items of their lives, such as toys, a violin, research books, food, pots, tools, and laundry, together with the then six-year-old Chloé, on one side, and herself, a mother/artist, on the other. The mother is constantly checking the balance between the two sides. How much can she hold? How can she achieve balance? At this point in time, 2012, balance is impossible between mother and six-year-old daughter alone. There are other items surrounding the child. The child is in between all the other items of the mother's life. The mother is the main player here, the protagonist, whose story we are to follow. This is mostly her stuff, her life. Chloé is a part of it. She might be the most precious item on the other side of the seesaw, but she cannot be alone. All the other items, all the other stuff, are making her comfortable as well as enabling her to balance with her mother, and therefore to play... to go up and down, to collaborate. This is an affair between two women, a mother and a daughter, albeit in different positions of weight, frame, and power.*

I am reminded of Iris Marion Young's term 'asymmetrical reciprocity' (1997), *which she developed when discussing language, communication, and moral discourse, in essence, the idea and desire that humans have for understanding each other's point of view, putting oneself in the other person's place. Young claims that '[e]ach participant in a communication situation is distinguished by a particular history and social position that makes their relation asymmetrical'* (p. 341). *In her development of this concept and her drive towards the acceptance of difference and asymmetry, Young is drawing on Irigaray's 'wonder' and Arendt's 'enlarged thought' which we can arrive at through ethical encounters with others, a sense of distance from one another and an amazement at each other's difference. Young concludes that it is only by listening to others' experiences and perspectives from a distance that we are open and able to learn and understand them* (1997, p. 350). *She writes:*

> *A condition of our communication is that we acknowledge difference, interval, that others drag behind them shadows and histories, scars and traces, that do not become present in our communication. Thus we each must be open to learning about the other person's perspective, since we cannot take the other person's standpoint and imagine that perspective as our own.* (p. 354)

Clearly, Young privileges difference over symmetry or sameness and insists that '[u]nderstanding across difference is both possible and necessary' (p. 354). *It is difference that should be the guide, that should enable a desire for understanding.*

The crucial term is 'reciprocity', which might be understood as akin to gift giving, never a commercial transaction, never the same gift, but rather a kind of openness towards an acceptance of another's gift, and each gift being a new opening, a new asymmetry in reciprocity. Young is not discussing parents and children, but non-disabled and disabled people, cultural, class, and sexual differences. She asserts that 'this reciprocity of equal respect and acknowledgment of one another, however, entails an acknowledgment of an asymmetry between subjects' (1997, p. 351). *I believe that in our discussions of performances which involve mothers and children, this concept of asymmetrical reciprocity between subjects might be useful. Kessel's piece makes it very obvious. The balance is managed, played with, questioned, negotiated* (Fig. 7.3).

In Balance With *was concerned with two subjects and many other inanimate items, the representative stuff of maternal, childlike, and creative life. Yet, upon closer analysis of the work, it is clear that the piece is about the mother/artist here. She is the one seeking balance in her life. She is the one struggling to find the equilibrium. She stages her struggle. It is through that staging, through maternal performance, that the mother/artist enacts and takes control of the artistic process and form, if not of the act of mothering itself, which might not be resolved, but exposed. This piece is about asymmetry rather than balance. Is the piece also about ethical relations and reciprocity; are those important here? A different performance, which seems more firmly based in public space, might address that issue of reciprocity more tightly, with clearer intent.*

Fig. 7.3 Courtney Kessel, *In Balance With* (2012) (Image courtesy of the artist)

A Blessing, A Wish, A Spell for the Next Generation *was a one-off durational performance, performed by Kessel and her daughter, Chloé, created for her thirteenth birthday. Emily and I saw it together during a wet October evening in 2017 at Astrid Noacks Atelier's courtyard in Copenhagen, Denmark, as part of the 'The Mothernists II: Who Cares for the 21st Century?' conference organized by Deirdre Donoghue and Lise Haller Baggesen. This piece marks a particular time, a birthday, a child becoming a teenager. The performance acknowledges itself as an art/life conflation. This is not only an art event, a happening, but also the actual birthday celebration.*

This was a long, risky, emotional, open (and rather boring given its duration) coming together of a community of women, all presenting gifts and words of wisdom to a young teenager over some three hours. The women involved had prepared gifts and words well in advance of the piece. The mother/artist had sent requests to her friends and colleagues for this celebration in the summer. The women had posted their presents to Athens, Ohio, US, and now all of them were presented to Chloé in Copenhagen, Denmark. I had personally sent Chloé a notebook from Dubrovnik, my hometown, together with a short note about the importance of women's writing, with an intention to inspire Chloé to keep a journal of her teenage years. Most of the gifts had travelled from afar, and would be travelling again, back to the USA. These gifts became props in the performance, and it took as long as it did (over three hours) for them all to be opened, considered, delivered as presents. Chloé was a receiver, thanking the women, her mother's friends and colleagues. Some of them were close to her, and some emotional hugs and words were exchanged in front of this small audience of Mothernists in Copenhagen.[10]

While the daughter was put on the spot here, receiving the gifts, it was actually the mother, in her role as a curator and a producer, who ensured this birthday celebration was special and memorable. The mother had laboured hard towards it, engaged in meticulous preparations, and opened up a public coming-together celebration for her daughter. Of course, the question, which becomes pertinent, is whether the daughter longed for this kind of public celebration, whether the birthday party was to her liking, appropriate for her age, for her teenage sensibility, but that kind of public generational clash on stage is possibly exactly what is needed for the development of intergenerational sensibility. Quite similarly, this issue relates to the question of whether Buckley's grandmother was only going along with the performance for the sake of her granddaughter's will and success, effectively to please the granddaughter. Young talks of Arendt's notion of the public realm:

> *Publicity in Arendt's sense is maintained only if the plurality of perspectives that constitutes it is preserved. The people who appear to one another in a public situation of communication each have a perspective on the world that lies between them, as well as on one another.* (Young 1997, p. 359)

Considering children's, mothers', and grandmothers' plurality of perspectives as exemplified in these performance works allows us to better understand the complexity of building a public sphere which is based on that plurality and difference. It was the birthday and its public celebration that was a medium here in A Blessing, A Wish, A Spell for the Next Generation, *a thing between all of us that invited a plurality of perspectives. The mother carried the work, and the daughter was its recipient, and the main protagonist; the women who participated in the gift-giving ritual were all connected to the mother-daughter duo to a differing degree. All of us, there and then, engaged in this gentle and at times unnerving performance celebration, with a multiplicity of perspectives. All were negotiating in the medium of participatory maternal performance.*

The piece was durational and enduring. Chloé, in this case, possibly due to the duration of the performance, in comparison to In Balance With, *was more of an active participant in the piece. She took on the role of a collaborator. She obeyed the script, at times protested, tensed, and cringed, unnerved the mother. They both verged on the brink of exiting the frame of the performance. This was art, but it was also real life; therefore, it was important that the piece did not fail as not only the performance but Chloé's birthday was at stake. As spectators we became invested in its success. While my spectator position stayed with them both, the mother and daughter, towards the end of the piece and right now in this writing I am aligned with Kessel, the mother/artist, a woman of my generation, exposed in her vulnerability and her risk in front of us. I am drawn to her attempt, to sympathy, to maternal compassion, and all these complex feelings have been enabled and revealed through the frame of maternal performance which conflated art and life.*

Intergenerational Reciprocity

We have attempted to understand generations through the work of three artists who inhabit different generations; horologically, Shaw is our senior, Kessel our contemporary, and Buckley belongs to the generation that follows us. Each artist addresses their own intergenerational relationships in the work they present, and each offers us a unique perspective; however, they are all united in an approach which acknowledges the interdependence they have with their 'other' generations. The generations in these artworks do not rebel against, consume, or become subsumed by their other. Instead, they are able to reconstitute themselves and raise one another to new levels of understanding through an intergenerational encounter, which follows the model espoused by Howie (2010). Buckley and Shaw openly work against the stereotypical misunderstanding of the older generation, its ridicule, and often contempt. Kessel's performances push us towards the acknowledgement of asymmetrical reciprocity and a new kind of exchange not only between the mother and daughter, but also a community of women/mothernists, as was made clear at Astrid Noacks Atelier's courtyard public performance gathering.

On 28 September 2020 Courtney Kessel and Chloé Clevenger performed a new *In Balance With* (Kessel 2020).[11] In this restaging of the work we see Chloé and Courtney more or less equally weighted on the scales, demonstrating the physicality of Chloé's transition to young adulthood while also asserting their equality and difference, or their asymmetry to follow Young. Unlike the *In Balance With* from 2012 discussed by Lena above, Kessel is not in sole charge of this piece anymore. She may have once been the initiator of the work but she now collaborates with her daughter, who exerts agency in her consent to make this new version and who often takes a lead in the conversation that mother and daughter have throughout the forty-five minutes of the work. The evolving relationship of mother and daughter is clearly articulated by Chloé, who opens *In Balance With 2020* with the statement: 'this is the first time that we have ever really been able to balance together' (Kessel 2020). Mother and daughter here are still separated, acknowledging their individuality at either end of the balance, but also able to play with their relationship as the seesaw is now free of the weight of objects once required to centre it. Free of the detritus of everyday life, the balance now more easily serves as a seesaw, allowing one or the other to ascend in turn, in a poetic representation of intergenerational exchange.

We began by marking that intergenerational thinking can be difficult and can challenge us to new ways of engaging with the world, yet our personal and political thinking can only be enhanced by these encounters with our others, be they the others within our communities, queer families of choice, nuclear families, or the feminist, political, activist, and performance making generations with whom we share the spaces and ideas we inhabit. What is important to recall is that intergenerational maternal performances are always political; they push us to imagine a different kind of social order; they entice us to enlarge our understanding of the world by considering interrelations beyond those, which are our closest.

One particularly poignant moment from Courtney Kessel's *A Blessing, A Wish, A Spell for the Next Generation* was when Kessel presented Chloé with a gift from Chloé's grandmother, Kessel's mother. Emily described the moment:

> One box, sent by Kessel's mother, was unwrapped to reveal an empty space and a small mirror. The mirror was accompanied by a letter containing the words 'in this box you will find the only thing you need!' The granddaughter was encouraged to look at herself, to see that all she might require can be found within. (Underwood-Lee 2018, p. 424)

Kessel's mother speaks to her young grandchild and reflects her back to herself; through the eyes of her grandmother Chloé is invited to see herself more clearly. The leap from grandmother to grandchild is enabled by the mother that sits between them. When all three come together a hope for the future is made manifest.

Notes

1. The narrative of compulsory progress that might be implied by notions of 'raising to new heights' is countered by Jack Halberstam's propositions on unbecoming, counter-productivity, and radical negativity as feminist strategies (Halberstam 2011). We examine various notions of intergenerational futures in our Futures chapter.
2. For more on 'Praisesongs: Honouring our elders in Wales' see https://vimeo.com/254707091.
3. For more information see https://performanceandthematernal.com/maternal-forums/ (Performance and the Maternal, n.d.).

4. See Kim Solga, *Theatre and Feminism* (2016) for a discussion of the evolution of feminism and its waves with a specific focus on theatre and performance.
5. The psychoanalytic understanding of the rejection of the mother of which we speak here is derived from Freudian thinking and the Oedipus Complex, a theory in which the rejection of the mother is central to human psychological development. This theory was developed extensively by Sigmund Freud throughout his writing, and is perhaps most clearly articulated in his 1913 work *Totem and Taboo* (Freud 1919).
6. Margolin formally collaborated with the company until 1992 (Case 1996, p. 6). For an early history of Split Britches see Case (1996). For a later history of the company see Shaw (2011) and Harvie and Weaver (2015) as well as Split Britches' performance *Retro-Perspective* (2007).
7. Shaw rejects descriptions of her butch identity as masculine, instead she claims, 'I am a new kind of femininity' (Shaw 2011, p. 41).
8. For more information about *Accumulation* (1971) note this description by Trisha Brown: 'One simple gesture is presented. This gesture is repeated until it is thoroughly integrated into my kinesthetic system. Gesture 2 is then added. Gesture 1 and 2 are repeated until they are assimilated, then Gesture 3 is added. I continue adding gestures until my system can support no further addition. The first 4 gestures occur on the first 4 beats. The subsequent gestures are packed into that one measure.' From https://trishabrowncompany.org/repertory/accumulation-1.html.
9. For more information about 'The Lived Female Body in Performance' symposium and downloadable programme please visit https://ahc.leeds.ac.uk/performance/events/event/1262/the-lived-female-body-in-performance.
10. For more information about 'Mothernists' please see Lisa Haller Baggesen's *Mothernism* (2014).
11. *In Balance With* (2020) can be viewed at https://youtu.be/wBlWwee3OCI (YouTube 2020).

References

Baggesen, Lisa Haller. 2014. *Mothernism*. Chicago: Green Lantern Press.

Baraitser, Lisa. 2020. Foreword. In *The Maternal in Creative Work: Intergenerational Discussions on Motherhood and Art*, ed. Elena Marchevska and Valerie Walkerdine. London, New York: Routledge.

Baraitser, Lisa, and Denise Riley. 2016. Lisa Baraitser in Conversation with Denise Riley. *Studies in the Maternal* 8 (1).

Case, Sue-Ellen. 1996. *Split Britches: Lesbian Practice/Feminist Performance*. London: Routledge.

Case, Sue-Ellen. 2009. *Feminist and Queer Performance: Critical Strategies*. Basingstoke: Palgrave Macmillan.

Dolan, Jill. 2011. Introduction. In *A Menopausal Gentleman: The Solo Performances of Peggy Shaw*, 1–38. Ann Arbor: University of Michigan Press.

Freud, Sigmund. 1950 [1919]. *Totem and Taboo*. London: Routledge.

Halberstam, J. 2011. Unbecoming: Queer Negativity/Radical Passivity. In *Sex, Gender and Time in Fiction and Culture*, ed. B. Davies and J. Funke. London: Palgrave Macmillan.

Harvie, Jen, and Lois Weaver. 2015. *The Only Way Home Is Through the Show: Performance Work of Lois Weaver*. London: LADA.

Howie, Gillian. 2010. Feminist Histories: Conflict, Coalitions and the Maternal Order. *Studies in the Maternal* 2: 1–12.

Irigaray, Luce. 1996. *I Love to You*. London, New York: Routledge.

Irigaray, Luce, Stephen Pluháček, and Heidi Bostic. 2008. Thinking Life as Relation. In *Conversations*, ed. Luce Irigaray. London: Continuum.

Kessel, Courtney. 2013. In Balance With. *Studies in the Maternal* 5 (1): 1.

Kessel, Courtney. n.d. *Courtney Kessel*. https://courtneykessel.com/artwork/2366241_BIO.html. Accessed 11 Feb 2021.

Loveless, Natalie, and Mary Kelly. 2020. Feminist Intergenerational Inheritance: A Conversation. In *The Maternal in Creative Work: Intergenerational Discussions on Motherhood and Art*, ed. Elena Marchevska and Valerie Walkerdine. London, New York: Routledge.

Marchevska, Elena, and Valerie Walkerdine, eds. 2020. *The Maternal in Creative Work: Intergenerational Discussions on Motherhood and Art*. London, New York: Routledge.

McCloskey, Paula, and Mary Kelly. 2012. In Conversation: Mary Kelly Speaks to Paula McCloskey. *Studies in the Maternal* 4 (1): 1–10.

Performance and the Maternal. n.d. Maternal Forums. *Performance and the Maternal*. https://performanceandthematernal.com/maternal-forums/. Accessed 4 Feb 2021.

Pollock, Griselda, and Laura Mulvey. 2010. Laura Mulvey in Conversation with Griselda Pollock. *Studies in the Maternal* 2 (1): 1–13.

Prior, Jaclyn. 2014. 'When Elephants Are in Must': Peggy Shaw, Acts of Trans/fer, and the Present Future of Queer Desire. *TDR* 58 (4): 68–79.

Ryan, Miffy. 2017. Motherhood and Live Art 2 [Report]. Liverpool: The Institute for the Art and Practice of Dissent at Home. https://issuu.com/twoaddthree/docs/motherhood_and_live_art_2. Accessed 16 Nov 2020.

Segal, Lynne, and Lisa Baraitser. 2009. Lynne Segal in Conversation with Lisa Baraitser. *Studies in the Maternal* 1 (1): 1–19.

Shaw, Peggy. 2011. *A Menopausal Gentleman: The Solo Performances of Peggy Shaw*. Ann Arbor: University of Michigan Press.

Shaw, Peggy with Emily Underwood-Lee. 2020. An Interview with Peggy Shaw. *Performance and the Maternal*. https://performanceandthematernal.files.wordpress.com/2020/10/peggy-shaw-.pdf. Accessed 5 Nov 2020.

Šimić, Lena, and Emily Underwood-Lee (Eds.). 2016. *Live Art and Motherhood: Study Room Guide on Live Art and the Maternal*. London: Live Art Development Agency.

Šimić, Lena, and Emily Underwood-Lee. 2017. On the Maternal—Editorial. *Performance Research* 22 (4): 1–4.

Solga, Kim. 2016. *Theatre and Feminism*. London: Palgrave.

Split Britches. n.d. *Split Britches*. http://www.split-britches.com/. Accessed 5 Nov 2020.

Underwood-Lee, Emily. 2018. On Openings. *Performance Research* 23 (4/5): 422–424.

Weaver, Lois, and Peggy Shaw. 2007. MAKE SOMETHING: A Manifesto for Making Performance About Making Change. In *Staging International Feminisms*, ed. Elaine Aston and Sue-Ellen Case. Basingstoke: Macmillan.

Young, I.M. 1997. Asymmetrical Reciprocity: On Moral Respect, Wonder, and Enlarged Thought. *Constellations* 3 (3): 340–363.

YouTube. 2020. *In Balance With 2020*. https://youtu.be/wBlWwee3OCI. Accessed 12 Feb 2021.

Performances and Artworks Cited

Baker, Bobby. 2015. *Drawing on a Grandmother's Experience* [performance].

Buckley, Hannah, Brown Elsie, and Rowland Hill. 2015. *Untitled (Elsie and Hannah)* [film].

Dahlsveen, Mimesis Heidi. 2016. *Frigg Lost Her Son, So Did I* [performance].

Greenhalgh, Jill. 2011. *Daughter* [performance].

Kessel, Courtney. 2012 *In Balance With* [performance].

Kessel, Courtney. 2017. *A Blessing, A Wish, A Spell for the Next Generation* [performance].

Kessel, Courtney. 2020. *In Balance With* [performance].

Saltus, Roiyah, and Solange Saltus. 2020. *What I Want* [digital story].

Shaw, Peggy. 1993. *You're Just Like My Father* [performance].

Shaw, Peggy. 2003. *To My Chagrin* [performance].

Shaw, Peggy. 2008. *Must—The Inside Story* [performance].

Split Britches. 2007. *Retro Perspective* [performance].

CHAPTER 8

Futures (8 months)

Letters to an Unknown Future

In this, our penultimate chapter, we turn to maternal futures, which must always be potential and open. We attempt to imagine the kind of futures we want for the maternal communities that follow us. In Beginnings we identified Imogen Tyler's 'maternal commons' as a way of engaging politically with society through collaboration, collectivity, and care (Tyler and Baraitser 2013, p. 23). We began to explore what could be learned from thinking communally across age-groups and familial and intellectual lineages in our previous chapter, Generations, but there we looked to our maternal forbearers in order to consider how an intergenerational sharing might be enacted. Now we look to our children and to those generations who will succeed us (and we hope that they will succeed both chronologically and in terms of achieving something that we have neither managed nor imagined). The future is always impossible to pin down—it is, by its nature, unknown. We are reminded of Jacques Derrida's concept of *l'avenir*, which is about the unpredictable and unexpected future which carries the Other. In Derrida's words:

L. Šimić and E. Underwood-Lee, *Maternal Performance*, Contemporary Performance InterActions, https://doi.org/10.1007/978-3-030-80226-4_8

> But there is a future, *l'avenir* (to come) which refers to someone who comes whose arrival is totally unexpected. For me, that is the real future. That which is totally unpredictable. The Other who comes without my being able to anticipate their arrival. So if there is a real future, beyond the other known future, it is *l'avenir* in that it is the coming of the Other when I am completely unable to foresee their arrival. (Derrida in Dick and Ziering 2002)

It would be impossible to predict who or what the Other is, and its coming. We do not want to simply align the Other with the child. They are unknown, unforeseen. Lee Edelman provides a strong critique of the child figure who 'remains the perpetual horizon of every acknowledged politics, the fantasmatic beneficiary of every political intervention' (2004, p. 3). While there is a kind of dependence between maternal identities and the child figure, in this chapter we are primarily concerned with maternal futures that might take us beyond the dualistic configuration of mother and child. Instead, we turn to feminist perspectives on maternal future matters. How unknown and unforeseeable are they, individually and collectively? It has strongly transpired that choice in terms of biological mothering, as well as alternative caring structures, are crucial in terms of how we organize our futures, while at the same time allowing for *l'avenir* to unfold.

In this particular moment in time, the early 2020s, amidst the Coronavirus pandemic (*l'avenir* of its own kind), we feel questions about the future more pressingly than we ever have in our own lifetimes as we face climate crisis. The world is in need of revolutionary thought to achieve equality for all and to secure the survival of our planet. We recognize here that equality does not mean sameness, but the embracing of our differences, as we have discussed in connection with Iris Marion Young's (1997) notion of asymmetrical reciprocity in Generations. We turn to a diverse range of scholars and artists to imagine just a few of the infinite possible maternal futures that might come to be. In particular, we are inspired by Sara Ruddick's (1989) invitation to think how maternal care for all children might be found through action and legislation. We also turn to Donna J. Haraway's (2016) call to imagine a future where maternal links are forged through a rejection of the production of more humans; instead of biological mothering we are invited to make 'oddkin' across species. We are invited to think beyond mothering as it has been previously understood and to think about the mother as a m/other, a term employed by many mother artists and scholars, but most notably in this context by Bracha L. Ettinger, who develops it in relation to her project of rethinking the mother within psychoanalytic discourse as a subject with agency and to whom we should express compassion rather than disavowal or rejection (2006, p. 73). The performances we examine are *Dear Daughter* (2016–2019) by Nanna Lysholt Hansen, which we watched at the conference 'The Mothernists II: Who Cares for the 21st Century?', the maternal works of Lynn Lu, *Adagio* (2013), *The Hand that Rocks the Cradle* (2015), and *Tend* (2015), and *TheBabyQuestion* (2019) by Paula Varjack, Luca Rutherford, Catriona James, and Maddy Costa.

We employ letter writing as a formal means to address our concerns in this chapter. Margaretta Jolly (2008) notes that letters are often a central part of political movements, and in particular of feminist movements and our aims throughout this book have certainly been both political and feminist in that we hope to reimagine and bring to attention the maternal through performance. It is not surprising that the letter form is a central device for building knowledge and community in order to create a political movement. As Liz Stanley notes, letters are dialogic, they are a coming to knowledge through exchange (2004, p. 201). This is an exchange that moves from the singular 'I' to the 'we' of community. We (Lena and Emily) speculate together on an imagined future and hope these letters enable you to postulate on the future alongside us, building a larger 'we' of maternal practitioners. The letter form allows for a more open and uncertain tone, one where we can contemplate and come to understanding in relation to one another (Lena and Emily) and also in relation to our imagined reader (you). Phyllis Chesler opens her beautiful work *Letters to a Young Feminist* (1997) with an invocation of her imagined reader: 'Here I sit, head bent, writing you an intimate letter. I sense your presence, even though I don't know your name' (1997, p. 1). The intimacy Chesler speaks of is one we also feel here.[1] The letter form we adopt in this chapter feels rather private, close, or secret, even though we are writing our letters for a reader, who takes on an imaginary role of the unknown Other. These are the letters towards them, and the future, possibly even *l'avenir*. Of course, we (Lena and Emily) know one another's names and have a long history of collaboration and friendship, but in writing to one another we also write to you, our anonymous reader. The letters we write are somewhat confessional. We have chosen to edit them minimally and to allow our uncertainty to remain, in recognition of the inherent uncertainty of the future, *l'avenir* (to come). Our letters are full of questions and hopes, in writing about the future they could perhaps be nothing else, but we are satisfied that questions are enough.

On Nanna Lysholt Hansen's *Dear Daughter*, Lynn Lu's *Adagio*, *Tend*, and *The Hand that Rocks the Cradle*, and Paula Varjack, Luca Rutherford, Catriona James, and Maddy Costa's *TheBabyQuestion*

Dear Emily,

> *We are the chthonic ones. The not-yet-finished ongoing abyssal and dreadful ones, generative and destructive.* (Haraway quoted in Lysholt Hansen 2016–2019)

Do you remember? It was hot, it was sweaty, even when this was October 2017 in Copenhagen. All the bodies huddled together in a tiny performance space of the Astrid Noacks Atelier, creating certain intimacies between strangers, all too close.

A singular body, in white talcum powder, or chalk, a whitened body, almost robotic, technological, and naked at the same time, was out there in space away from us, audiences, a multitude of critters. She was alone. Naked and alone, her body covered with video imagery, a microphone in front of her, with sound recording as well, but also, importantly, lots of space around her, so much space. This white chalked body, this naked techno woman was saying something, or possibly it was a recording that was saying something… to the future, to her daughter.

Later on, I found out that most of the text in Dear Daughter/Anatomy of the Chthulucene (2016–2019) *is directly taken from Donna J. Haraway's inspirational and ground-breaking book* Staying with the Trouble (2016), *which addresses our multi-species conditions and relations on the endangered planet. In the opening paragraphs of the book, Haraway explains her concern for the trouble and a desire to stay with it: 'Staying with the trouble requires making oddkin; that is, we require each other in unexpected collaborations and combinations, in hot compost piles. We become-with each other or not at all'* (p. 4). *This was certainly a different kind of collaboration in terms of what is usually expected of a theatre audience. We were transformed into a hot compost pile all huddled together, and the creator, mother/artist was, to use Haraway's terminology, becoming-with her daughter.*

We witnessed a version of Dear Daughter,*called* Dear Daughter/Anatomy of the Chthulucene (2016–2019). *Nanna Lysholt Hansen has been making a series of* Dear Daughter *performances since 2013. Her previous versions included* Dear Daughter/Organic Cyborg Stories (After Donna Haraway) (2013–2015), *first performed when pregnant and once she felt herself to be in a cyborg-like, machine-like production line, and* Dear Daughter/Motherboard Theories of Evolution (w/ Braidotti, Plant et aliae) (2014–2018), *which was a speech to a newborn child, through the laptop, motherboard. The most recent reiteration is* Dear Daughter/Sen_sing_inannainanna (Russ, Shiva, Klein) (2019–2020), *which is concerned with climate crisis and the questions of mythologized pasts and futures of the planet. This particular version of the performance, which we witnessed, is set within the* Chthulucene, *a term proposed by Haraway in* Staying with the Trouble (2016). Chthulucene *replaces the term 'Anthropocene', moving us away from the primacy of the human, anthropos.* Chthulucene *'is a compound of two Greek roots (*khthōn *and* kainos*) that together name a kind of timeplace for learning to stay with the trouble of living and dying in response-ability in a damaged earth'* (Haraway, 2016, p. 2). Khthōn *is a Greek word for earth and* kainos *means now.*

In the chapter 'Making Kin' Haraway writes: '"My" Chthulucene, even burdened with its problematic Greek-ish rootlets, entangles myriad temporalities and spatialities and myriad intra-active entities-in-assemblages—including the more-than-human, other-than-human, inhuman, and human-as-humus' (p. 101). *What is our maternal relation to anythingother-than-human? Can our maternal thinking encompass terms such as more-than-human, other-than-human, inhuman and human-as-humus? Given the current environmental and ecological crisis including the increasing number of humans, estimated to be eleven billion by the end of the twenty first century, Haraway's proposition to the human critters, and particularly feminists, comes in the form of a slogan: 'Make Kin Not Babies!'* (p. 102).

What do you make of that, Emily? How do we, as feminist scholars and biological mothers, with a concern for maternal studies and performance, organize ourselves in this new configuration of oddkins? Do we make kin and not babies?

In her writing Haraway continues: 'Making – and recognizing – kin is perhaps the hardest and most urgent part' (p. 102). *Is it challenging to think about making kin, oddkin, or in her own words kin as 'something other/more than entities tied by ancestry or genealogy'* (pp. 102–103)? *How does such oddkin making sit in the context of maternal studies and in particular maternal performance? What is it that the pregnant and later on post-partum maternal body of Lysholt Hansen, the mother/performer, brings to the debate on oddkin? What is the message to the 'dear daughter'? What is the feel of the performance?*

> *Do you see how I am pulsing? A little bit forward. A little bit back. Spreading and searching for other bacteria or fungi.* (Lysholt Hansen 2016–2019)

While watching the piece, I was among hot and sweaty bodies in a space, with too much proximity of the other, with all others as accidental kin, not as babies, and yet with the mother/performer cast aside from these bodies, in space, alone and naked. The mother/performer figured as only in relation to her 'dear daughter' via *her voice, but certainly away from us, the spectators. And us, the audiences, we were all huddled together because of her, her baby-making body. We were making-with each other, becoming a kind of assemblage, placed in a position to connect otherwise. This was an odd kind of intimacy among strangers, all of us reframed as oddkin.*

Being a part of this performance, in this particular crammed space in the Astrid Noacks Atelier (ANA), the space full of intention to provide a different kind of living, performing, and being, felt somehow distinct. It caused me to wonder if the space itself has given us the potential of 'staying with the trouble'? Let us be reminded of the present and history of the ANA. On its website ANA describes itself in relation to Astrid Noack, as:

> *an association of artists, art workers, architects, composers and local residents who since 2009 has been committed to bring new life to the old studio of Astrid Noack in Rådmandsgade at Nørrebro in Copenhagen. Walking into the backyard of Rådmandsgade 34 is like entering a time warp that takes you back to a very different Copenhagen – pre-gentrification. The Danish sculptress and dedicated communist Astrid Noack (1888–1954) lived and worked here from 1936–1950 and took part in everyday life in the area.* (Astrid Noacks Atelier n.d.)

The commitment to the place and its past is evident and palpable in the performance event itself. And, so I ask in this particular space with its history, with its otherness, can I love the other, the oddkin that is too close to me? Can I love all these bodies around me, all these human critters, with their breath and sweat and smell and heat and otherness (all that is not mine)? What is it that connects this crowd in this performance space, this kind of bodily desire in the making, in thinking together? How are we different to strangers on the Tube, during rush hour, forced to be together?

Of course, there is a choice in having committed ourselves to see Lysholt Hansen's performance in the ANA, to carefully and collectively think through an issue of body and technology and supremacy of the humans above all other species in the Anthropocene, which we are renaming Chthulucene for the sake of non-hierarchical inter-species harmony. But naming is a gesture—we need to act such inter-species justice beyond the performative acts as presented in writing, art, and performance. Yet, staying with the reality of this performance, and particularly its bodily experience, allows for some kind of emergence between us all in the space, and metaphorically on the planet, into new feminist relations, which must embrace both the mother and the daughter not as biological entities but as a new kind of kin, oddkin in a newly emergent configuration. The daughter might have to stay with a task of non-reproduction. It is up to her to think planetary relations differently. Haraway reminds us that:

> *Gaia does not and could not care about human or other biological beings' intentions or desires or needs, but Gaia puts into question our very existence, we who have provoked its brutal mutation that threatens both human and nonhuman livable presents and futures. ... Gaia is an intrusive event that undoes thinking as usual.* (2016, p. 44)

It might be that intrusion is the form that is needed to open us up into new feminist relations; it might be that recompositioning ourselves through performance, feeling hot and uncomfortable, too close to one another, brings about a much-needed difference in relations. Maybe it is through maternal performance that we arrive at a recomposition of kin and care. After all, 'the stretch and recomposition of kin are allowed by the fact that all earthlings are kin in the deepest sense, and it is past time to practice better care of kinds-as-assemblages (not species one at a time)' (Haraway 2016, p. 103).

The performance ends with these lines:

Dear Daughter,
Here is no mother. Here is mothering
here is caring for others, caring for the chthonic, for the self-with-others.
Care. Dear Daughter. The future is female. Now you take over.

What is this attempt at framing the future as female about? Is it about sympoiesis—making-with her daughter, thinking their future together, taking response-ability for the current state of ecological affairs, remaking of one's own baby as kin? What kind of being-with can we as an audience of Mothernist m/others, as co-inhabitants of Gaia, envisage? What remains after the event for you, Emily? (Fig. 8.1).

Love

Lena

Dear Lena,

I do remember. So hot I could hardly breathe! So many bodies crammed together, I could feel the collective sweat that condensed on the walls and ceiling dripping onto my head, neck, and shoulders. I so desperately wanted to move but was too afraid to venture too near to the performer, who we now call by her name, Nanna Lysholt Hansen, but at that point was a terrifying more-than-human presence in the space. When I watched the show, I did not yet know about Haraway's notion of the human-as-humus but I lived it in that space, where I was afraid and unable to breathe. How I longed to stick with my position as 'sky-gazing Homo' as Haraway would have it (2016, p. 2). *I did not want to inhale that stagnant air, in that tiny space, with those people, and that technology, and the wires that came too close to my feet.*

You ask if the maternal space that was created as part of the conference we attended, or the nature of maternal performance, might make this particular physical crush of bodies different from the crowded space of the rush hour Tube train. In the performance space we are expected to identify as part of the crowd and to acknowledge the 'us and them' of the audience and performer; we are asked to become part of the mob in opposition to our collective other—the performer. In the Tube train everyone strives to keep isolated, head in a book to block sightlines, or headphones to mask sound. Do not catch the other's eye. In the performance space we are one mass of audience—a group, not individuals here.

Fig. 8.1 Nanna Lysholt Hansen, *Dear Daughter/Anatomy of the Chthulucene* (2016–2019) (Image courtesy of the artist)

On the whole I do not like to touch, or be touched by, others' bodies; and yet my connection to my biological children is so visceral and intimate. I squeeze them, hold them, and feel their breath on my face as they sleep next to me still. I would hate this kind of intimacy with kin; I only want it with babies.[2] *I am afraid of the physical intimacy with the other audience members in Lysholt Hansen's performance (my kin) and I love the physical intimacy I share with my children (my babies). I am afraid not only of the intimacy caused by proximity to other audience members in* Dear Daughter, *I am also challenged by the visual intimacy created in the invitation to look at this particular masked yet naked body of the performer. It feels an intrusion to look at this body with its face covered, even when we have been invited into the space for exactly this purpose.*

I understand the sense of Haraway's call to make kin not babies and I understand the urgency to break down barriers between human and non-human. We must treat other species, the Earth, and each other with respect if we are all to survive, but at an emotional level I find it troubling. Haraway invites us to stay with this trouble—it is of course the whole subject of her book Staying with the Trouble. *I am a rebellious child, though—I do not want to stay with the trouble any more. You and I have an easy get-out clause now: neither of us will have more biological babies and have moved on from that point in our lives. My salpingo-oophorectomy means that I am unable to biologically produce more children and, even without the surgery, I would probably be too old now anyway. It is easy for me to say 'OK, from here on, I will follow Haraway and make no more babies' but what a cheat that makes me! How can I espouse this view? How could I deny another woman the joy I have felt from my biological parenting? How can I align my intellectual and political knowledge that we should not make more babies with my feminist ideals that I cannot deny another woman pleasure or privilege or dictate her choices?*

You suggest Lysholt Hansen's closing line 'the future is female' might be a making together with her daughter, a sympoiesis as Haraway would have it (2016). *It might also be a recognition that our generation has failed: we made the babies and now we leave our children to sort out our problems, 'now you take over'. The school strikes for climate are perhaps symptomatic of this—here come the children to provoke the adults and to sort out the mess. We have been inspired by Ukeles' question 'After the revolution, who's going to pick up the garbage on Monday morning?'* (1969). *I thought the answer to Ukeles' provocation was obvious: it was to be 'the mothers'; well maybe, as we look to our maternal future, the answer is instead 'the children'.*

Lysholt Hansen's performance, which we watched back in 2017, was made before Greta Thunberg's extraordinary speeches and action had changed the way we think about children's role in politics, but I cannot help now but bring the two things together. Maybe the 'dear daughter' invoked by Lysholt Hansen is all our daughters and it is this new generation who can make kin together and sort out our mess? Perhaps it is time we handed over the Chthulucene? But what a future we are condemning our daughters to.

I want to think about what we might need to do to support and enable our children to take forward the future. What is our responsibility if we are handing the problems over to them? Lynn Lu's performance The Hand that Rocks the Cradle (2015) *deals with the mess that we hand down to our children in a different way. She notes that a mother's peri-natal depression increases a child's chances of developing their own depression. Lu created* The Hand that Rocks the Cradle *to address this inheritance, and, in her own words, to 'metaphorically break this vicious cycle of depression and neglect, by making up for our lost opportunities to be nurtured'* (Lu n.d.). *Audience members were cared for by Lu during a four-hour participatory performance commissioned as part of the 'Couldn't Care Less/Cross-Cultural Live Art Project' in Deptford, London. Anyone who chose to participate would be wrapped in a blanket and rocked in a hammock while listening to a soothing audio track on headphones. Similarly, in* Tend (2015) *Lu invited audiences into a space for a one-to-one encounter, where she offered them a variety of soothing actions including 'back scratching with fingernails on bare skin, ear cleaning, hair brushing, storytelling from memory, lying down side by side'* (Lu n.d.). *Lu takes her adult audience back to a childlike experience of being cared for and looked after, and, in doing so, better equips them to go out and take on the world. I read this performance as another example of Haraway's call to make kin not babies. Lu's kin become the audiences she works with, her maternal acts extending beyond her own biological family and into her wider communities.*

Sara Ruddick asks us to think of the maternal as an ethical approach; she states: 'we must work to bring a transformed maternal thought into the public realm, to make the preservation and growth of all children a work of conscience and legislation' (1980, p. 361). *Lu, in* Tend *and* The Hand that Rocks the Cradle, *gives all her audience members a chance to be mothered. Quite simply, we cannot hand over our Chthulucene and expect our children to sort out our mess without first enabling them through our mothering within and beyond our families, through our kinship making with and for those who will follow us. It is not so simple to transfer the problem to them. We are back to the reciprocal relationship of care that we have explored throughout this book.*

Ruddick's call for reciprocal care that is not only the responsibility of individuals but also of the state reminds me of the Well-being of Future Generations (Wales) Act, 2015. This act makes it a legal requirement for public bodies in Wales to consider the implications of their actions for future generations of children—both those children who are with us now and those who are yet to be born (Well-being of Future Generations [Wales] Act 2015). *This act foregrounds sustainable development, particularly in relation to economic, social, environmental, and cultural well-being. In this piece of legislation, public bodies are legally required to think maternally as Ruddick proposed and Lu models. What kind of futures might be created if we take seriously Haraway's invocation to make kin and Ruddick's call to think maternally, and we truly take care to enable a new generation to change the world?*

Love

Emily

Dear Emily,

One of the things I remember Lynn Lu telling us in the interview that we conducted with her is that she allowed audience members in both Tend *and* The Hand that Rocks the Cradle *to be taken care of for as long as they wanted* (Lu with Šimić and Underwood-Lee 2020, pp. 19–20).*There was no time limit on the audiences' desires and needs. Lu mentioned that the needs of an artistic community in search of an aesthetic experience and pleasure in the Palais de Tokyo in Paris, where* Tend *took place as part of the 'Secret Archipelago' exhibition, were not as great as those of a local community of people in Deptford who might be older, lonely, or homeless, and who might have stumbled across the live art invitation and* The Hand that Rocks the Cradle *participatory performance, as an act of tenderness. In the latter case Lu talked of having to ask the curators to manage the needs of the participants, to tell the audiences to consider others in the queue, to reflect on each other. Why is there so much need in this community, so much desire for acts of care? Why is it that it is up to the mother/artist, yet again, to call for setting the limits and therefore encourage acting responsibly?*

Who are the people who can manage themselves, and put limits on their desires and needs, people who know when to say 'this is enough', and who are those, possibly reminiscent of needy newborns, insistent crying babies, who have no limits, whose needs are so excessive, beyond the accepted norm? Are we returning to the questions of jouissance here, 'always in excess' as Jacqueline Rose and Juliet Mitchell note when introducing Lacan's Seminar XX (1985, p. 137)?[3] *Furthermore, are mother/artists placed as figures who are courageous enough to address the issues of care, not necessarily as the ones who will provide it, but frankly note and therefore address its inadequacies, as Lu has dared? Is that kind of openness, seeping through jouissance and excess, also a way forward to understanding and enacting new ways of relating to one another, while taking into consideration our differences in terms of class, race, gender, sexuality, social privilege, and age? A sense of heightened awareness that mother/artists bring into their performance making might just be able to offer a new set of feminist relations.*

Lu's work is provocative. It pushes the borders of the accepted. It risks judgement and invites us to accept the radical body of the other, oddkin among us. Lu talked of her post-partum depression and her own difficulty in accepting becoming the mother (Pariante 2016), *losing her sense of self, her happy life. We wondered how and why it was that learning how to care, how to tend in exactly that difficult stage of her life, the period after birth which we had named aftermath, when she first became the mother, happened through performance art practice and the two aforementioned projects.*

Emily, I agree with you about a slight repulsion towards others' bodies, the smell and heat of oddkin around us, about not wanting to be touched by others. And I, like you, embrace the visceral with my biological children. I adore squeezing them, feeling them, sensing their breath and smell. I am still provoked by their otherness, their difference, which is nevertheless mixed in with the complexity of feeling and knowledge that they are mine, of my body, of my creation, the biological within, flesh and blood. I am surprised at Lu's intimate offer to strangers, to enact those motherly bodily pleasures, such as the cleaning of ears, scratching of the back, brushing hair, telling a story while lying next to one another… and to extend that action that she remembers her mother only gave her for a short time, for as long as they desire. Lu wanted to extend the care she felt she missed out on. She said while she did not mind adults who she could engage with, it was the children who were more difficult. Yet she also admitted that some adults are harder to please than others—some did not know their limits. Effectively it was upon Lu to place limitations again, even when she did not want to do that, to start with. Should we rely on adults to know their limits, to behave themselves?

How long am I to cradle that stranger? Shouldn't they know their limits and thank me for the one-to-one performance after the respectable fifteen minutes (max.) have passed? Surely, they ought to be responsible for their own time, their own pleasure, their own life, in relation to all others around them. How does such a responsibility come about and at what age? Do we ask the state to ensure it through legislation, such as the Well-being of Future Generations (Wales) Act, 2015? Is it our collective responsibility, and, if so, to which degree do these small acts of care provided by individual artists come to matter? Do they teach us, push us, provoke us into action? Do we see them as instances of the avant-garde, a utopia to be achieved yet out there somewhere in the future, or are they already creating the here/now of a more compassionate and just society? Sara Ruddick (1980, 1989) *frames mothering as a practice. In an interview with Andrea O'Reilly* (2009), *she talks of outlining 'maternal thinking' with 'a practicalist view of reason', reminding us that it is not adult humans who are 'inherently motherly' but human children who are 'inherently vulnerable in ways that demand what we call "mothering"'. Ruddick continues: 'The aim of maternal practices is to meet the demands of vulnerable "children" for safety and well-being'* (O'Reilly and Ruddick 2009, p. 17).

It is the doing that makes us a mother, it is the labour, the practice, but it is also the vulnerability that demands, that drives us to act towards the safety and well-being of the children, of the others. 'Make kin not babies' connects with this practice thinking, but it also puts primacy on kinship, on making kin, not on the body and biological babies, which might be made accidentally, without intention. Babies happen to us; do friends, do kin? And yet, the body and the visceral will throw themselves again and again into the picture, into the sensual; they will demand recognition, as is made clear through a number of maternal performances we consider.

Adagio (2013) *was Lu's forty-minute performance/installation withher newborn daughter, the only piece in which she performed with her child.* Adagio *was a part of the 'In Confidence: Reorientations in Recent Art' symposium which contemplated art making in the Southern Hemisphere at Perth Institute of Contemporary Arts (PICA) in Australia. While Lu imagined the piece to last longer,* Adagio *had to be disrupted, finished prematurely, for the baby was crying too much. The baby does not know her limits—it is the mother who has to set them. Somehow it is always the mother who is held responsible. Jacqueline Rose puts it beautifully: 'With the suffering of the whole world etched on her face, she carries and assuages the burden of human misery on behalf of everyone'* (2018, p. 12). *Of course, Rose is critical of this understanding of mothers. Now I would like to turn from the human misery of the whole world to one singular moment in Lu's* Adagio *performance.*

On one side of the stage there was a mother hooked up to a breast pump; on the other, in the wash basin, there was a baby, playing with her dummy; in the middle of them, there was a suspended block of ice, with blossoming Corymbia frozen in it, melting… The performance happened only once. I watched its documentation on a privately shared unlisted YouTube link. 'Is that the real baby crying or is it recorded sound over the footage? If recorded, when was the crying of the baby recorded?' I found myself asking, judging while, at the same time, recognizing that I also made art pieces with my own babies and recorded them crying, their insistent crying, still resounding in my ears, the melody of early motherhood, its shrilling sound, its claustrophobic hold. Why do we so easily judge mothers? Why do we allow them to carry the burden of human misery? Why are mothers there for us, to be judged, to carry the world, to set the limits?

At one moment at PICA in Perth, Lu decided to stop the performance and pick up the crying baby. She tells us that she made this decision because there were sounds of disapproval from audience members. The audience sat there as judges, their ears pierced with the baby's cries. Here arrived a moment of interruption, of crisis, of conformity, of finding and knowing one's limits, as a mother, as a performer, as a mother/artist. What is enough is enough. Here came a moment of interruption, on stage, a showcase of mothering practice. Here was an impulse to act, to step away from the performance, a break in the representation, a cut into the frame of the performance. A mother tending to her crying child, with compassion, with anger, with annoyance, with love…

From a maternal performance point of view, I am interested to ask what happens to the representation then, at that very moment? Have we moved to the realm of action, of everyday mothering practice, of material reality, which was of course always there, but had then at that moment become more visible? And I am also keen to ask what does the practice of mothering actually entail? Attention? Bodily care? Endless thoughts about one's children? Daily-ness? Repetition? The everyday? The body? The presence? Love?

Fig. 8.2 Lynn Lu, *Adagio* (2013) (Image by Renae Coles)

Ambivalence? How do we describe the practice of mothering? Is it possible and desirable to enact it on stage as well? (Fig. 8.2).

Love

Lena

Dear Lena,

You ask questions that I do not know how to answer. Our whole motivation, when we set about researching this book and our wider project on Performance and the Maternal, was to address these questions. What is it to mother? What is it to enact motherhood on stage? What kind of new understandings might we gain from listening to how mothers tell their stories in performance? And what kind of maternal futures do we want to create? We are nearing the end of our research and yet I still cannot answer these questions. All I have are individual instances of mothering: my own, yours, Lynn Lu's, Nanna Lysholt Hansen's, and all the other artists whose work we have encountered over these last years. You and I are so similar in our approach—we both laugh at our similarly squeamish reactions to the prospect of tending to the other, so different to Lu's capacity to offer care, or being crammed in as part of a human humus audience in Lysholt Hansen's performance. And yet, here, in our consideration and idealization of a maternal future, we are drawn to these performances and have these intellectualized ideals about creating oddkin—creating maternal empathy across physical, temporal, generational, racial, biological, and other boundaries and points of difference. We are both inspired by Haraway's propositions about the maternal future where we care for more than ourselves and our insular, nuclear families, and yet we both chose to have biological children.

Do you think we are drawn to these theories and performances precisely because they allow us to think about a maternal future that does not come naturally to us and is not our lived daily reality? When we interviewed her, Lu told us how she delights in sharing these moments of intimacy with strangers; when she talked to us about these very intimate acts of care for the other in Tend, *she spoke of the genuine pleasure she found in doing this. Her connection with the other adults in the space is both physical and intellectual. Lu spoke to us about how this pleasure was driven primarily by language—when she works with adults, she can converse with them. In contrast, she stated that her baby daughter, in her pre-linguistic state, felt more like a prop than another human being with whom Lu could have a genuine encounter; instead, Lu performed the necessary actions that constitute a good mother, caring for her baby and meeting all the child's needs, but not feeling it. Lu told us how she used performance to work through these problems and to come to a better understanding of her maternal position* (Lu with Šimić and Underwood-Lee 2020, p. 5). *Perhaps this complicates Ruddick's assertion that we can come to a maternal way of thinking through action? Lu was certainly carrying out the actions of mothering but stopped short of the thinking in relation to her own child. It seems to me that Lu found her maternal way of thinking through performance precisely because she did not find this way of thinking through maternal action in the home. Of course, Ruddick asserts that motherwork is intellectual work and that maternal thinking cannot be so simply divided from the everyday labours of mothering. Ruddick states that the decisions and judgments we make about our mothering are an essential part of our labour, and thus our work and thinking are inherently intertwined* (1989, p. 24). *When I consider Ruddick's propositions on maternal thinking through Lu's work here, it seems to me to be usefully developed through performance. I am not dismissing the importance of Ruddick's work—it is only through the lens that she creates (i.e. that mothering is a practice that leads us to different ways of thinking) that I am able to come to these ideas; however, I wonder if Lu's work gives us a chance to take Ruddick's argument further in relation to performance. It is when Lu makes a performance of her motherwork, and thus separates her action from her consideration and uses performance to reframe that action, that Lu is able to come to maternal thinking. Lu then generously makes this consideration of the maternal public through exhibiting her work, which also allows us to refigure our own thinking alongside her. Lu's experiences are, of course, different from yours or mine, the particularities of each of our maternal exploits and understandings are unique. My own predisposition makes me find intimate acts of care with my own babies easy and creating oddkin (to return to Haraway) very hard, but through Lu's work I am enabled to refigure my maternal thinking through a consideration of performance. Performance allows us to step aside from our maternal action and engage with a very consciously considered and aesthetically framed representation of that action. Lu demonstrates a care beyond the biological family; she is carrying out that care but is also representing that care and thus creating a more conscious thinking about the maternal. Lu shows me a glimpse of the utopian maternal thinking evoked by Haraway and Ruddick, in their very different but complementary propositions—Haraway asking us to consider what a future beyond simply biological reproduction might mean and Ruddick asking us to think about what it would mean if we took an attitude of maternal care towards all the children, not just our own.*

In order to further understand maternal perspectives, and imagine maternal futures, beyond my own I have also turned to TheBabyQuestion (2019) *by Paula Varjack, Luca Rutherford, Catriona James, and Maddy Costa. In this piece, shown as a work in progress at the 'Calm Down Dear' festival at Camden People's Theatre, London, and other venues, the performers ask questions about what it means to choose not to be a mother. They start in the 1970s with glam rock and the NHS roll-out of the pill to 'single women' and move through the decades to eventually explore their own choices and the maternal futures they might want to create. At one point in the show Catriona James discusses the break-up of her relationship with a partner and how her care for their dog has moved from a shared endeavour to a solo one. She notes that looking after her dog is perhaps the closest she will come to parenting. It is at once a ridiculous and deeply moving statement. James is accompanied by sentimental music and adopts a performance style that conveys 'authenticity' to the audience—she stands close to the audience and drops the gestures and high camp that have accompanied other parts of the show. The dog comes to stand in for all recipients of maternal care and for all the care that this particular performer has to offer. As the speech develops, James reveals to us that she understands that family and maternal care can be constituted in whatever form we choose. James removes her wig and fluffs out her hair as she states, 'I believe that families can take any shape we want them to'* (Varjack et al. 2019). *In taking off her wig James is signifying her transition from performance to more honest, candid telling. It is a gesture that we are familiar with reading in contemporary performance and which has come to stand as part of the linguistic shorthand of contemporary British experimental theatre and dance. We are asked to think of this as an honest and revealing moment, but we are also aware that this is still a performance and the candid nature of the telling is just as much a construct as anything else in the show. Nonetheless, in this moment of mixed honesty and artificiality, James reveals a hope that seems to me to contain some sort of truth for her and, by extension, for me. I am asked to imagine a future where the choice to remain childfree is embraced and a new formulation of family, in whatever form we choose to make it, could be possible. When we interviewed Varjack, James and Rutherford, they talked about the extensive research they carried out to create* TheBabyQuestion, *speaking to various women who, for whatever reason, were childfree. James notes that this is nothing new—queer communities have long challenged compulsory heteronormative family structures:*

> *I was interviewing women who, in many other ways, were totally aligned with heteronormative ways of being, but were in fact making quite queer choices … I thought – that's a queer commune … I align to this because it's not just about fighting for female choice but it's about dismantling the whole structure that says this is the way you have to be, and it's questioning and it all comes back to patriarchy in the end.* (James in Varjack, James, and Rutherford with Šimić and Underwood-Lee 2020, pp. 17–18)

TheBabyQuestion *does not take on this imagining of the future lightly; they acknowledge the great social stigma of choosing to remain childfree or being forced by circumstance or biology to be childless (a distinction they make clear throughout the show). They also explore how this is only possible because of advances in reproductive and contraceptive medicine and because of the hard-won fights of generations of feminists. The show is framed as a timeline from 1974 to today and into the future, complete with news-style announcements about the relevant medical, legal, and social changes that took place in each year, alongside references to the chart-topping hits of whatever year they are exploring. The chronological frame constantly reminds me of the groundwork that enables some to choose not to have biological children or to form alternative maternal relations. And through these performers I project myself into an imagined maternal future where these choices are possible.*

I hope that the creators of TheBabyQuestion *are right. I hope that how we express our maternal care is a choice that people will be able to make in future. I turn again to my initial response to Haraway's battle cry of 'Make Kin Not Babies', which so upset me when I first read it. Yes, of course that is one option, and it is perhaps the most responsible option given the climate chaos and inequality of our times, but I prefer the gentler suggestion of* TheBabyQuestion. *In* Letters to a Young Feminist (1997) *Phyllis Chesler states, 'Feminists envisage a variety of families, not just one … We all need an extended family – a network of people who will extend themselves to each other … If we want one – we must often create it for ourselves'* (1997, pp. 105–109). *Chesler proposes we make our families through those we reach out to. James, in* TheBabyQuestion, *also suggests we can choose and create the family we want or need. Ruddick calls for the state to take on the role of care and safeguarding of the future (as it has to some degree here in Wales in the context of the Future Generations Act) and Haraway encourages us to extend our families to the more-than-human. Chesler goes on to point out the difficulties of the utopian ideal she presents, citing examples drawn from her own experience in women's collectives in the 1970s. She issues a provocation to those that follow her: 'Try to see if you are better at this than we were'* (1997, p. 110). *Do you think the families we make and the maternal care we extend can realistically be conceived of as a question or a choice? Do you think a maternal future might simply be one in which having children, extending care across our communities and to the more-than-human world is something we consider consciously and really engage in deep thought about?* (Fig. 8.3).

Fig. 8.3 Paula Varjack et al. *TheBabyQuestion* (2019) (Image by Field and McGlynn)

With Love

Emily

Dear Emily,

We have been contemplating questions of maternal practice, the practice of mothering. I appreciate your thinking about Lu's performance piece and understanding that it is through a performance of motherwork that Lu is able to come to maternal thinking. This newly discovered maternal thinking, through the medium of performance making, expands our biological borders, extends our care beyond our own children only, and helps us imagine the world of oddkin, of the expansion of maternal care to others, including the more-than-human. A dog appeared in Elina Brotherus' artwork as well.[4]

I have found myself in a new transitional space in my own life, having separated from my former husband, and the father of my four children. While we still share childcare across two households, a new system of mothering or parenting appeared. A lot more negotiation with his new partner, and subsequently her former partner, dependent on the care they share for their two children; all this negotiation is around childcare arrangements, work conferences, COVID-induced home schooling matters, holiday dates. More people are now present and actively involved in the upbringing of the children; relationships are complexified. I am sometimes affronted with a fearful thought about not wanting to be considered a 'part-time Mum', who sees her children less, and yet, I enjoy the time for myself, when I am childfree, when I am free to think and create, research and write. A sense of choice and agency is crucial here, just as TheBabyQuestion *instigates. What is it that we choose to do in our practice of mothering? What are we 'obliged' to do? How can we configure desire in the maternal?*

As an experiment and provoked by our correspondence, I asked my children what constitutes being a mother. My six-year-old started listing all the 'important work', like cooking, putting the kids to bed, home schooling, and taking the kids to school… He was also quick to protest: 'How am I supposed to know? I'm just a kid watching TV.' Finally, he remembered me 'doing Labour', us delivering political leaflets together, door to door. 'Is that mothering?' I asked him. 'Yes, us leafleting', he replied, confident. I was lifted by such a political response, especially given my role as a local councillor (which has in my six-year-old's eyes become a more visible job that I perform in the local community than my academic work, which has mostly moved online). The twelve-year-old answered sharply: 'Answering the phone.' 'Do I not answer the phone?' I enquired. 'Yes, you do; you are the only person that does.' So, I conclude that mothering is about being there, being available. The seventeen-year-old was clever in his response: 'Living someone else's life rather than your own.' This touches on the questions of identity. We, Emily, both know that being a mother carries a struggle for one's identity, and that maternal performance and art is a kind of assertion of the mother/artist identity, often artist over mother.

Discussing what constitutes a mother got me and my nineteen-year-old, a first-year philosophy student, into an exploration of gender and its margins, and a quick realization that 'mother' is a contested term. We wondered to what degree it was useful, since the acts of care were more important than biological ties. Our conversation started with his protesting words: 'Do you really think that after all your years of research I'm just going to come up with a suitable answer?' and then a kind of trick 'let's please everyone' answer: 'Mother's anyone who declares themselves to be a mother; that way everyone is happy.' Choice, once again, seemed important here. Our conversation soon moved to the questions of essentialism, the birthing body and death (is someone still a mother if a child dies?), and his refusal to assign being a mother on the primacy of care over biological connection. We returned again and again to the question of the body (pregnancy and birth), the body which is so often present in performance practice too. 'So, if you are saying that it is about practice and care of the child, what is the difference between a mother and a father? So basically, you are saying that a mother is a father?', my nineteen-year-old challenged me when I was insisting on the labour and practice of mothering being the predominant feature of what constitutes being a mother. 'What about all those mothers whose children are away for some reason?', he continued, 'Are they less a mother than you?' At the same time, we understood that the term 'parent' erases motherwork, that it is still predominantly mothers who perform the care and upbringing of the children. We did not find a suitable definition.

During the pandemic, artist and curator Helen Sargeant (2020) *gathered artwork from twenty mother/artists for* Maternal Art Magazine, *issue one, 'Stay at Home'. I participated in this new venture. What I find moving about this attempt is a creation, yet again, of a new network of mother/artists, a sense of support, a place of holding one another, and each other's practices in this time of need. You ask me: 'Do you think the families we make and the maternal care we extend can realistically be conceived of as a question or a choice? Do you think a maternal future might simply be one in which having children, extending care across our communities and to the more-than-human world is something we consider consciously and really engage in deep thought about?' I think there are instances of that care in the present, in the past… I do not think it is purely a question of the future. I think the maternal and care always need to be renewed, with each new collective, each new network, each new family (in whatever form). I don't think that heteronormative nuclear family units are sustainable; they must overspill into extended families, which might consist of friends too, childcare professionals, neighbours and babysitters, dogs, pets, the natural world, trees and plants. It is policies and politics that help the work of mothering. It is the whole planetary environment that holds the mothers and their ability to practise, work, and make choices. And it is childfree women, mothers, and artists working through maternal themes who help shape the political perceptions and policies on this troubled planet.*

Love

Lena

Notes

1. The bent head that Chesler invokes might be considered another attitude of maternal inclination as proposed by Adriana Cavarero (2011) and discussed in our Maintenance chapter.
2. This aversion to touch might be considered even more pressing in these current times in the midst of a global pandemic when government advice is to avoid contact with the other, who is framed as a potential threat of infection.
3. See our Aftermath chapter for a discussion of excess and jouissance.
4. See our Loss chapter for a discussion of Elina Brotherus' work.

References

Astrid Noacks Atelier. n.d. *Astrid Noacks Atelier*. https://astrid-noack.dk/en/. Accessed 9 Nov 2020.

Cavarero, Adriana. 2011. Inclining the Subject. In *Theory After 'Theory'*, eds. Jane Elliott and Derek Attridge. London and New York: Routledge.

Chesler, Phyllis. 1997. *Letters to a Young Feminist*. Chicago: Lawrence Hill Books.

Edelman, Lee. 2004. *No Future: Queer Theory and the Death Drive*. Durham and London: Duke University Press.

Ettinger, Bracha L. 2006. Fascinance and the Girl-to-m/Other Matrixial Feminine Difference. In *Psychoanalysis and the Image: Transdisciplinary Perspectives*, ed. Griselda Pollock, 60–93. Oxford: Blackwell.

Haraway, Donna J. 2016. *Staying with the Trouble: Making Kin in the Chthulucene*. Durham, NC: Duke University Press.

Jolly, Margaretta. 2008. *In Love and Struggle: Letters in Contemporary Feminism*. New York: Columbia University Press.

Lu, Lynn. n.d. *Lynn Lu*. https://lynnlu.info/. Accessed 9 Nov 2020.

Lu, Lynn with Lena Šimić, and Underwood-Lee, Emily. 2020. *Interview with Lynn Lu*. https://performanceandthematernal.files.wordpress.com/2020/10/lynn_lu-.pdf. Accessed 9 Nov 2020.

Mitchell, Juliet, and Rose, Jacqueline. 1985. Introduction. In Lacan, Jacques, *Feminine Sexuality*, eds. Juliet Mitchell and Jacqueline Rose, trans. Jacqueline Rose. New York and London: W. W. Norton.

O'Reilly, Andrea, and Sara Ruddick. 2009. A Conversation About Maternal Thinking. In *Maternal Thinking: Philosophy, Politics, Practice*, ed. Andrea O'Reilly, 14–38. Toronto: Demeter Press.

Pariante, Carmine M. 2016. Seven Things Lynn Did Not Know About Pregnancy, the Postpartum, and Why She Became Depressed. *HuffPost*, 29 February. https://www.huffingtonpost.co.uk/carmine-pariante/postpartum-depression_b_9338354.html. Accessed 9 Nov 2020.

Rose, Jacqueline. 2018. *Mothers: An Essay on Love and Cruelty*. London: Faber.

Ruddick, Sara. 1980. Maternal Thinking. *Feminist Studies* 6 (2): 342–367.

Ruddick, Sara. 1989. *Maternal Thinking: Toward a Politics of Peace*. Boston: Beacon Press.

Sargeant, Helen (ed.). 2020. Stay at Home. *Maternal Art Magazine* 1 (1). Available at https://maternalart.com/shop/p/magazine-issue-1-digital. Accessed 4 Feb 2021.

Stanley, Liz. 2004. The Epistolarium: On Theorizing Letters and Correspondences. *Auto/biography* 12 (3): 201–235.

Tyler, Imogen, and Lisa Baraitser. 2013. Private View, Public Birth: Making Feminist Sense of the New Visual Culture of Childbirth. *Studies in the Maternal* 5 (2): 1–27.

Ukeles, Mierle Laderman. 1969. *Manifesto for Maintenance Art 1969!* Proposal for an Exhibition 'Care', originally published in Jack Burnham. 1971. Problems of Criticism. *Artforum*, 41. http://www.queensmuseum.org/wp-content/uploads/2016/04/Ukeles_MANIFESTO.pdf. Accessed 19 Sept 2020.

Varjack, Paula, James, Catriona, and Rutherford, Luca with Šimić, Lena, and Underwood-Lee, Emily. 2020. An Interview with Paula Varjack, Catriona James, and Luca Rutherford (the makers of *TheBabyQuestion*). *Performance and the Maternal*. https://performanceandthematernal.files.wordpress.com/2020/11/the-baby-question-interview-final-1-1.pdf. Accessed 21 Dec 2020.

Well-being of Future Generations (Wales) Act. 2015. https://www.futuregenerations.wales/wp-content/uploads/2017/01/WFGAct-English.pdf. Accessed 9 Nov 2020.

Young, Iris Marion. 1997. Asymmetrical Reciprocity: On Moral Respect, Wonder, and Enlarged Thought. *Constellations* 3 (3): 340–363.

Performances and Artworks Cited

Dick, Kirby, and Ziering, Amy [directors]. 2002. *Derrida*. Zeitgeist Films [film].

Lu, Lynn. 2013. *Adagio* [performance].

Lu, Lynn. 2015. *The Hand That Rocks the Cradle* [performance].

Lu, Lynn. 2015. *Tend* [performance].
Lysholt Hansen, Nanna. 2013–2015. *Dear Daughter/Organic Cyborg Stories (After Donna Haraway)* [performance].
Lysholt Hansen, Nanna. 2014–2018. *Dear Daughter/Motherboard Theories of Evolution (w/ Braidotti, Plant et aliae)* [performance].
Lysholt Hansen, Nanna. 2016–2019. *Dear Daughter/Anatomy of the Chthulucene* [performance].
Lysholt Hansen, Nanna. 2019–2020. *Dear Daughter/Sen_sing_inannainanna (Russ, Shiva, Klein)* [performance].
Varjack, Paula, Rutherford, Luca, James, Catriona, and Costa, Maddy. 2019. *TheBabyQuestion* [performance].

CHAPTER 9

New Beginnings (9 months)

> *Audre Lorde*: The one thread I feel coming through over and over in my life is the battle to preserve my perceptions, the battle to win through and to keep them – pleasant or unpleasant, painful or whatever.
>
> *Adrienne Rich*: And however much they were denied.
>
> *Audre Lorde*: And however much they were denied. And however painful some of them were. When I think of the way in which I courted punishment, the way in which I just swam into it: 'If this is the only way you're going to deal with me, you're gonna have to deal with me this way'.
>
> (Lorde and Rich 1981, p. 714)

New Contexts and New Questions

In this discussion between Adrienne Rich and Audre Lorde, they highlight the need to keep going, to bring to light that which is important, and to keep on swimming towards the problem no matter how difficult. The cultural perceptions of the ideal mother, the good mother, the self-sacrificing mother, and the realities of the ambivalent mother, bad mother, or the monstrous mother have been exposed by the performance makers and artists we have looked at in the previous chapters. Perceptions are hard to shift, and it is difficult to hold onto those that we might find meaningful. The 'good mother' continues to dominate many

L. Šimić and E. Underwood-Lee, *Maternal Performance*, Contemporary Performance InterActions,
https://doi.org/10.1007/978-3-030-80226-4_9

of the cultural dialogues around motherhood. Jacqueline Rose notes that the dominant cultural representations of motherhood, which she analyzes with particular reference to the portrayal of mothers in tabloid newspapers, can never fully grasp or pin down motherhood, which is far more nuanced than the clichés might suggest (2018, p. 18). Mother/artists help us to diversify the narratives around the maternal. The portrayals of the maternal we have encountered in the artworks we have engaged with over the course of this book suggest to us that the maternal is infinite, complex, and multiple.

In autumn 2020 we organized a series of maternal fora under the title 'ENGAGE… conversations across performance studies and the maternal' which explored a number of themes: aesthetics, storytelling, gender, climate, futures, migration, citizenship, and health, policy and impact.[1] All of these events opened new questions and connections that we will continue to explore, including the prevalent contemporary topics around maternal performance in connection to envisioning of alternative maternal futures beyond the biological reproductive function, social and ecological activism, as well as emphasis on kin and more-than-human relations. It is clear that questions about the maternal and its performance are ongoing and this book does not conclude our research on maternal performance. We are both keen to yet again address its interdisciplinary aspects and develop further research gatherings and outputs in collaboration with other scholars and artists. Maternal performance is open to new beginnings. We must ask who these new beginnings are open to. We must recognize our situated position, our various privileges, and the places where we can support other mothers, artists, and scholars beyond our immediate frame of reference. Questions of race, class, culture, embodiment, gender, disability, illness, reproductive rights, access to economic support, and many other issues have been raised.

We have titled this final chapter New Beginnings. The title is somewhat perverse as this is the ending of our book; however, the never-ending, interconnected, and re-performed nature of the maternal is what has come through most strongly throughout our research in maternal performance. We have also made a conscious decision to quote poets and scholars from an older generation who have previously engaged with maternal matters. Concerns and struggles to keep our perceptions, in this case for a complex maternal sensibility and approach, are cyclical. We note that the maternal is one of those eternal topics to which new generations of scholars, artists, and mothers will always come back, anew. The fight for more nuanced readings of maternity will continue. Yet, regardless of this repetitive quality of the maternal, if we had to summarize one narrative that might be useful in relation to the maternal it is probably this—that the maternal is always *more than*, exceeding itself and reinventing itself anew at every turn. The maternal allows for newness, to go back to our beginning and Hannah Arendt's discussion of the human capacity to initiate, to act, to begin, as we outlined in our first chapter Beginnings.

To its credit, the maternal is often critical as to how we create meaningful engagements with the world beyond ourselves. Because of its encapsulating and overwhelming qualities, its too-muchness and jouissance, the maternal pushes us to our limits, inside and outside, forcing us to engage with the other, sometimes violently, sometimes with care. We have seen how it is through maternal performance that the maternal is brought to matter—both in terms of marking the maternal as worthy of public consideration and action as well as making the maternal materially visible, through body, flesh, and otherwise, and thus challenging the dominant popular perceptions and representations of the maternal, the sacrificial, the beautiful (morally, aesthetically, or artistically), the pleasing, the meek and sweet.

We open this, our final chapter of the book, with a quote from two women in conversation, just as we began the first chapter, Beginnings, with an extract of a conversation between our contemporaries Deirdre M. Donoghue and Paula McCloskey.[2] Moreover, these two quotes, from the first and final chapters, are both taken from conversations between two mother/artists. The process of researching and writing this book, and thoughts we have arrived at, would not have been possible without numerous conversations with women artists in the forms of interviews, research gatherings, online fora, as well as correspondence with one another.[3] We are keen to foreground the reciprocity of thought and the interconnected nature of the maternal. A maternal way of thinking necessitates us to always be aware of, and in conversation with, our other, be that one another as co-authors, our children as constant reminders of our lived and experienced mothering, those who have mothered us, the artists who we have engaged with, our wider communities, or you—our reader. The artists whose work we have examined through this book also bring this awareness of their connected but separate, interdependent other to light in their work. Thus, it is through conversation, through keeping going, and through interdependence that we come to a maternal understanding together and bring the maternal to light in and through performance—the maternal here becomes an ethical feminist relation. To bring the maternal to matter through aesthetic endeavours is to claim a position, to place the mother/artist at the centre, and is intrinsically linked with what we might call the realm of political action after Arendt (1958). In our interview with Nathalie Anguezomo Mba Bikoro she noted that it was through her experience of becoming a mother that she was able to bring a more interconnected relational encounter into her artworks, creating a political community through aesthetic endeavours. She states:

> Doing this work to inform and empower my community here is integral to the movement of the maternal body, accountability and responsibility … Those currents in the relationship of maternal force to our own children enable the ability for a poetry of radical mutation. My whole work for eighteen years has been a preparation for this trajectory to learn new definitions of myself, unlearning violence and embracing unknowns. (Anguezomo Mba Bikoro with Šimić and Underwood-Lee 2020, p. 23)

Bringing to matter is what we see in all the works we have explored throughout this book; all might be said to be engaging in what Anguezomo Mba Bikoro refers to as 'a poetry of radical mutation'. In order for such 'radical mutation' to take place, mother/artists courageously place themselves into the public realm through maternal performance, not only to forge new connections in their communities and networks but also in order to embrace the unknowns and learn about their own new identities. By marking the complexities of bringing the private realm of the maternal to appearance within the public sphere through performance and in opening out a more nuanced and complex maternal, we are able to bring a maternal politics of feminist relations to light.

We wonder about the position of the mothers in society, in both the private and public sphere. As Jacqueline Rose notes, and as we have explored throughout this book, mothers are often placed within the domestic realm and considered those who do not appear to count, their role simply being to propel the child into the world (2018, p. 37). Mothers do not matter as subjects in their own right but simply function to serve others. Rose aims to counter this narrative of the mother. Throughout this book we have tried to do the same, not by forgetting those others that mothers might be in relation to, but by paying particular attention to mother/artists, mothers on stage, mothers/performers, and artists who tackle maternal themes. In this, the final chapter of our book, we return to some of our key arguments about what maternal performance specifically has to offer to this debate about mothers' visibility and inclusion within representation. Furthermore, we offer new ways of thinking and feeling the maternal in and through performance practices.

Maternal performance centralizes the mothers, their experiences and understandings and refuses to be confined to the domestic realm. It is useful here to re-rehearse Simone de Beauvoir's definition of immanence and transcendence in relation to motherhood. De Beauvoir aims to counter what she terms the 'misfortune' of motherhood (1988 [1949], p. 96). For de Beauvoir, to be born a woman is to be biologically predestined to be confined to the private, domestic sphere, to the immanent rather than the transcendent (p. 97). The maternal performance that we have examined in the previous pages collapses the immanent and transcendent spheres—it is precisely from that immanent position that mother/artists demonstrate that transcendence can be sought. Maternal performance, which happens in the public sphere, becomes about the movement from the immanent to the transcendent. And yet, maternal performance asserts the maternal as an immanent, embodied, experiential, and political way of thinking, feeling, and understanding the world beyond ourselves. Moreover, maternal performance presents us with a means of re-examining the maternal as the basis of a new political perspective and reimagined social relations, from which we can move into action, or, to continue using de Beauvoir's terminology, transcend. Through this artform, generations of performance makers claim their politics, and thus assert themselves as a political generation (Baraitser 2020, p. xxii). Importantly, maternal performance, while moving the mother/artist towards public and political action, often remains deeply grounded in and immersed in our everyday relations. The maternal is of the daily; it is messy and unruly. Baraitser (2009) connects it with the notion of interruption, and argues for a new understanding of subjectivity which is based on our relation with others, an ethics of interruption. While such interruptions happen in everyday life, and most often with babies, toddlers, and small children, we are keen to point out public examples through maternal performances.

Emily on Performance and Maternal Interruptions

On 28 November 2019 Lena and I travelled to Manchester, UK to watch I'm a Phoenix, Bitch! *by Bryony Kimmings. I was expecting to see a performance that dealt with Kimmings' experience of post-natal depression and her recovery. I had heard lots about the performance—it had been much lauded in the press* (Eaton-Lewis 2019; Gillinson 2018). *We arrive early at the venue, Home, laptops ready in bags. We find a table in a quiet(ish) bar and work together. This is a public performance of academic life but this also somehow feels more like my true academic life: being in a theatre, watching shows, researching, and conversing about the maternal. It is so different from the daily marking and admin of my normal academic routine. While having a pre-show drink in the bar, we discuss love and desire and being away from the children and our offices—these escapes from the daily to allow us to think more clearly, these chosen interruptions from interruptions.*

We move into the auditorium, filled with earnest young people with esoteric hairstyles and serious older women with their statement glasses (like us). The usher tells us that there is a 'technical issue' and the show is delayed. We wait about half an hour and then the performance starts. Kimmings enters the stage to grand operatic music, performs a kind of magnificent pregnancy routine making gestures that signify the changes that her body underwent during pregnancy, and then stops suddenly and states: 'Imagine if I started the show like that!' (or words to that effect). Kimmings employs those usual experimental performance tropes to introduce herself, tell us she works in autobiographical performance, explain what the show is about, and let us know we are in safe hands: 'I process my trauma and then I make art about it' (Kimmings 2019). *She begins to do a routine about all the shows she has done before, asserting her performance credentials, letting us know that her previous shows were 'notorious' and important, that she is a 'professional'. And then the performance stops. Mid-sentence. Kimmings puts her hands to her mouth and runs off stage. The music cuts. The house lights come on. We are left in the audience wondering if this is part of the performance. The longer we are left the less certain we become. Is this some clever device to push us to our limits as audience members? Is this the aforementioned 'technical issue'? It looked like she was going to be sick—is she too ill to perform? After a very long pause a man enters the stage, and he introduces himself as the stage manager. He tells us that Kimmings has had 'a family emergency' and explains that she cannot perform. He tells us how this is a 'difficult' show on a good day and today is a 'really bad day'. The show will not go on but Kimmings is active on Twitter and we will find out more later.*

Lena and I decide to stay in the venue to try to process what has happened in this space. We go up to the restaurant to have a meal. We keep checking Twitter. Kimmings soon tweets—her son is in hospital but okay. She 'couldn't perform knowing he was there without me' (@BryonyKimmings 2019). *This is maternal performance wrenched open by the reality of maternal life. As Kimmings has already stated, it is only after processing trauma that we can perform it. The trauma of maternal life writ large on the performer's body is unperformable, too much, beyond representation and language. We ask why they lied. Why frame maternal life as a 'technical issue'?*

That same evening Kimmings has already returned to Twitter to perform herself to her extensive public audience of 19.8K followers. The public maternal rupture is soon mended; even though the lived experience of Kimmings may not align with her public performance, she is clearly managing how this moment of interruption is received and presenting herself and her son as recovered to some degree, reassuring her audience that her son is 'okay' and that we will be reimbursed for the cost of our tickets. Audience members are performing their maternal solidarity right back at her: 'Don't be sorry. Go home. Cuddle Frank. The show and the audience can and will wait until the time is right. Sending♥' (@MrsGdrama 2019). *A conscious performance of the maternal played out in the public domain of social media replaces the public performance in the theatre.*

This interrupted performance by Kimmings opens up many questions: Should we perform our maternal ruptures? Should we value rawness, trauma, and excess as the central qualities of the live art encounter that somehow separate it out from the more prosaic or safe theatrical experience? When does the maternal become unperformable? Can a child's illness be a technical issue? When do our children call us back from our artistic and academic endeavours—their urgent needs taking precedence over our artistic or scholarly goals? Kimmings did not perform the show that night but returned to the space of social media to perform her maternal story. The Real is rent open and made visible. Afterwards we can reframe our encounters with the visceral Real: we make art, we 'process our trauma and then make art about it'.

This was a true maternal interruption, made public, in the theatre. This was an example where, in public, we were reminded that maternal performance interrupts and thus creates new relations, new ways of being with one another in public space. We glimpsed this briefly through Kimmings' exit from the stage and the frame of representation before her performance was restored on the digital stage provided by social media.

As we have seen in so much work by mother/artists, maternal performance brings us to the limit. It collapses the realities of the personal and the political, private and public, immanence and transcendence. Here again, Kimmings' performance remains immanent in its transcendence. In this particular example, it cannot transcend 'properly' from its domestic or family emergency matters and this is precisely where its power lies.

Lena on Performance and Maternal Liberation

We have, like numerous other scholars and artists, highlighted the shock of the maternal, and how maternal aesthetics carry 'the surprise of the Real' (Liss 2013). *Becoming a mother inevitably interrupts one's life; it propels you into an unknown relation, not only with the tiny screaming infant, and the surrounding world, but also oneself. A new mother deals with the unknown relation to oneself. I remember those fragile times. But I also remember such a powerful sense of agency and control, which felt as if it was granted to me, just through the act of giving birth and my subsequent becoming a mother. In conversations with Bill Moyers, Toni Morrison talks about a sense of liberation experienced upon motherhood:*

> *There was something so valuable about what happened when one became a mother. For me it was the most liberating thing that ever happened to me, having children. ... Liberating. Because of – the demands the children make are not the demands of a normal other.* (Morrison with Moyers 1990)

In Sid Jonah Anderson by Lena Šimić (2008), *a live art event created during one of my maternity leaves, I called my child a revolutionary. I wrote:*

> *He is so disruptive.*
> *He cares not for time.*
> *He is a revolutionary. He has no proper behaviour. Sid carries my dissent.*
> *I get threatened by his disobedience, his constant carrying-on, his crying, his pooing, his eating and sleeping patterns.*
> *Sid and I do not belong here.* (Šimić 2008)

There was something powerful in not belonging, in finding a different kind of time, and rhythm to my days and nights, in disruptions, and interruptions to my everyday life. The demands of an infant are so different, so other-worldly. A new world opened up upon stumbling into the intense experience of mothering. And it might be that given these new surprising and highly demanding living conditions, mixed in with the sense of agency and power of becoming a mother, an aesthetic expression of a new kind of daring appeared. This was for me evident through the act of art making and a public performance of mothering in Sid Jonah Anderson *by Lena Šimić. This is also evident in Courtney Kessel's* In Balance With *(2010–ongoing) series of performances with her daughter, or Grace Surman's* Performance with Hope *(2017) to name a few of the examples of 'the public performance of mothering' that we have discussed in this book.*

Long before starting to work on this research project, Emily and I exchanged secret thoughts on motherhood. I remember us confessing to one another that we felt having children was selfish, selfish in a sense of our accumulation of further love. It was naughty somehow, and irresponsible. It was a kind of hunger for more love. Who doesn't want to have these little beings that utterly adore you? At least for a while. There is a compulsiveness in our desire for mothering, for care even, for love. Are the two of us, then, with our love of reproduction and biological children, appropriate scholars for this complex topic of maternal performance? What are the themes that we have missed? Have we been overly subjective in our choice of mother/artists? What is our responsibility as feminist mothers and artists? We ought to dissipate the tensions between motherhood and feminism, and we hope that this book has helped with the task by profiling a number of critical maternal performance practices with love and care. Yet, I cannot help but ask if mothers can ever live up to the ideal of being critical feminists, or if they are doomed to be perceived as soft, caring, and giving entities, framed through their biological reproductive function, somehow acritical and full of love and cuddles? A big task remains in terms of getting rid of such a set of preconceptions, and, to go back to Lorde, battling to preserve our own.

I want to reveal another well-known secret: an old childhood friend of mine told me that becoming a mother was the best thing that ever happened to her. This was following a fairly difficult fertility journey. She said: 'But I never knew it would be this good, the best thing in the world… If I did, I would have done it years before. Why doesn't anyone tell you this? How good it is to feel so much love.' I feel guilty writing this. Because of course, not all women are mothers, nor do they want to be mothers, or cannot be mothers. And of course, having an informed choice is crucial here. There is no liberation without a sense of agency over the decision.

I have been reading Sheila Heti's Motherhood (2018), *an autobiographical account about her decision whether to become a mother. One particular passage resonates so strongly, as it summons up in such powerful ways some of my disjointed thoughts in the previous paragraphs. Heti writes:*

> *On the one hand, the joy of children. On the other hand, the misery of them. On the one hand, the freedom of not having children. On the other hand, the loss of never having had them – but what is there to lose? The love, the child, all those motherly feelings that the mothers speak about in such an enticing way, as though a child is something to have, not something to do. The doing is what seems hard. The having seems marvellous. But one doesn't have a child. One does it.* (pp. 21–22)

Here we have it: it is about mothering, and doing. It is about maternal enticement that I and other mothers are guilty of. The lived reality of mothering is truly complex—joy and misery combined.

At the end of this book, I must be harsh with myself and pose a question: Have we achieved our aim of delivering a complex book deserving the title of Maternal Performance: Feminist Relations? *A multiplicity of performing maternal voices have been represented, although I am less sure about feminist relations, about the working ethics we have encountered in all different performances, scholarship, and the process of writing this book. Are secretive exchanges among women and mothers, as my examples with Emily and the old childhood friend indicate, and the creation of networks of mother/artists, curations of maternal art exhibitions, publications, and performances in exclusive contexts, a way forward towards an understanding of mothering? Is there not something stifling in this secrecy still? A kind of shame? Shouldn't we get out from our enclave of maternal art and performance? How can we speak up firmly, with agency from our maternal positions, whatever they happen to be, without fear, and with a sense of liberation? Can the sense of liberation that Morrison expresses upon becoming a mother be transferred onto maternal performance scholarship too? Can we align the demands and methodologies of feminist scholarship, which might translate as feminist relations, as those of not a normal 'other', to go back to Morrison's expression? Is there liberation in this kind of performance criticism or in the way that all the artists who address maternal themes carry with their work? A liberation of expression into the public sphere, as a form of action towards new maternal feminist relations.*

Maternal Openings

We began this research with many questions.[4] We stated that we did not attempt to answer these questions but instead open them up as areas for conversation. Perhaps not answering is something of a cheat, a refusal to pin down the maternal and its artistic forms, particularly performance. And perhaps turning this final chapter, which in traditional academic construction should be an ending, into a discussion of the never-ending, never fixed nature of the maternal, located in the imminent sphere yet allowing us to transcend, is yet another 'dodge'. And yet, this eternal extension of the maternal, and in particular maternal performance, might be exactly the right answer to our questions. We need to keep extending the maternal, taking its delicate intimacies and vulnerabilities and opening it up to the public, to the other. It is through the other that the maternal is framed. We begin anew each time, with each new mother, each new child, each new maternal performance. The maternal comes in all forms, shapes, and sizes, and maternal performances can help us see it and experience it in its differences: the maternal as messy and unruly, abject and loving, compassionate and ambivalent, complex and unnerving. Such extension and opening of our lived maternal conditions link us to our place and our moment in history, just as they link us to those other places and moments and the beings that have inhabited them. Maternal openings allow us to think not just of our small and personal biological families but on a wider more public and global scale.

The ephemerality of performance—moreover, the specificity of its artform—allows us to share these thoughts with fleeting communities of audiences without ever having to fix the maternal. Nanna Lysholt Hansen notes this reciprocity and mutability of maternal performance. She states:

> This is why I'm interested in performance. It fits really with mothering as well because there are all these things you cannot control. I do different versions of the same work. I don't say 'Here's my stage and I'm going to go and do this and that etc.' I avoid this element of control. Each performance really has so much to do with who and what the space, the situation, the context and the audience are, and how many people are going to be there as well. Like the performance you saw was packed, you couldn't move, you were a compost pile of bodies. Imagine if there had only been five people there. Maybe I would have moved closer to these five people. It would have been a very different experience. (Lysholt Hansen with Šimić 2020, p. 12)

Maternal performance is primarily about openings, endless possibility, the refusal of endings. The maternal is always about new beginnings.

Maternal Performance Relations

Writing this book took us through in-depth explorations of the maternal including loss (Elina Brotherus) and grief (Fern Smith and Patrick Fitzgerald), embodied pregnant bodies on stage (Hannah Ballou, Aleksandra Nikolajev-Jones, Quarantine), live birth (Marni Kotak) as well as its representations (Third Angel), and birth story contemplations (Tracy Breathnach-Evans). We moved through the aftermath of birth and a variety of maternity leave performances (Lenka Clayton, Lizzie Philps, Lena Šimić, Grace Surman, Megan Wynne), all set to a tight temporal frame and searching for their aesthetic expressions, to somewhat more considered and calmer maintenance works, both durational (Jessica Olah) and studio theatre formats (Grace Surman and Liz Clarke). Intergenerational relations have been crucial to maternal ethics as evident in the works of Hannah Buckley, with her grandmother, Courtney Kessel, with her daughter, and Peggy Shaw, with her grandson and the queer performance community she creates. Thinking beyond blood ties and extending a maternal relational sensibility has featured prominently in the works of Nanna Lysholt Hansen and Lynn Lu, as well as Paula Varjack, Luca Rutherford, Catriona James, and Maddy Costa, who formed a collective to address *TheBabyQuestion*.

We have realized that maternal performances have a concerned relation to time as well as a deep inclination towards intergenerational sensibilities. The maternal body featured in some of the works, predominantly those that had to do with pregnancy and birth, and yet others focussed on relations, and thus gave prominence to maternal ethics and care. Performance and the maternal are allied as durational, embodied, relational practices. Maternal performance aesthetics could be defined as carrying some of those qualities in the content of the performance as well as its format. As has been made evident in our analysis of various maternal performances, often the pieces are about participation and engagement with the other, and they are time-based, durational, and enduring.

In terms of its relation to time, maternal performance might include interruptions and unpredictability, especially if dealing with children on stage or video (Kotak, Clayton, Lu, Kessel, Philps, Surman, Šimić,

Wynne). A mother might deliberately be putting herself into a position of maternal alertness, a kind of public test or performance of 'good/bad' mothering. At times maternal performance is also about embracing the real time of life and action. It might be worth noting here a short online performance delivered by Lynn Lu and Dyana Gravina for our 'Maternal Performance (Artist Forum)' on 6 October 2020 which involved pre-recorded audio narration on maternal matters while the artists were both performing maternal time while putting their children to bed. By making their performance of the mothering public through the forum, they were highlighting the demands placed upon mothers of small children, particularly at bedtime; this was especially pertinent in the light of the timing of the forum at 7 p.m. (Performance and the Maternal n.d.). Maternal time often remains undervalued and invisible, slow and stretched out time which also belongs to others, notably small children, living and breathing beside us. In other cases maternal time expands in order to become intergenerational (Buckley, Kessel, Olah, Shaw), layered with past traumatic events (Smith and Fitzgerald, Clarke), or future-orientated (Brotherus, Lysholt Hansen, Quarantine, *TheBabyQuestion*).

Maternal performance also works from the rupture of the body (Ballou, Nikolajev-Jones, Kotak, Lysholt Hansen, Smith and Fitzgerald, Ballou, Third Angel). It is embodied and visceral, be it through birth and breastfeeding, thriving on the narration of leakages, bodily crisis, trauma or body memory, sensuality, and in some cases overt proximity to flesh and exposures.

Primarily, all maternal performance inevitably has to consider ethics and its relation to others, situated as it is and working from the artists' everyday contexts and connecting to what Imogen Tyler has named 'a maternal commons' (2013, p. 107), the collective thinking invoked by a maternal engagement with the world which extends to collaboration and solidarity networks formed between mother/artists, activists, scholars, programmers, and curators. Thinking of ourselves as beings who are intrinsically linked to one another and to the planet we inhabit makes the maternal the pre-eminent frame for thought. We have a reciprocal maternal responsibility to all those we gestate and those who have gestated us, either through biology or through committed engagement to care for another over the long-term, including the more-than-human. A politics informed by feminist relations, by care and reciprocity, and in which we extend our thinking beyond ourselves and our immediate surroundings, has the capacity to challenge all of the crises we find ourselves living through and those that we will leave behind for the generations that chronologically follow us. Interconnected thinking as linked with care for the other, and offered by a maternal perspective, is more pressing now than ever in our COVID-19, climate chaos times which are causing us to rethink who our other might be and what responsibilities we have as care-takers and allies.

Theoretically, we began this book exploring the public as the space of freedom, drawn from Arendt, and immanence and transcendence, as outlined by de Beauvoir. We then moved to the related propositions from Arendt regarding the transformation from labour and work to action. We explored maternal loss, and the early years of mothering a young baby through the lens of feminist philosophers from a broadly psychoanalytic perspective, including Melanie Klein, Julia Kristeva, and Luce Irigaray. We examined the construction of identity as presented in relation to another through Adriana Cavarero's notion of life stories and Iris Marion Young's discussion on asymmetrical reciprocity. We wove a path through Lisa Baraitser's concerns with interruption and time that pools rather than flows and Gillian Howie's intergenerational wave-like exchange, and finally moved to Donna J. Haraway's conception of a future based on oddkin relations. All of these concerns are linked by a desire to move away from finality and, if we are to follow de Beauvoir's terminology, into a 'transcendent' future where we exceed ourselves in some way and escape dissipation or mortality.

The maternal turns us towards the future, to the legacies we leave behind and the possibilities we open up, but at the same time the maternal keeps us grounded. It is widely accepted that it is the children who represent the future, while the mothers labour in the present, doing the maintenance work; however, the refusal of generational inheritance can also be a feminist tactic to create an alternative future. Jack Halberstam proposes that we can reject the mother–daughter inheritance that we take from those who come before us and, further, that we can deliberately not reproduce the status quo by consciously resisting the cultural expectation that a mother will labour to produce the new generation. Halberstam proposes: 'a feminism grounded in negation, refusal, passivity, absence, and silence, offers spaces and modes of unknowing, failing, and forgetting as part of an alternative feminist project' (2011, p. 124). We read Halberstam's provocation not as a refusal of the maternal but instead as a proposition of an alternate maternal. Ana Grahovac analyzes Aliza

Shvarts' 2008 documentation of her deliberate repeated potential conceptions and chosen terminations, facilitated through the use of donor sperm and the morning-after pill, to argue that performance can be employed to help us imagine an alternative maternal future where women can resist compulsory biological reproduction (Grahovac 2013). Grahovac employs Shvarts' controversial artwork to presents us with a complex model of bodily autonomy that challenges what Grahovac terms the 'reproductive narrative of "natural" womanhood' (p. 13). Schvarts' artwork was never exhibited (p. 2); however, through the heated discussion that it provoked, Grahovac is able to reconfigure the maternal. The maternal, and maternal artworks, then allow us to renegotiate the future, to resist productivity and future orientation, and to challenge the configuration of the mother as the biological producer of new subjects. As we have explored throughout this book, as mother/artists we leave behind enduring works of art (de Beauvoir 1988), changed political or legal frameworks (Arendt 1958), generations that can go beyond us through maintenance, care, or exchange (Baraitser 2017; Howie 2010), or a renewed global interconnectedness and responsibility (Haraway 2016; Ruddick 1980, 1989). We have argued that the maternal is about thinking beyond ourselves and making connections across generations and borders and this desire takes us back to where we began—to the yearning to transcend the limits of ourselves and our maternal daily role while at the same time committing to the exploration of the everyday lived experience of maternal immanence.

Yet, if the maternal is always about thinking of ourselves in relation to our many others, be they our biological or chosen family or our global or inter-species kin, and maternal performance is about expanding this thinking into the public domain and creating further relational encounters with the other that is the audience, the maternal must always be about what extends, remains, and endures beyond ourselves; maternal performance is about creating these extensions and openings within the public realm. We have called this final chapter 'New Beginnings' because what we are really interested in throughout this book is the maternal's capacity to take us beyond endings and to think of a constant beginning anew, or to focus on natality, to employ an Arendtian turn of phrase. We are taken back to thinking about what it would mean for the human condition to align itself more with natality and not death. How can we always stay open rather than closed? What is it about maternal performance that offers us a capacity towards the natal and living?

It is frequently and popularly argued that we create culture or works of art in order to be remembered beyond death or to escape our mortality. This search for immortality through the things we create is one of the central goals of humanity according to Arendt.[5] For de Beauvoir this has been confined to the realm of the masculine by the patriarchy (1988, p. 45). And yet, the maternal artists that we have considered have positioned themselves both as artists and as mothers, exceeding the confines of the domestic and making significant artworks that are considered in the public domain. As we have argued throughout this book, the maternal performances we have examined create relations with their audience and enable the performers to translate and frame their maternal experience within the realm of art and thus move from the domestic to the political. By creating artworks in a performance medium, which are deliberately about exploring relationships rather than centring the creative genius of the individual, we move away from the patriarchal notion of artwork that de Beauvoir critiques and towards a feminist maternal relationality that transcends, endures, and remembers the maternal state.

Our maternal condition pushes towards a constant renewal, a never-ending. The common maxim 'A mother's work is never done' suggests something of the endless endurance and inescapability of the maternal. Thinking maternally might allow us to think not of this endurance as an act of sufferance but as a committed way of living that obliterates linear chronology and private individualism. Making maternal thinking public through maternal performance brings it into the domain of the political.

Birth marks the end of pregnancy and also the beginning of new life, a capacity to start again. We are renewed with each new life. We begin anew. We have drafted this book in nine months, starting on 4 November 2019, finishing on 4 August 2020. This was our pregnancy, our gestation period, our time of writing. We wrote each chapter in a month. We decided to mimic an idealized pregnancy. We know this nine-month period is a fallacy—as we stated in our opening chapter, where we detailed how just one of the ten pregnancies we have bodily held between us has lasted for the predicted time. We did not begin to count the many false starts and evaded pregnancies that we may not even be aware of, the times we might have miscarried before knowing of the gestating embryo or the many morning-after pills that we have sought out. Perhaps in constructing a neat, pregnancy metaphor to help us along in our writing we are aiming for a kind of maternal embodiment that we never actually had in our 'real-life' pregnancies. However, this nine-month first draft draws on years of research, and was many times and extensively revised over a further nine months. Our thinking will continue to be revised long after publication, just as our maternal sensibilities are to grow further. There is no finality; therefore, following our maternal sensibility, it is fitting to call this final chapter New Beginnings.

While approaching the end of this book, Emily asked her daughters about their understanding of the maternal. One child stated, 'I don't want to be a mummy, it means you always have to put someone else before yourself'. We hope a maternal future will be opened up where a new kind of maternal understanding comes to prominence, where women do not face a future where they are condemned by their choice to mother or not, do not have to sacrifice themselves on the altar of motherhood. We dream of maternal sensibilities, thinking, actions, and experiences that are ever beginning anew, and, as Audre Lorde encourages in the quote at the opening of this chapter, we keep swimming towards the problem.

Notes

1. Documentation of the 'ENGAGE' series is available at https://performanceandthematernal.com/maternal-forums/.
2. See https://www.mothervoices.org/art-research-and-theory.
3. Our ENGAGE fora were initially conceived as a two-day conference; the events, however, had to move online due to the lockdown initiated in response to the global COVID-19 pandemic. We wonder what the new maternal relations will be as we enter an age where face-to-face engagement is replaced by online encounters.
4. As we outlined in Beginnings, our questions included: What is specific about maternal performance, as opposed to other artforms? What processes, strategies, and methodologies are used by performance practitioners and mother/artists working with maternal themes? What, if any, are distinct maternal performance aesthetics? What is the history of the relationship between motherhood and feminism? How is the maternal life/art dyad informed by both performance practice and theory? How is maternal subjectivity framed in both representations of motherhood and of being mothered? What can a maternal sense of subjectivity offer in performance encounters? How are the maternal and ecology connected? What are our maternal futures? How is maternal art able to contribute

to change in the material and social conditions in which women mother?

5. Hannah Arendt states 'The task and potential greatness of mortals lie in their ability to produce things – works and deeds and words – which would deserve to be and, at least to a degree, are at home in everlastingness, so that through them mortals could find their place in a cosmos where everything is immortal except themselves. By their capacity for the immortal deed, by their ability to leave nonperishable traces behind, men, their individual mortality notwithstanding, attain an immortality of their own and prove themselves to be of a "divine" nature' (1958, p. 19).

References

Anguezomo Mba Bikoro, Nathalie with Šimić, Lena, and Underwood-Lee, Emily. 2020. An Interview with Nathalie Anguezomo Mba Bikoro. *Performance and the Maternal*. https://performanceandthematernal.files.wordpress.com/2020/12/nathalie-anguezomo-mba-bikoro.pdf. Accessed 17 Dec 2020.

Arendt, Hannah. 1958. *The Human Condition*. Chicago: The University of Chicago Press.

Baraitser, Lisa. 2009. *Maternal Encounters: The Ethics of Interruption*. London: Routledge.

Baraitser, Lisa. 2017. *Enduring Time*. London: Bloomsbury.

Baraitser, Lisa. 2020. Foreword. In *The Maternal in Creative Work: Intergenerational Discussions on Motherhood and Art*, eds. Elena Marchevska and Valerie Walkerdine. London, New York: Routledge.

Beauvoir, Simone de. 1988 [1949]. *The Second Sex*, trans. H.M. Parshley. London: Picador.

@BryonyKimmings [Bryony Kimmings]. 2019. I am so so sorry to have to cancel tonight's show. I am on a train home to Brighton. Frank is in hospital. He's ok. But I couldn't perform knowing he was there without me. I promise to sort your tickets and I love you. I'm sorry I couldn't go on. Twitter, 28 November, 8.57 p.m. https://twitter.com/BryonyKimmings/status/1200156659307417600 [tweet].

Eaton-Lewis, Andrew. 2019. Theatre Review: Bryony Kimmings: I'm a Phoenix, Bitch Pleasance Courtyard. *The Scotsman*, August 21.

Gillinson, Miriam. 2018. I'm a Phoenix, Bitch Review: Wacky, Warped and Wonderful. *The Guardian*, October 9.

Grahovac, Ana. 2013. Aliza Shvarts's Art of Aborting: Queer Conceptions and Resistance to Reproductive Futurism. *Studies in the Maternal* 5 (2): 1–19.

Halberstam, Jack. 2011. *The Queer Art of Failure*. Durham, NC: Duke University Press.

Haraway, Donna J. 2016. *Staying with the Trouble: Making Kin in the Chthulucene*. Durham, NC: Duke University Press.

Heti, Sheila. 2018. *Motherhood*. London: Harvill Secker.

Howie, Gillian. 2010. Feminist Histories: Conflict, Coalitions and the Maternal Order. *Studies in the Maternal* 2 (1).

Liss, Andrea. 2013. Maternal Aesthetics: The Surprise of the Real. *Studies in the Maternal* 5 (1).

Lorde, Audre, and Rich, Adrienne. 1981. An Interview with Audre Lorde. *Signs: Journal of Women in Culture and Society* 6 (4): 713–736.

Lysholt Hansen, Nanna with Šimić, Lena. 2020. An Interview with Nanna Lysholt Hansen. *Performance and the Maternal*. https://performanceandthematernal.files.wordpress.com/2020/09/nanna-lysholt-hansen-.pdf. Accessed 28 Sept 2020.

Morrison, Toni with Moyers, Bill. 1990. Toni Morrison on Love and Writing. https://billmoyers.com/content/toni-morrison-part-1/. Accessed 24 Nov 2020 [interview].

@MrsGDrama [Charlotte Grovesnor]. 2019. Don't Be Sorry. Go Home. Cuddle Frank. The Show and the Audience Can and Will Wait Until the Time Is .... Twitter, November 28, 9.04 p.m. https://twitter.com/MrsGDrama/status/1200158539353927682 [tweet].

Performance and the Maternal. n.d. Maternal Forums. https://performanceandthematernal.com/maternal-forums/. Accessed 2 Feb 2021.

Rose, Jacqueline. 2018. *Mothers: An Essay on Love and Cruelty*. London: Faber.

Ruddick, Sara. 1980. Maternal Thinking. *Feminist Studies* 6 (2): 342–367.

Ruddick, Sara. 1989. *Maternal Thinking: Toward a Politics of Peace*. Boston: Beacon Press.

Tyler, Imogen. 2013. *Revolting Subjects: Social Abjection and Resistance in Neoliberal Britain*. London: Zed.

Performances and Artworks Cited

Ballou, Hannah. 2016. *goo:ga* [performance].

Breathnach-Evans, Tracy. 2016. *Cord* [performance].

Brotherus, Elina. 2009–2013. *Annonciation* [photography series].

Buckley, Hannah, Brown Elsie, and Hill, Rowland. 2015. *Untitled (Elsie and Hannah)* [film].

Clarke, Liz. 2017–2018. *Cannonballista* [performance].

Clayton, Lenka. 2012–2014. *An Artist Residency in Motherhood* [art project].

Kessel, Courtney. 2012. *In Balance With* [performance].

Kessel, Courtney. 2017. *A Blessing, A Wish, A Spell for the Next Generation* [performance].
Kimmings, Bryony. 2019. *I'm a Phoenix, Bitch!* [performance].
Kotak, Marni. 2011. *The Birth of Baby X* [performance and installation].
Lu, Lynn. 2013. *Adagio* [performance].
Lu, Lynn. 2015. *The Hand That Rocks the Cradle* [performance].
Lu, Lynn. 2015. *Tend* [performance].
Lysholt Hansen, Nanna. 2016–2019. *Dear Daughter/Anatomy of the Chthulucene* [performance].
Nikolajev-Jones, Aleksandra. 2012–2020. *Gravida* [performance series].
Olah, Jessica. 2016. *2 340 Peanut Butter and Jelly Sandwiches* [performance].
Philps, Lizzie. 2013. *Maternity Leaves* [photography series].
Quarantine. 2016–2017. *Summer. Autumn. Winter. Spring.* [performance].
Shaw, Peggy. 2003. *To My Chagrin* [performance].
Šimić, Lena. 2007–2008. *Contemplation Time* [mixed media].
Šimić, Lena. 2014. *Friday Records* [mixed media].
Šimić, Lena. 2008. *Sid Jonah Anderson by Lena Šimić* [performance].
Smith, Fern, and Fitzgerald, Patrick. 2003. *This Imaginary Woman* [performance].
Surman, Grace. 2010. *I Love My Baby and My Baby Loves me* [film].
Surman, Grace. 2017. *Performance with Hope* [performance].
Third Angel. 2015. *Partus* [performance].
Varjack, Paula, Rutherford, Luca, James, Catriona, and Costa, Maddy. 2019. *TheBabyQuestion* [performance].
Wynne, Megan. 2018. *Affirmation (I Am A Professional Artist)* [film].

Index

L. Šimić and E. Underwood-Lee, *Maternal Performance*, Contemporary Performance InterActions,
https://doi.org/10.1007/978-3-030-80226-4

N

FSC
www.fsc.org
MIX
Papier | Fördert
gute Waldnutzung
FSC® C083411